Douglas DC-3
60 Years and Counting

Douglas DC-3 60 Years and Counting

Ed Davies • Scott A. Thompson • Nicholas A. Veronico

Library of Congress Catalog Card Number: 95-76183

ISBN 0-9637543-4-3

First Printing August 1995

The authors would like to dedicate this book to Dan Reid and Roland Halter who died December 15, 1994, when their turbo DC-3 tragically crashed soon after takeoff from a small strip near Lobito in Angola. They and their unique aircraft were on a humanitarian relief mission, one of many they had flown in Africa in the past several years. They will be sadly missed.

Front cover photos by Nick Veronico
Rear cover photos by Scott Thompson, Ed Davies, and FAA

Book production by Scott Thompson

Aero Vintage Books
P.O. Box 1508
Elk Grove, California 95759-1508
Phone or Fax: (916) 684-7028
see ordering information on last page of book

Contents

Acknowledgments

The authors wish to thank the following individuals for their contributions to this book, both in photos and information:

Ed Davies: Don Brooks (for inviting me to fly the North Atlantic) and all the great people I flew with on that trip, Bill Dause, Peter Davies, Jim Findlay (Otis Spunkmeyer Air), John Havers, Paul Howard, Peggy Vanden Heuvel (Basler Turbo Conversions), Dan Kitley, Geoff Macfee (Otis Spunkmeyer Air), Harry Moore, Michael Prophet, Steve Tournay, Patrick Vinot Prefontaine, Ron Wilson, and Morfydd Davies.

Scott Thompson: Stan Cohen, Owen Gassaway (Florida Airmotive), Todd Hackbarth, Norm Thompson, John Wegg, and especially, my understanding wife and patient sons.

Nick Veronico: A. Kevin Grantham, W.T. Larkins, Milo Peltzer, Dale Collier (Otis Spunkmeyer), Taigh Ramey, Luis Hernandez, Mike Bossert, Robert D. McSwiggan, Paul Salerno, Steve Franklin, Maria Guerrero, Pamela Veronico, Kathy Markowski, Todd Hackbart and Armand H. Veronico.

The authors would also like to acknowledge the following sources: Air Britain's excellent *The Douglas DC-3 and its predecessors*, and both Updates 1 and 2, as edited by J.M.G. Gradidge; Douglas *DC-3 Survivors*, Volumes 1 and 2, by Arthur Pearcy, *U.S. Military Aircraft Designations and Serials*, by John Andrade, and *The DC-3: 50 Years of Legendary Flight*, by Peter M. Bowers.

Notes about the text..

Because of the wide variety of identification marks assigned to most DC-3s in their half-century utilization, we have included the manufacturer's serial number (msn) as the base identification for individual aircraft. The msn, also commonly referred to as constructor's number (c/n) is that number assigned to individual airframes by Douglas as they were being assembled. With DC-3s, this method does not eliminate confusion because some DC-3s were assigned, in error, two manufacturer's serial numbers. We have chosen, as a method to reduce confusion, only to provide the corrected msn for each aircraft. Also, those R4D-8/C-117D airframes remanufactured by Douglas were assigned a new msn, but this is explained, where appropriate, in the text. Finally, we included the msn wherever possible to assist serious students of the DC-3.

Preface

"Oakland Center, Douglas niner six bravo foxtrot checking on at Flight Level two six zero."

"Douglas niner six bravo foxtrot, Oakland Center, roger...are you showing a ground speed readout?"

"Center, Douglas six bravo foxtrot is showing two hundred knots."

"Roger, six bravo foxtrot. Verify your type aircraft again."

"Oakland Center, Douglas niner six bravo foxtrot is a Douglas DC-3."

Sixty years after the first flight of the Douglas DC-3, Douglas N96BF was encroaching upon the high-flying, high-speed territory of the modern jetliner. The pilot of this newly modified, turboprop-powered antique and his puzzled controller friend hadn't been born when N96BF was rolled from the Douglas-Oklahoma City plant in May 1944. Neither had their parents.

The longevity and exploits of the Gooney Bird are legendary. Replaced in the 1940s by the Martin 202 and Convair 240, more of the famous Douglas airliners are still flying than both of these types combined. During the subsequent decade, the DeHavilland Comet, the Boeing 707, and the Douglas DC-8 ushered in the jet age. These aircraft are already endangered species, seen far less frequently than the plane that is justly credited with giving birth to the entire air transport industry. When the last supersonic Concorde has long been relegated as a museum curiosity, Douglas DC-3s will still be flying somewhere in this world.

Douglas DC-3: 60 Years and Counting takes a close look at some of the more obscure uses of this veteran transport through the years, with a particular emphasis on a few of the special tasks the DC-3 has performed in its service. Also included is a special focus on its more recent activities: where and why more than 1,000 DC-3s continue to ply the skies around the world, and how new technology is transforming this timeless airframe into a modern, solid performer that will keep some of them in the air well into the 21st century and, quite possibly, to the DC-3's own centennial date of 2035.

As the authors of this book, we were trying to avoid producing just "another DC-3 book." Rather, we were quite intentional on looking at the DC-3 from a fresh perspective and somewhat apart from the type's much-documented use as a passenger-carrying transport. So, we have examined the DC-3 in the historical light of its service with the U.S. CAA and FAA, as well as other obscure but significant uses. We have taken a close look at the numerous efforts to modernize the DC-3 with new engines and airframe modifications, and some of the successes those efforts are producing. We looked around the world to see where a person can still catch a ride on a DC-3 and, also, where a person can even grasp a throttle full of Pratt & Whitney to actually fly one. We've gathered as many photos of interesting DC-3s as we could find, and added enough detailed appendices about a variety of DC-3s to hold even the most dedicated DC-3 enthusiast's attention. Much of the information and most of the photos you see here won't be found published anywhere else, which also was our intent. We think we have succeeded in the above, and hope you agree.

Ed Davies, Scott Thompson, and Nicholas Veronico

Ed Davies

Chapter 1

Where in the world...

...can you catch a ride in a DC-3?

The development of the world's air transportation system and the story of the Douglas DC-3 are inexorably intertwined. During the years immediately prior to World War II, the DC-3 had revolutionized air travel and was carrying 95 percent of the world's airline passengers. During the war, countless Allied soldiers, sailors and airmen were introduced to this relatively new form of transportation. For many of them their first flight in a plane was aboard a rugged *Gooney Bird* or *Dakota*.

Though already obsolete after World War II, converted C-47s were thrown into stop-gap service by the airlines to meet the needs of the explosive expansion in civilian air travel. After only a few years, they were displaced on the long-haul routes by the newer, faster, more comfortable four-engined airliners that were rolling off the peacetime Douglas and Lockheed assembly lines. Still, the DC-3s lingered on in airline service, handed down to work the short-haul scheduled routes or to fly for the many non-scheduled operators that had sprung up all over the world.

New turboprop equipment eventually relegated the big taildraggers from even the short-haul passenger market. But still plentiful and cheap, and with many hours left on the rugged airframes, DC-3s found yet another niche in the airplane marketplace. Fitted out with luxurious interiors, some became executive aircraft with major corporations. Others, with their interiors gutted, became freighters and eventually joined the rapidly developing express parcel business. A few remained in military service, funneling a supply of low time airframes into the civilian market up through the 1980s. A few countries, notably Israel and South Africa, still have significant numbers of DC-3s in their air force's inventory.

The number of airworthy DC-3s dwindled rapidly in the late 1980s. Engine overhaul costs, mandated inspection schedules for older aircraft, and the availability of newer equipment have all made DC-3s less attractive in North America and Europe for even the low utilization freight routes. Inevitably, many were exported to South America or for relief work in Africa where their low cost, short rough-field capability, and simple maintenance remain overwhelming advantages.

When seemingly doomed to extinction or reduced to museum status, some of the best examples of the enduring DC-3 were acquired and refurbished for a boom in nostalgia tour-type operations. Unfortunately, the high cost of insurance, particularly in the United States, has lately threatened even this type of flying. However, it is still possible (though not easy) to purchase a ride in the plane that changed the world. Information on some of the remaining DC-3 operations is listed for the benefit of the enthusiast and/or adventurer. Frequent changes in South America have precluded a listing from this area still rich in DC-3s. Even for those operators in the following listings, however, it is always advisable to call ahead for the current schedule or status.

North America

Air Cruise America

1 Via Pasa
San Clemente, CA 92673-2750
Phone: (800) FLY DC3S or (714) 661-8410
Fax: (714) 240-0498

Offers champagne flights over the Southern California coastline from the Long Beach Airport. Also offers group flights, private charters, *Temecula Valley Wine Flights*, and special events (such as weddings) as requested.

DC-3s:
N7500A (msn 11693), C-53D 42-68766, delivered to the USAAF in April 1943. Surplus in August 1945 and acquired by Eastern Airlines as NC45332. Converted to a corporate transport by L.B. Smith Aircraft and flown by Ramapo Foundry, Triangle Construction, and Hecht Construction companies. Returned to passenger flights with Mercer and Pacific American Airlines before being bought by actor John Travolta in 1977. Bought by the present owner, Jan Aarvik, doing business as Britt Odin Air in 1983. Used for skydiving out of California City, and participated in the DC-3 Air Rally, Vancouver, Canada in June 1986.

Stan Cohen

Air North

P.O Box 4998,
Whitehorse, Yukon Y1A 4S2, Canada
Phone: (403) 668-2228
Fax: (403) 668-6224

Offers scheduled air service from Whitehorse to Juneau, Dawson City, Fairbanks, and Old Crow.

DC-3s:
CF-CUG (msn 9891), C-47A 42-24029, delivered to the USAAF in July 1943. Surplus in March 1946, registered CF-CUG to Canadian Pacific Airlines in May 1947. Eldorado Aviation of Edmonton in February 1958, and leased to pacific Western and Echo Bay Mines. Sold to Air North in December 1979.
CF-IMA (msn 13070), C-47A 42-93186, delivered to the USAAF in April 1944. Surplus in June 1946, registered NC88740 to the Gulf Research and Development Company. Became CF-IMA in 1961, registered to Canadian Aero Services in Ottawa. Flew with Survair, Questor Surveys and the Gestalt Corporation before being acquired by Air North in 1988.
C-GZOF (msn 20833), C-47B 43-16367, delivered to the USAAF in August 1944. Converted to an SC-47D for search and rescue missions. Surplus in 1961, sold to Aero American Corporation and stored near Tucson, Arizona, until 1974. Registered C-GZOF to Contact Airways of Fort McMurray, Alberta, in August 1975. Purchased by Air North in 1986.

Ed Davies

Michael Prophet via Ed Davies

Nick Veronico

Alexander Airplane Company

118 Huff Daland Circle
Griffin, GA 30223
Phone: (800) 831-2949
Fax: (401) 227-7298

Offers one day DC-3 adventures, including ground school and two hours flight time, from Spalding County Airport, GA. Private pilots license required.

DC-3s:
N28AA (msn 2239), DC-3-314A, delivered to Braniff in June 1940, registered NC25666. Sold to Trans Texas Airlines in 1953, to Tradewinds in February 1969 and Air Mid America in 1971. Served briefly with Cryderman Air Services before being bought by Provincetown-Boston Airlines in June 1978 and registered N139PB. When PBA collapsed, Starflite Corporation, a well known broker of DC-3 type aircraft bought several of the fleet, including N139PB. Sold to Alexander Airplane Company, and re-registered N28AA in August 1992.

Brooks Aviation

P.O.Box 610
Douglas, GA 31533
Phone: (912) 384-7818
Fax: (912) 384-1849

Offers ground instruction and flight time in an historic Dakota that took part in the Normandy invasion.

DC-3s:
N99FS (msn 12425), C-47A 42-92606, Dakota III KG395, delivered to the RAF in February 1944. Took part in the Normandy invasion, June 1944 (See Chapter 6, *Return to Normandy*, for a detailed account of the history of this aircraft). Acquired by Don Brooks in April 1989.

Ed Davies

N99FS (msn 12425) shortly before embarking on its historic "Return to Normandy" in May 1994. Brooks Aviation continues to offer flight time in their DC-3. (Ed Davies)

N99FS in an earlier paint scheme, this view taken at Oshkosh in August 1992. (Nick Veronico)

Buffalo Airways

Box 4998
Hay River, NWT XOE ORO Canada
Phone: (403) 874-3333
Fax: (403) 874-3572

Scheduled passenger and freight services from Hay River to Yellowknife and Ft. Simpson.

DC-3s:
C-GPNR (msn 13333), C-47A 42-93423, Dakota III KG602, delivered to the RAF at Montreal in May 1944. Served with 437 Squadron in the U.K., returning to Canada with the RCAF after the war. Declared surplus, it was purchased by Buffalo Airways Ltd., and registered C-GPNR in April 1981.
C-GWZS (msn 12327), C-47A 42-92518, Dakota III KG330, delivered to the RAF in Montreal February 1944. Served with 437 Squadron in the U.K., returning to Canada with the RCAF after the war. Declared surplus it was bought by Can-Air Services and registered C-GWZS in May 1976. Acquired by Buffalo Airways Ltd. in June 1988.
C-FLFR (msn 13155), C-47A 42-93263, Dakota III, KG563, delivered to the RAF at Montreal in May 1944. Served with 436 Squadron in the U.K., returning to Canada with the RCAF after the war. Declared surplus, it was acquired by St. Felicien Air Services and registered CF-LFR in December 1969. Flew for Survair and Bradley Air Services before being bought by Buffalo Airways.

Steve Tournay via Ed Davies

Classic Airlines

P.O. Box 246
Collingwood, Ontario L9Y 3Z5 Canada.
Phone: (705) 445-1616
Fax: (705) 445-6503

Based at Collingwood, Ontario, Canada. Late word at press time indicates that this successful operation was forced to suspend its DC-3 service on January 31, 1995, when its annual insurance premium was tripled to nearly C$100,000 per year. This enormous increase being levied upon operators of aircraft the size of the DC-3 has also forced Island Airways of Nantucket, Massachussetts to shut down what was the last remaining scheduled DC-3 passenger service in the United States.

DC-3s:
C-FWGO (msn 4932), XC-53A 42-6480, delivered to the USAAF in July 1952. Retained by Douglas at Santa Monica for conversion to full span flaps with an engine exhaust deicing system. Surplus in 1949, it was fitted with standard C-47 wings and registered N69032 to the Brinkerhoff Drilling Company. Flew with Corning Glass as N48CG and N480G. Went to C.W. Millard in Canada as CF-WGO in June 1967. Registered to Spartan Air Services and Airdale Ltd in Canada, before being acquired by John Worts of Collingwood Air for his nostalgia charter business.

Otis Spunkmeyer Air

14390 Catalina Street
San Leandro, CA 94577
Phone: (800) 989-1900
Fax: (510) 352-5680

Offers one hour nostalgic air tours over San Francisco from Oakland International Airport, North Field.

DC-3s:
N97H (msn33613) C-47B 44-77281, delivered to the USAAF in July 1945. Acquired by Bill Celli Leasing for Otis Spunkmeyer Air in June 1988.
NC41HQ (msn 2053), C-41 38-502, delivered to the USAAC in October 1938. Acquired by Bill Celli Leasing for Otis Spunkmeyer Air in May 1989. For more detailed history on both of these aircraft see *Return to Normandy*.

Ed Davies

Vintage Air Photo via Ed Davies

Vintage Airways/South Florida Sea Ventures, Inc.

2 Marco Lake Drive, Suite 6
Marco Island, FL
Phone: (800) 835-9323
Fax: (813) 642-1080

Orlando-based Vintage Air Tours, the brainchild of Virgin Atlantic's Richard Branson, ceased its nostalgic flight operations in October 1994. The two DC-3s have since been acquired by Terry Fansone, and the reborn Vintage Airways runs from Naples and Ft. Meyers to Key West, operating in conjunction with South Florida Sea Venture's high-speed ferry boats. Special packages offer service to Ft. Lauderdale and connections with a Laker Boeing 727 to Freeport in the Bahamas.

DC-3s:
N12RB (msn 20401), C-47A 43-15935, delivered to the USAAF in May 1944 for service in the South Pacific. Surplus to requirements after the war and sold to Silver City Airways in Australia, being registered as VH-BHC. Re-registered in the U.S. as N94529 and operated by Standard Industries beginning in December 1950. Served with a number of companies as both executive transport and cargo hauler before being registered in October 1992 as N12RB to Dakota Aircraft for operation by Vintage Air.
N22RB (msn 4926), C-53 42-6474, delivered to the USAAF in April 1942 and serving with the U.S. during the war. Released as surplus after the war and operated in Mexico by a commercial carrier. Returned to the U.S. in the early 1950s and operated by the Eastman Kodak Company as N46TE. Later owned by serveral corporations before being ferried to Hawaii to operate both sightseeing and scheduled inter-island service for Air Molokai-Tropic Airlines. Registered as N22RB to Dakota Aircraft for operations by Vintage Air in August 1992.

Europe

Air Atlantique

Hangar 5
Coventry Airport
Coventry CV8 3AZ U.K.
Phone: 0203 307 566
Fax: 0203 307703

Day return flights from Coventry to various U.K. air displays and special events.

DC-3s:
G-AMPZ (msn 32872), C-47B 44-76540, Dakota IV KN442, delivered to the RAF at Montreal in March 1945. Served in the U.K. with 525 and 46 Squadrons RAF. Declared surplus, it was registered G-AMPZ to Starways in March 1952. Flew for British United and Silver City Airways, among a host of other owners. Served with Harvest Air's off-shore pollution control fleet before eventually being acquired by Air Atlantique in September 1990.
G-AMRA (msn 26735), C-47B 43-49474, Dakota III KK151, delivered to the RAF at Montreal in December 1944. Served in the U.K. with 525 and 238 Squadrons RAF. Declared surplus and registered as G-AMRA to Starways in March 1952. Purchased and leased by a number of operators before becoming an Air Atlantique acquisition in October 1981.

Geoff Hill via Ed Davies

Air Atlantique is operated by the Atlantic Group, which also operates seven DC-3s under contract with the U.K.'s Marine Pollution Control Unit. The DC-3s are used to spray an oil detergent and disperser. (Phillips Petroleum)

Airveteran OY

Finnish Helsinki-Malmi Airport
Office 55,
00700 Helsinki, Finland
Phone: 358 0-379060
Fax: 358 0-889719

Scenic flights, restricted to shareholders and DC-3 Association members only.

DC-3s:
OH-LCD (msn 19309), C-47A 42-100846, delivered to the USAAF in December 1943, serving with the 8th Air Force in Europe. Made available to the Government of Finland, it was converted by Fokker to a civil DC-3C-S1C3G airliner and registered OH-LCD in April 1947. Converted to a freighter in 1966 and assigned to the Finnish Air Force Transport Wing in 1969. Given serial number DO-8, it was used mainly for aerial photography. Sold to Airveteran Ltd. in January 1986. Stored and awaiting restoration.
OH-LCH (msn 6346), C-53C 43-2033. Built originally for Pan Am, it was requisitioned and delivered to the USAAF in December 1942. Served in Europe with the 8th Air Force. Made available to the Government of Finland after the war and converted to a civil airliner by the State Metal Factory at Tampere. Withdrawn from service in 1960, it was used for parts until rebuilt as a freighter in 1963. Sold to the Finnish Air Force in 1970, serving in the Transport Wing at Utti AFB as DO-11. Bought by Airveteran Ltd in 1986, restored, and given its old call sign OH-LCH.

Flygande Veteraner DC-3 SE-CFP (msn 13883) in color scheme of SE-BAA in 1990. (C. Munk via Michael Prophet and Ed Davies)

Classic Air

Post Box 276
CH-8058 Zurich-Flughafen
Switzerland
Phone: 01 814 30 85
Fax: 01 814 19 04

Luxury tours and charters throughout Switzerland and the rest of Europe.

DC-3s:
HB-ISB (msn 4666), C-47D 41-18541, delivered to the USAAF in September 1942 and subsequently served in North Africa. Surplus in November 1945 and acquired by Canadian Pacific Airlines. Converted for passenger operation by Douglas and registered as CF-CPW. Sold to Trans Air Ltd. in August 1957 and re-registered CF-TAS. Owned by several other Canadian companies before being bought by Classic Air in October 1985. Ferried to Switzerland via the North Atlantic route in November 1985. Operated Classic Air's first commercial flight on May 10, 1986.
HB-ISC (msn 9995), C-47A 42-24133, delivered to the USAAF in August 1943 serving domestically in the U.S. Surplus after September 1945 and sold to Salem Engineering Company and registered as NC65266 and later, NC6K. Bought by National Lead in 1953 and re-registered as N88Y in 1966. Operated by various owners in the U.S. until acquired by Aces High in the U.K. and registered as G-BMCR in 1985. Purchased by Classic Air in March 1986, refurbished, and registered as HB-ISC. Operated its first commercial flight in March 1987.

Dakota Norway

Sandefjord Lufthaven
N-3200 Sandefjord
Norway
Phone: 34 70 300

Tours and flights to European air displays. All passengers are enrolled as members of the society.

DC-3s:
LN-WND (msn 11750), C-53D 42-68823, delivered to the USAAF in June 1943 and taken on charge by the 8th Air Force in Europe in October of that year. Surplus to requirements, it was ferried to R-13 at Oberpfaffenhofen in Germany for storage in January 1948. Delivered to the Finnish Government in June 1948 and refurbished, registered as OH-LCG, and operated by Finnair. Sold to the Finnish Air Force in 1969, flown as a VIP transport, serial number DO-9, until retirement in 1985. One of two Finnish DC-3s bought by Arne Karlsen, Tom Karlsen, and Thore Virik in January 1985. One was resold to Aces High, and DO-9 acquired the temporary U.S. registration of N59NA prior to certification in Norway. Finally registered LN-WND in July 1986.

Michael Prophet via Ed Davies

Flygande Veteraner

Flygplatsinfaren 41
S-161 69 Bromma
Sweden
Phone: 08 764 5208

Flights to air shows and special events for members of Flygande Veteraner and their guests.

DC-3s:
SE-CFP (msn 13883), C-47A 43-30732, delivered to the USAAF in October 1943, operating with the 7th Air Force in North Africa. Returned to the U.S. and declared surplus in October 1945. Converted to airliner configuration by Canadair and served with Norwegian Airline DNL, registered LN-IAF. Transferred to the newly formed SAS in 1948, remaining with them until transferred to the Swedish domestic airline Linjeflyg in 1957 and registered as SE-CFP. Acquired by the Swedish Air Force in 1960 and assigned serial number 79006, taking part in many Red Cross relief missions. Phased out in 1983 and purchased by the Flygande Veteraner Association, founded specifically to maintain and operate the DC-3. First flight for the society took place in June 1984.

Dutch Dakota Association

P.O.Box 75090
1117 ZP, Schiphol Airport
Netherlands
Phone: 31 20 6010132
Fax: 31 20 6010858

Formed in 1982 to "purchase, maintain and fly historic aircraft." Operates moonlight cruises and day trips to European air shows, and offers weekend packages.

DC-3s:

PH-DDA (msn 19109), C-47A 42-100646, delivered to the USAAF in November 1943 and serving with both the 8th and 9th Air Forces in Europe. Surplus to requirements, was stored in Germany until acquired by the Finnish Government. Converted to airliner status by Fokker Aircraft and registered OH-LCB for operations with Finnair. Sold to the Finnish Air Force in 1962 as DO-7, remaining in military service until 1983. The Dutch Dakota Association was formed in March 1982 with the object of acquiring and operating a Dakota aircraft. They bought DO-7 and, after a major overhaul in Finland, it was flown to Schipol where it was registered PH-DDA in January 1984.

PH-DDZ (msn 19754), C-47A 43-15288, delivered to the USAAF in March 1944. After surplus, transferred to the U.S. CAA and, later, FAA for government use. (See Appendix 2 for a detailed history of this aircraft.) Originally acquired by the Dutch Dakota Association to be preserved for study by future generations of engineers, it was decided in 1991 to refurbish this Dakota to flying status as a back up for PH-DDA.

Paul Horst via Ed Davies

Africa

Air Kenya Aviation

Wilson Airport
P.O. Box 30357
Nairobi, Kenya
Phone: 254 501601
Fax: 254 500845.

Ron Mak via Ed Davies

Scheduled and charter flights from Wilson Airport, Nairobi.

DC-3s:
5Y-AAE (msn 32844), C-47B 44-76512, Dakota IV KN418, delivered to the RAF at Montreal in March 1945. Ferried to the U.K. and assigned to 187 Squadron at Merryfield, being used for troop flights to India. Transferred in May 1946 to 525 Squadron, then to 1381 Transport Conversion Unit.The last operational service was with No. 1 Parachute Training School at Ringway in Manchester, after which it was mothballed at 22 Maintenance Unit in Siloth in July 1950. Two years later it was purchased by the East African Airways Corporation and registered as VP-KJQ. Re-registered 5Y-AAE in 1964 and sold to Caspair/Sunbird Aviation in 1977. Joined Air Kenya when they took over Sunbird in November 1987.
5Y-BGU (msn 4890), C-53 41-20120, delivered to the USAAF in March 1942. Declared surplus to requirements in May 1945 and sold to Iberia Airlines in Spain, being registered as EC-DAL and later, EC-ABQ. Transferred to the Spanish Air Force as T3-58, which operated the aircraft at the IFR training school at Matacan AFB in the northwest of Spain. Bought by Fairoaks Aviation Services in 1978 and registered in the U.K. as G-BFXA. In November 1978 it was sold to to the Kenana Sugar Corporation and registered in the Sudan as ST-AHK. Ownership transferred to Caspair/Sunbird Aviation in 1979, and to Air Kenya after the take-over in November 1987.

Avia Air Charter

P.O. Box 14471
Sinoville 0129
South Africa
Phone: 27 12 543 0824
Fax: 27 12 543 0683

Freight and passenger charters from Wonderboom to destinations throughout Africa.

DC-3s:
ZS-MRU (msn 4363), R4D-1 BuNo 04703, delivered to the U.S. Navy in May 1942. Struck off charge in November 1946, it briefly served with Expreso Aereo as C-900 before beginning a long career as a corporate aircraft with several U.S. companies. In August 1979, this plush aircraft was acquired by HRH Prince Talal Bin Aboul Aziz El Saud of Saudia Arabia and registered as HZ-TA3. DC-3 ferried from Houston to Jeddah, arriving September 12, 1979. The prince donated the aircraft to UNICEF in the early 1980s for use in Africa, and it eventually appeared back on the U.S. registered as N234Z in March 1987. Acquired by Avia in October 1990.
ZS-GPL (msn 9581), C-47A 42-23719, delivered to the USAAF in May 1945. Stored surplus to requirements at Ontario, California. In August 1946 it was sold to General Airways of Portland, Oregon, and registered N47573. Decorated with a distinctive rose on its tail, the DC-3 flew ad hoc passenger and freight charters in the Pacific Northwest and Alaska. Between 1966 and March 1971 it was operated by North American Aviation, American Rockwell, and the Elbee Company in the U.S. Ferried to Africa, it was registered as ZS-GPL to Grinair, A2-ACH to Air Services Botswana and back to ZS-GPL with United Air Services. Extensively damaged while flying for Sandriver Safaris in a takeoff accident in February 1985. It was subsequently rebuilt and later registered to Avia Air Charter.
ZS-PTG (msn 13331), C-47A 42-93421, Dakota III KG600, delivered to the RAF at Montreal in May 1944 and ferried to the U.K. Taken on strength by the RCAF in June 1946 and initially loaned to Trans Canada Airlines. Converted to an instructional airframe in 1953 and struck off in November 1960. Registered in the U.K. as G-ASDX to Standard Telephone and Cable in November 1962. Went to South Africa in 1974, registered ZS-PTG to United Air Services and later transferred to Avia Air Charter.

New Zealand

Pionair Adventures

Sightseeing and charters from Queenstown, New Zealand.

DC-3s:
ZK-AMS (msn 9286), C-47A 42-23424, delivered to the RAAF as A65-9 during May 1943, one of 124 Dakotas turned over to the RAAF under the Lend-Lease program. Acquired by Quantas Empire Airways after the war and registered as VH-EAM in December 1946. Joined East-West Airlines in 1953 when DC-3s replaced the airline's Ansons for scheduled service in New South Wales. Re-registered VH-EWF in 1959 and leased to Airlines of South Australia in June 1965. Operated for a number of Australian airlines during the next decade and was again re-registered VH-PWN. Bought by Dick Lang in August 1992 for use as for nostalgia tour flights, but sold to Pionair Adventures in New Zealand for sight seeing and charter work in November 1993.

via Ed Davies

Warbird Dakota

GeostarTravel
1240 Century Court
Santa Rosa, CA 95403 (U.S.)
Phone: (800) 624 6633
Fax: (707) 579 2704

Offers Sunday sight seeing tours from Aukland's Ardmore Aerodrome and luxury air tours of New Zealand.

DC-3s:
ZK-DAK (msn 26480), C-47B 43-49219, delivered to the USAAF in October 1944. After surplus, converted to an airliner and transferred to Philippine Airlines as PI-C486. In December 1969 it was purchased by Papuan Air Transport and registered as VH-PNM, remaining with the airline when it was taken over by Ansett in July 1970. Leased and later bought by Bush Pilots Airways, Ltd., and based at Cairns. Purchased by the Mackay Air Museum in November 1983 and re-registered as VH-SBT. Purchased by the Warbird Dakota Society in 1987 and registered as ZK-DAK.

Australia

Ansett Australia

501 Swanston Street
Melbourne, VIC 3000
Phone: 03 668 1211
Fax: 03 668 1144
Charters and airshow appearances for Ansett staff, from Melbourne/Tullamarine Airport.

DC-3s:
VH-ABR (msn 2029), DC-3-202A delivered to Australian National Airways Pty Ltd. in October 1938, named *Kanana*. Conscripted into the Royal Australian Air Force in September 1939 as A30-3, serving briefly with 8 Squadron based in Canberra. Returned to the airline in May 1940. Withdrawn from use in October 1975, this aircraft was restored to flying condition by Ansett for the 1988 Bicentennial Air Show at Richmond.

South Pacific Airmotive's VH-MIN (msn 13459) in November 1993 while based at Cairns. The company's name was recently changed from Dakota Downunder. (Paul Howard via Ed Davies)

South Pacific Airmotive

263 Connells Point Road
Connells Point NSW 2221
Phone: (060) 21 1136
Fax: (060) 41 2293

Outback tours from Albury and Cairns Airports. Named changed from Dakota Downunder in 1995.

DC-3s:
VH-MIN (msn 13459), C-47B 42-93536, Dakota III KG647, delivered to the RAF in Montreal in June 1944, and leased briefly by BOAC as G-AIAZ. Transferred to Australia in 1946 as VH-SMI for the Sydney Morning Herald. Registered VH-MIN and operated by the Bureau of Mineral Resources in December 1954. Several other operators, including Northern Airlines, Setair, Rebel Air and Splitter's Creek Airlines.
VH-CAN (msn 13506), C-47A 42-93579, delivered to the USAAF in June 1944. Operated by Dakota Downunder before being sold to Vincent Aviation in New Zealand in August 1994 as ZK-AMY.
VH-MMA (msn 9583), C-47A 42-23721, delivered to the USAAF in May 1943. Transferred to the Dutch Marine Luchtvaartdeinst during 1946. Converted to a civil DC-3 and registered as VH-MMA to MacRobertson Miller Aviation in October 1947. Later flew for Ansett Airlines. Acquired from Air North in 1994.
VH-SPY (msn 33113), C-47B 44-76781, delivered to the RAAF as A65-102 in May 1945. Registered to South Pacific Airmotive in January 1995.

Dakota National Air

Office 3, Building 483
Airport Avenue
Bankstown Airport, NSW 2200
Phone: 043 24 6451
Fax: 043 23 3422

One of the largest DC-3 civil operators, Dakota National Air operates scenic Australian air tours, champagne night flights, specialty adventure flights, corporate and private charters from Bankstown airport.

DC-3s:

VH-SBL (msn 12056), C-47A 42-92274, delivered to the Royal Australian Air Force as A65-29 during January 1944. After the war, it was sold to Trans Australian Airlines and registered as VH-TAE in September 1946. Leased to New Zealand National Airlines in 1960 and re-registered as VH-SBL on its return to TAA. Sold to Air Niugini in November 1973, registered first as P2-SBL, and later as P2-ANR. Returned to Australia in October 1976, regaining the registration of VH-SBL with Forrester Stephen Pty Ltd. After a period of storage at Essendon, it was acquired by CranwaysPty Ltd., doing business as General Cargo in November 1981. Several transactions later, it was purchased by Travair, refurbished, and began operating nostalgia flights for them in 1987. Acquired by Dakota National Air in 1992.

VH-DNA (msn 27130), C-47B 43-49869, delivered to the Royal Australian Air Force as A65-68 in January 1945. One of six Australian Dakotas presented to the Papua New Guinea Defense Force, it was transferred in January 1976 and assigned serial number P2-004. Surplus to requirements and released for disposal in 1993. Subsequently purchased by Dakota National Air.

VH-ATO (msn 33109), C-47B 44-76777, delivered to the Royal Australian Air Force as A65-100 in May 1945. Another one of the aircraft transferred to the PNGDF, this one as P65-001, and similarly acquired by Dakota National Air in the 1993 auction. Currently stored at Warnervale.

VH-UPQ (msn 33300). C-47B 44-76968, delivered to the Royal Australian Air Force as A65-105 in May 1945. Withdrawn from use at the Woomera Rocket Range in 1973 and operated, in turn, by Connair, Northern Air Lines, and Setair. Registered to Colbinra Transport, doing business as Rebel Air before being acquired by Dakota National Air in 1993.

VH-BPN (msn 32945), C-47B 44-76613, Dakota IV RAF KN470, delivered in March 1945. Assigned to the Pakistani Air Force after World War II as serial number H-717. First registered in Australia in April 1954 to MacRoberston Miller Aviation as VH-MML. Recently acquired by Dakota National Air from Dick Lang's Desert Air Safaris.

VH-PWN (msn 26001), C-47B 43-48740, Dakota IV RAAF A65-63, delivered to 38 Squadron in September 1944. One of six operational Dakotas presented to the Papua New Guinea Defense Force where it assumed serial number P2-005. Surplus to requirements and bought by Dick Lang in 1993 and recently sold to Dakota National Air.

Dakota National Air's VH-PWN (msn 26001) in the finish of a previous owner. (Paul Howard via Ed Davies)

via Ed Davies

Shortstop Jet Charters

Hangar 5
Wirraway Road, Essendon Airport
Victoria, VIC 3041
Phone: 03 379 9299
Fax: 03 379 3643

Twilight, Bistro, and elegant Silver Clipper dinner flights from Essendon, flying over Port Phillip Bay and Melbourne. Charters and flight training.

<u>DC-3s</u>:
VH-OVM (msn 33102), C-47B 44-76770, delivered to the RAAF in May 1945 as A65-98. Served with the Transport Support Flight at Butterworth, Malaysia and for apprentice training at Wagga Wagga. Retired to the RAAF Museum at Point Cook as VH-JXD, then registered to Shortstop Jet Charters in June 1990.

Ed Davies

Chapter 2

Where in the World...

...can you skydive from a DC-3?

On June 6, 1944, an armada of C-47s and C-53s dropped thousands of paratroopers into France to spearhead the Allied seaborne invasion. Skydiving has since become a popular civilian sport, and for years DC-3 survivors have served as a popular launch platform this exhilarating pastime. As recently as August 1990, five Gooney Birds were assembled at Lodi, California, in an attempt to break the state record for the number of people joining up during the free-fall portion of the jump. Slowly, however, the Twin Otter has supplanted the DC-3 as the aircraft of choice for competitive skydiving, leaving but a handful of locations where the DC-3 is still used. Following is a listing of those centers in the United States that still make available the big taildragger as a jump ship. However, because of the ever changing situation, readers would be well advised to call ahead for current information.

Eddie Gibson via Ed Davies

United States

Dallas Skydive Center

8324 Lake June Road
Dallas, TX 75217
Telephone or Fax: (214) 398-2360 or, on weekends, (214) 957-4801

DC-3s:
N408D (msn 2247), built as a DC-3-201D and delivered as NC15596 to Eastern Airlines in September 1940. Acquired by Capital Airways in 1952. Subsequently flew with Mohawk where it was re-registered N409D, finishing its scheduled airline career when it was retired by North Central in 1964. Painted in desert camouflage after it was purchased by Jack Ormes in 1983. Earned a red cross on the tail after flying mercy missions in El Salvador during 1986. Flew skydivers for Larry Hill out of Coolidge, Arizona, before being acquired and refurbished by "Doc" Linden.

Remarks:
Based near Sherman, Texas, approximately 75 miles north of Dallas and operated by Richard "Doc" Linden.

N408D operates as Lady Luck *for the Dallas Skydive Center.(Ed Davies)*

Mr. Douglas

P.O. Box 1119
De Leon Springs, FL 32130
Telephone: (904) 736-3539

DC-3s:
N129H (msn 4126), built as DC-3A-197E and delivered to United Airlines in April 1941 as NC33647. Acquired by Western Airlines in 1942, continuing as part of their fleet until 1958. Registered as N129H to H.W. Jamieson Enterprises in 1963 and, later, several civil operators. Purchased by Mark Borghorst in late 1981. This aircraft was featured recently in the movie *Drop Zone*.

Remarks:
Skydiving from DeLand Airport, which is operated by Mark Borghorst.

Scott Thompson

Parachute Center

P.O. Box 423
Acampo. CA 95220
Phone: (209) 369-1128

<u>DC-3s</u>:
N4991E (msn 12106), C-47A 42-92319, Dakota III FRZ571, delivered to the RCAF at Patricia Bay, Canada, in January 1944. Converted by Canadair during 1946 for service with Trans Canada Airlines as CF-TDU. Re-registered as N4991E to Frontier Airlines in the U.S. in 1958. Several civil operators after 1968. Acquired by Bill Dause Sr. in 1976.
N45366 (msn 11757), C-53D 42-68830, delivered to the USAAF in July 1943. Declared surplus to requirements in August 1945. Converted to airliner configuration and registered as NC45366, first to Penn Central. Later became *Capitaliner Toledo* when the airline's name was changed in 1948. When Capital's DC-3s were displaced by Viscounts in 1959, it was sold to the Crucible Steel Company, serving as an executive aircraft. Eventually arriving at Lodi, it was totally rebuilt by Dan Kitley and test flown in 1991. Currently registered to the Lodi Airport manager, doing business as DC-3 Flights Inc.

Remarks:
Operated Bill Dause.
Jump center at Lodi Airport, located just off Highway 99 north of Lodi, California.

N45366 (msn 11757) being rebuilt at Lodi, California. (Ed Davies)

Paralift, Inc.

P.O. Box 332
Perris, CA 92572
Telephone: (909) 657-7185

DC-3s:
N20TW (msn 2236), built as a DC-3-201C and delivered to Eastern Airlines as NC25648 in June 1940. Flew for Mackey, North Central, and Galaxy Airlines through 1970. Registered as N20TW to Tri-World Enterprise in 1976, then passed through several owners. Began carrying skydivers from Perris Valley Airfield in California in 1987. Registered to Skip Evans, doing business as Paralift Inc.
N26MA (msn 2169), built as a DC-3-313 for Penn Central Airlines and delivered in November 1939 as NC21781. Titled *Capitaliner Detroit* when the airline's name was changed to Capital Airlines in 1948. Briefly flew for United Airlines when they absorbed Capital in June 1961. Converted to an executive aircraft by Remmert Werner and then flew for a number of owners as N180W and N180WK. The aircraft was re-registered as N26MA when it was acquired by Mercy Air Lift in 1977. N20TW began its career as a skydiving DC-3 in 1979 and is currently registered to Paralift Inc.

Remarks:
Skip Evan's two DC-3s are based at Bear Creek Airport (Murrieta, California), and used mainly for promotional and movie work; however, groups calling ahead can still book one of the big twins.

N20TW loading skydivers in the Wright-powered ex-Eastern airliner at Perris Valley in July 1989. (Ed Davies)

Skydive Arizona

4900 N. Tumbleweed Road
Eloy, AZ 85231
Telephone: (602) 466-3753
Fax: (602) 466-4720

DC-3s:
N86584 (msn 4935), C-53 42-6483, delivered to the USAAC in May 1942. Served in Britain and the Middle East during World War II. Declared surplus to requirements and converted by Canadair in Montreal. Registered as NC86584 and entered airline service with Eastern during 1946. Converted by Aerodex to a Wright-powered DC-3-G202A in 1953, it went to Mackey Airlines where it was named *City of Palm Beach*. Currently registered to Aerospecialists Inc., it flew skydivers out of Coolidge, Arizona, before recently being moved to Eloy. Operated as *Colonel Joe*.

Remarks:
Company operates one DC-3 and four Twin Otters out of Eloy, Arizona.
Owned and operated by Larry Hill.

Indonesia

Federation of Air Sports Indonesia (FASI)

Pondok Cabe

Air Force 4752 (msn unknown)
Air Force 4775 (msn 13334)
Air Force 4776 (msn unknown)
Air Force 4777 (msn unknown)
Air Force 4790 (msn unknown)

FASI, sponsored by the Indonesian armed forces, is believed to be open to civilian participants. The venue and FASI base is located at Pondok Cabe, an airfield approximately 40 km south of Jakarta.

Paul Howard via Ed Davies

Nick Veronico

Chapter 3

Where in the world...

...can you learn to fly a DC-3?

For any pilot with a tinge of high-octane running through his or her veins, the thought of firing up a pair of Pratt & Whitney radials shivers the skin and brings forth the kind of faint smile often mistaken for inner peace. One can imagine deft hands switching pumps to life, tickling primers, engaging starters, and counting prop blades until that satisfying belch of smoke from a cold exhaust stack signals the impending thunder of fourteen cylinders pumping out many hundreds of horsepower.

Flying the airplane attached to these two particular engines is within reasonable reach of those pilots with the desire and a few discretionary dollars. Training to competency and an airplane type rating is a step beyond, but well within reach of a determined DC-3 driver-to-be. Whether it's for commercial gain or personal satisfaction, any pilot who takes a particular affection toward the DC-3 should figure out a way to spend a little time in the cockpit of the fabled classic.

Fortunately, for those of us without any really good friends who own DC-3s, there is a simple way into the left seat. Dotted across the country are a number of flight schools that offer training in the type. It's much easier to get some flight time or serious training in a DC-3 than some other classics with a little more pizzazz, say a B-25. Part of the reason is that there is a commercial outlet for the type-rated DC-3 pilot beyond scaring birds and impressing friends at airshows. There are still dozens of commercial operators of the DC-3 which might well find you desirable and employable, and perhaps your niche in life is really to fly Gooney Birds for some on-call Part 135 cargo operator rather than a three-holer for United. The established DC-3 schools cater to the professional pilot, the well-heeled airline pilot out to add another type rating, to the Douglas fanatic who really wants to learn how to fly a DC-3, and to anyone else who is qualified and has the cash.

When looking at DC-3 flight training, one has to consider the possibilities. Most of the DC-3 schools offer a variety of training options. For the curious of heart, familiarization training is available, which provides a rudimentary ground school and an hour or so in the left seat. For the old C-47 or DC-3 pilot from years past, a few hours of pay-as-you-go dual instruction might satisfy the appetite for flying the old girl again. For the committed "make me sweat" types, complete training to an airplane type rating will be just the ticket. For that level of training, a multi-engine rating is a necessity, an instrument rating is suggested (otherwise the type rating is restricted to VFR operations only), and some tailwheel experience is highly recommended. In other words, go get five hours of Citabria time.

For a certificated pilot to act as pilot-in-command of an aircraft with a maximum gross loaded weight in excess of 12,500 pounds (such as the DC-3), the Federal Aviation Administration requires the pilot to hold a specific rating for that type of aircraft. Part 61 of the Federal Aviation Regulations specifies those aspects of pilot certification. For pilot rating purposes, the FAA considers available variations of the DC-3 as three different types: the *DC-3*, which encompasses the DC-3, the C-47, and the C-117; the *DC-3S*, which encompasses the Super DC-3 and the C-117D; and

Nick Veronico

the *DC-3TP*, which encompasses the DC-3 turboprops. To fly all the variations requires three distinct type ratings and, necessarily, three check rides with an FAA designated examiner.

Training toward a type rating is rigorous. It starts with a thorough ground school covering all aspects of the various aircraft systems, the aircraft manual, aircraft checklists for normal, abnormal, and emergency procedures, and aircraft performance charts. Cockpit familiarization is then performed in the pilot seat with the instructor working through the cockpit reviewing dry-run starting procedures, emergency actions, and other checklist items. Finally, the flight training is started, which usually encompasses five to ten hours of intensive flying. Normal takeoffs and landings, stalls, steep-turns, emergency and single-engine procedures, and instrument approaches are all practiced and perfected until the flight instructor is satisfied that you have trained to at least the FAA requirement of performance. At that point, a designated examiner, representing the FAA, sits with you for a spell reviewing and watching you do all of the above in a check ride environment. Assuming the results are satisfactory, the designee types up a little temporary certificate that says you can now fly a DC-3 as pilot-in-command. *You are a DC-3 pilot!* Far out.

Of course, if you want to actually fly a DC-3 for a commercial operator, you have to do the above and then do it all again for the FAA when a company actually hires you to fly a DC-3. Usually, though, the company is picking up the tab for the second checkride.

Speaking of tabs, most of the DC-3 training schools surveyed offer their complete type-rating courses in the $3,000 to $7,000 range. The big variable is the amount of airplane time required; for straight VFR training a competent taildragger-experienced pilot could probably accomplish the training in five flight hours. IFR training adds another five hours, plus about two hours for the checkride. Additional flight hours might be needed at a cost of, usually, between $600 and $700 per hour. Prices obviously vary and can change as quickly as the cost of a gallon of aviation gas. There is also more to flight training than cost, with such factors as airplane availability, location, schedule, and general ambiance requiring consideration. In any event, the idea is to have some fun while acquiring some rare experience, so call around and find the school that best fits your individual situation. Set aside a week of time and buy a Ford Escort instead of that T-Bird. Then, go fly a DC-3.

Ed Davies

Nick Veronico

DC-3 Flight Training

Academy Airlines

P.O. Box 693
Griffin, GA 30224
Phone: (404) 227-2000
Fax: (404) 229-8991

DC-3s:
N130D (msn 19800), C-47A 43-15334, delivered to USAAF in March 1944. Operated for Parks Airlines and Ozark Airlines after the war, and a succession of civil owners afterwards. Operated from Griffin, Georgia, since 1973.
N143D (msn 2054), DC-3-227A built for Fokker and Swissair and delivered in October 1938. Operated in Europe through 1955 when sold to a U.S. owner. Operated by Ozark Airlines as N143D and sold through a succession of civil owners. Operated from Griffin, Georgia, after 1974.

Remarks:
Principal contact: Robert D. McSwiggan
Offers flexible flight training program based upon pilot's need.
Training toward a type rating and/or familiarization flying.
Provides recurrent and initial training to FAA inspectors requiring DC-3 authorization.
Operates in conjunction with on-call cargo operation.
One FAA designated examiner available.

Ed Davies

Airway Transport

22636 Airport Way #3
California City, CA 93505
Phone (619) 373-4287
Fax: (619) 373-3554

DC-3s:
N7500A (msn 11693), C-53D 42-68766, delivered to the USAAF in April 1943. Surplus in August 1945 and acquired by Eastern Airlines as NC45332. Further details are under Air Cruise America in Chapter 1.

Remarks:
Training conducted at the California City Airport near Mojave, California.
Two-week advance scheduling recommended.

Alexander Aeroplane

118 Huff-Daland Circle
Griffin, GA 30223
Phone: (800) 831-2949
Fax: (404) 227-7298

DC-3s:
N28AA (msn 2239), built as DC-3-314A for Braniff and delivered as NC25666 in June 1940. Post-war use with a variety of civil users, culminating in use with Provincetown-Boston Airlines as N139PB. Purchased by Alexander Aeroplane as the company's flagship.

Remarks:
Company can provide hotel, car rental, and restaurant information.
Offers "A Day in a DC-3" special.
Training toward a type rating also offered.

Nick Veronico

DKI Aviation Services

100 Court Street
Lehighton, PA 18235
Phone: (610) 377-4179
Fax: (610) 377-6805

DC-3s:
N25646 (msn 2234), DC-3-201C for Eastern Airlines as NC25646 and delivered in June 1940.
N88874 (msn 12693), C-47A 42-92847, delivered to the USAAF in March 1944. Assigned to 8th and 9th Air Forces. Surplus in October 1945 and operated by a variety of civil owners as N88874.

Remarks:
Principal contact: Doug Sellix (owner)
Flight training conducted at the Reading, Pennsylvania, airport.
Also operates Part 135 cargo operation with DC-3s and Beech 18s.
Performs mechanical and restorative work on DC-3s and Beech 18s.
Offers training toward type rating (typically 10 hours flight plus two-hour checkride).
Also offers familiarization flying and veteran flights for old DC-3/C-47 pilots.
Two FAA designated examiners available.

N6898D (msn 20082) is one of the Basler DC-3s utilized by Aviation Services for DC-3 flight training. (Scott Thompson)

Aviation Services

7745 Country Club Road
Oshkosh, WI 54901
Phone (414) 426-3131

<u>DC-3s</u>:
As leased from Basler fleet, including turboprop-powered DC-3.

Remarks:
Principal contact: Steve Davis (owner)
FAA designee on staff.
DC-3 Type rating course: 3-10 hours.
DC-3TP or DC-3 type rating available.
Familiarization course also available: 2 hours ground, 1 hour cockpit, 1 hour flight time.

One of DKIAS's DC-3s is N25646 (msn 2234), shown here at Chicago in July 1952 while operating with Eastern Air Lines. (Doug Olsen via Ed Davies)

Flight Data's C-117D while active with the USMC at El Toro in July 1976. Flight Data's owner, Glenn Hyde, flew this same aircraft for the Marines during this period. (Larry Smalley via Ed Davies)

Another view of N44GH (msn 43393), this taken while registered as N306SF and operated by Airpower, Inc., at Lakeport, California, in September 1990. (Ed Davies)

Flight Data

P.O. Box 1542
Ronoke, TX 76262
Phone (817) 430-1905
Fax (817) 491-2538

DC-3s:
N44GH (msn 43393), R4D-8 BuNo 12437, built as C-47A 42-23757/R4D-5 BuNo 12437 (msn 9620), and delivered to the USN in May 1943. Excess in 1979 and operated as N8538R for TBM, Inc. of Redmond, Oregon. Obtained by Flight Data in 1991.

Remarks:
Super DC-3/C-117D Type Rating.
Principal contact: Glen Hyde
Flight training conducted at Denton, Texas and Carson City, Nevada.
Training primairly geared for professional training of qualified pilots.
Three-day course (usually Friday-Sunday) with 3-6 hours of flight training.
Instructor was an aircraft commander of this same aircraft on active duty with the USMC.

Flight Data's Super DC-3, N44GH, airborne over Texas. The company splits its training operation between Denton, Texas, and Carson City, Nevada. (via Glen Hyde)

Southwind Flight Training Systems, Inc.

Brownsville-South Padre International Airport
495 South Minnesota Ave.
Brownsville, TX 78521
Phone: (210) 544-2300 or (800) 421-9847
Fax (210) 544-2673

DC-3s
N32MS (msn 4978), built as a DC-3A-453 for Northwest (NC30025) but impressed as C-53D 43-2023 in October 1942. Excess in October 1945 and leased by the DPC to United as NC19934. Various civil owners as N93C, N81R, N400RS.
N3906J (msn 43344), R4D-8 BuNo 39061, built as C-47A 42-23997/R4D-5 BuNo 39061 (msn 9859) and delivered in July 1943. Excess in 1977 and operated by several civil operators as N90628. Registered as N3906J in August 1981.

Remarks:
Super DC-3/C-117D and/or DC-3 training available.
Two FAA designees available for each aircraft.

Ed Davies

Chapter 4

More Power...
...from radials to jets

Throughout its long and distinguished career, the Douglas DC-3 and its many civilian and military variants have probably been fitted with more engine types and thrust augmentors than any other aircraft. Initially, the cost-effective derivative of the successful DC-2 came into being largely because of the simultaneous development of two competing air-cooled radial piston engines. The Pratt & Whitney Aircraft *Twin Wasp* and the Wright Aeronautical Corporation *Cyclone* provided Douglas engineers with powerful and reliable engines for their revolutionary airliner design. Sixty years later, it is not surprising that this rugged airframe has been adapted to use many of the aircraft power plants developed over the intervening years. Beginning with the original piston engines, this chapter traces the chronological use of developing technologies to power the enduring DC-3.

A note should be mentioned about the certification of aircraft. When a manufacturer proposes to build an aircraft, the prototype goes through a series of test phases until the Federal Aviation Administration or, in the DC-3's case, one of the FAA's predecessor organization (the Bureau of Air Commerce), awards an Approved Type Certificate (ATC). Then, as long as the airplane manufacturer builds aircraft to the specifications of the ATC, these aircraft are certificated as an approved type. Numerous ATCs were awarded to Douglas on the DC-3 design for various combinations of engines and equipment. If a subsequent operator wishes to modify an aircraft and use it with the approved type certificate limitations, a prototype modification is engineered and certified by the FAA, which then awards a Supplemental Type Certificate (STC). The modifications called for by the STC can then be performed to the STC standard on additional airframes with the FAA's blessing. If an STC is not granted, the aircraft must be operated under the limitations of a restricted or experimental airworthiness certificate and cannot be used for revenue or passenger-carrying operations. STCs are therefore required for any engine installations not originally approved for the DC-3 design if these aircraft are going to be operated under a standard airworthiness certificate.

Piston-Engined DC-3s

The first Douglas Sleeper Transport, which was built for American Airlines, was powered by two Wright SGR-1820-G5 Cyclones, each a nine cylinder, single-row radial with a displacement of 1,823 cubic inches. The specification called for a rating of 1,000 horsepower (hp) for up to five minutes at takeoff power, and a maximum continuous horsepower of 850 at 2,100 rpm to 5,500 feet altitude. Later, production American Airlines DC-3s used the GR-1820-G102, and 1,200 hp -G202 Cyclones.

A Pratt & Whitney R-1830 Twin Wasp in its rightful place. The engine configuration places seven cylinders in each of two rows. The competing Wright R-1820 was a single-row nine-cylinder radial engine. (Ed Davies)

Good view of the Aerojet-General JATO installation on a DC-3. Note the simplicity of the mounting brackets under the center section. (Larry Smalley via Ed Davies Collection)

United Airlines' first DC-3s were not delivered until a year later. Because of United's mountainous central transcontinental route and the need for a gimmick to recover market share from established DC-3 users, United opted for a different, higher-powered engine built by Pratt & Whitney. The airline paid Douglas for the certification and redesign of the mountings and engine cowling, the cost being added to the purchase price of United's initial aircraft order. Pratt & Whitney had previously introduced their R-1830 Twin Wasp in 1932, and their latest -SB3G version was rated at 1,000 hp for takeoff and a maximum continuous 900 hp at 2,450 rpm to 6,500 feet. This rugged engine had a twin- row, 14-cylinder configuration and displaced 1830 cubic inches. The cost per engine to Douglas was $10,005, plus $307.75 for additional accessories. United's Twin Wasp-equipped DC-3s were approximately 14 miles per hour faster than American's Cyclone-powered airliners of the same period.

By 1941, technical developments in both types had raised the available takeoff horsepower to 1,200 with no increase in the physical size of either engine. However, it was the R-1830 that was selected for the thousands of military transport versions of the DC-3 built during World War II. Most C-47, C-47A and C-53-type transports used the R-1830-92, military version of the S1C3-G, while -90B or -90Cs fitted with two-speed superchargers powered most of the C-47Bs.The final post-war production versions, the Super DC-3 and R4D-8 conversions for the Navy and Marine Corps, utilized the Wright Cyclone R-1820-80 rated at 1,475 hp for takeoff.

Over the half-century since the end of World War II, surviving DC-3 types have been retrofitted with a continuing variety of piston engines, including the Pratt & Whitney R-2000 as used on the bigger C-54. With the Pratt & Whitney R-1830s long out of production, Airtech Canada envisioned that there would be a market for a current replacement engine. They installed PZL ASZ-621R radials, still being built in Poland, on C-CJDM (msn 20721), together with four-bladed propellers. The first flight was in 1987, but the combination does not appear to have been a commercial success. Earlier in the 1950s, the Stewart-Davis Company at Long Beach, California, modified a number of corporate DC-3s by fitting them with surplus Navy PB4Y-2 Privateer R-1830-94 radials, each rated at 1,350 hp for takeoff. This engine and the similar R-1830-75 have continued to be popular replacement units when retrofitted in conjunction with the installation of a geared rudder trim tab. With one engine feathered, the rudder tab provides increased controllability, which enables the full 1,350 hp to be utilized on the remaining powerplant.

JATO-powered DC-3s

On August 6, 1941, an Ercoupe XPQ-13, followed by a huge lingering trail of smoke, hurtled down the runway at March Field in Southern California. This initial test of Jet (or rocket) Assisted Take Off (JATO) led to the production of thousands of short duration jet and rocket motors used with great success by many aircraft types during World War II.

After the war, rocket-motor builders Aerojet Engineering Corporation of Azusa, California, sought civil applications for their JATO units. One of the market segments they targeted was the large number of war-surplus DC-3 types being used for passenger and freight operations throughout the world. The addition of the JATO units could allow higher gross weight takeoffs from hot, high-altitude airfields and afford a greater margin of safety in the event

DST-A-207A N22Z (msn 1977) as operated by Aspen Airways at Denver in June 1967. Note the JATO installation on the belly under the wing fillet. The JATO was useful in the high altitude, warm temperature environment in which Aspen operated. (Clay Jannson via Ed Davies Collection)

of an engine failure during the critical takeoff and climb-out phase. To prove the viability of the project, Aerojet carried out a series of flights during April 1946 from the Ontario Army Air Field in Southern California. The Civil Aeronautics Administration monitored the tests, which were flown by C-47B 43-48273 (msn 25534), on loan from the Flight Test Division, Air Technical Service Command at Wright Field in Dayton, Ohio. Two Aerojet12AS-1000D-5 rocket motors were installed below the fuselage and controlled from the cockpit. Eighty units were expended while emulating various takeoff configurations. Each takeoff and the measured distance to clear a 50-foot obstacle were photographically recorded for future analysis.

A Douglas study recommended that the standby source of power receive serious consideration. Further operational testing in South America with TACA of Nicaragua's DC-3, AN-ACF (msn 25246), resulted in the JATO installation on a number of corporate DC-3s. The rocket manufacturer, now called Aerojet-General, quoted $4,000 in the mid-1950s for a complete DC-3 JATO installation including four rocket engines. Unfortunately, the expected demand never materialized, though at least two U.S. passenger carriers, Aspen Airways and Perdue Aeronautics Corporation, did equip their DC-3s with Aerojet's rocket motors.

The rocket-assisted DC-3 failed to become a commercial reality, though the concept dragged on until the early 1970s. Today one can only fantasize about a spectacular departure of a smoke and fire breathing DC-3, hurtling down the runway overtaking a tortoise-like 747 on the parallel.

Turbojet DC-3s

With the rapid post World War II development of the turbojet engine, it is not surprising that several efforts were made to utilize this form of controlled-thrust propulsion to enhance the performance and safety of the many surviving Douglas DC-3s. The first conversion appears to have been during 1950, when C-53D F-BEIS (msn 11746) was fitted with two Turbomeca Palas turbojets by SNCASO, in Toulouse, France. The jets were mounted under the wings outboard of the piston engines. Each turbojet engine weighed 132 pounds and had a static thrust of 352 pounds. For a while this Dakota was utilized as a flying billboard for an aperitif company.

C-53D F-BEIS at Toulouse, France in the early 1950s. Note the Turbomeca "Palas" turbojet mounted under each wing outboard of the radial engine nacelle. (Jean Delmas via P. V. Prefontaine and Davies Collection)

Armee de L'Air (French Air Force) C-47B s/n 349881 (msn 27142) with the "Palas" turbojets, each rated with a static thrust of 352 pounds, mounted under the wings. This aircraft was operationally tested in Central Africa with the French civil registration of F-SCHU applied. (Ed Davies Collection)

A variation on the French turbojet installations was this single Turbomeca "Palas" mounted under the wing center section. This aircraft (msn 6055) operated as F-BEFF with the turbojet installation between 1952 and 1954. (Jean Delmas via P.V. Fontaine and Ed Davies Collection)

A similar conversion was undertaken in 1958 on the French Air Force's C-47B s/n 349881 (msn 27142) by SFERMA. The aircraft was tested in Central Africa, but the French Air Force abandoned the project in 1959 and ordered the jet boosters removed.

Union Aeromaritime de Transport (predecessor of the French airline U.T.A.) had a single Turbomeca Palas mounted under the center of the fuselage of their DC-3 F-BEFF (msn 6055). The aircraft was used on scheduled routes in Central Africa between 1952 and 1954, after which the turbojet was removed and the aircraft sold to Autrex.

Perhaps the most interesting turbojet-augmented DC-3 was the Argentine Air Force's TA-05. A French Turbomeca Marbore 11C of 836-pound static thrust was mounted in the tail cone. The retractable air intake was positioned ahead of the vertical stablizer and could be closed when the jet was not in use. Used to support Argentina's Antarctic bases, TA-05 flew to the South Pole in 1965/66. The third engine significantly reduced the takeoff run, improved the climb performance and, above all, offered a comforting margin of safety in the forbidding polar region. This aircraft is now on display at the Museo Aerospacial in Buenos Aires and is thought to be msn 4365.

Stewart-Davis, earlier involved in DC-3 piston-engine retrofitting, also developed and offered their Jet-Pak 920 modification kit for the C-47 beginning in 1963. A housing containing the Continental J69-T9 turbojet, producing 920 pounds static thrust, could be mounted on the top forward section of the fuselage and run off the plane's regular aviation gasoline. Despite a promised marked improvement in performance, especially in hot, high airport conditions, none of the kits were sold for application on the DC-3.

Obviously, a limiting factor in the installation of turbojet engines on DC-3 airframes was the radically increased fuel demands while the jets were operational. Even limiting the use of the jets to augment departure performance significantly reduced the available range and payload of the DC-3.

Turboprop DC-3s

Though the turbojet engine became the propulsion unit of choice for military aircraft during the late 1940s, the high fuel consumption and noise levels of early engines predicated that the gas turbine and conventional propeller combination (turbo-propeller) would be the way to go for new civil airliners. Much of the turboprop development work was being done in the United Kingdom and, not surprisingly, the readily available Dakota was utilized as the test-bed for several of the new gas turbine powerplants.

The first of these test aircraft was Dakota KJ839 (msn 25623), leased from the RAF by Armstrong Siddeley Motors in 1949. The piston engines were replaced by two of the company's Mamba axial-flow turboprops, with a takeoff rating of 1,475 equivalent shaft horse power (eshp). The net dry-weight of each of the turboprop engines was only 800 pounds (versus 1,465 pounds for each R-1830-92), and they had to be mounted much farther forward of the wing than the piston engines in order to maintain the longitudinal balance of the aircraft. Though this engine was never used in a commercial civil airliner, the Double Mamba, using two Mamba engines mounted side by side and driving two contra-rotating propellers, was chosen for the Royal Navy's Fairey Gannet anti-submarine patrol aircraft. KJ839's Mamba turboprop installation was replaced by the original piston engines before 1958, and the aircraft is currently registered as N4797H to Coast Airways Inc., in Miami, Florida.

Vickers Armstrong Ltd., also in the United King-

The first known DC-3 piston-to-turboprop conversion was performed by Armstrong Siddeley on Dakota KJ839 (msn 25623) leased from the RAF in 1949. Two "Mamba" engines of 1,475 eshp each replaced the piston engines. Though commercial development of the installation was not pursued, the "Double Mamba" engine derivative later equipped the Royal Navy's Fairey Gannet. (McDonnell Douglas)

First scheduled freight service in the world to be operated with turbine-powered aircraft was performed by a BEA DC-3 conversion. Dakota G-ALXN (msn 26106) was modified with Dart turboprops for Vickers Viscount route tests. G-ALXN, one of two such conversions by BEA, flew the inaugural service between Northolt, England, and Hanover, Germany, on August 15, 1951. (BEA via Ed Davies Collection)

Details of the Dart turboprop installation on the BEA Dakotas. (via Ed Davies Collection)

dom, built the first and one of the most successful turboprop-powered airliners, the Viscount. The first production Viscount, registered G-ALWE, flew its maiden flight on August 20, 1952. The type 700 Viscount was powered by four Rolls Royce Dart 504 turboprops, each driving a four-blade Rotol fully-feathering 10-foot diameter propeller. The maximum output from each engine was 1,400 eshp, plus 365 pounds of exhaust jet thrust. The launch customer for the Viscount was British European Airways (BEA). Designed to facilitate a trouble-free introduction into service for the new design, BEA took the unusual step of converting two of their *Pionair* Dakotas to Dart engines. Placed into freighter service over the proposed Viscount routes, the airline hoped to obtain realistic information on ground and flight handling. Their pilots would obtain turboprop operating experience, while the freight service would enable the planes to earn their keep. Both airframes were modified by Scottish Aviation, then ferried to Rolls-Royce at Hucknall for engine mount design engineering and installation. G-ALXN (msn 26106), named *Sir Henry Royce*, was delivered to BEA on June 9, 1951, and flew the first-ever scheduled freight service by a civilian turboprop airliner on August 15, 1951, from Northolt, England to Hanover, Germany. The second Dart Dakota, G-AMDB (msn 26432), named *Claude Johnson*, joined the BEA fleet on September 5, 1951.

The airline gained almost 4,000 hours of valuable experience from the Dart Dakotas before the Viscount began the world's first scheduled civil turboprop passenger service on April 18, 1953. Both DC-3s were converted back to Twin Wasp piston engines. G-ALXN continued flying for BEA, East Anglian Flying Service, and Channel Airways, eventually being broken up in 1964. Reconverted to *Pionair* configuration, G-ALXN flew for BEA until 1962 when it was registered to British Westpoint Airlines. It was broken up for spares in late 1967.

The dubious record as the "Most Modified DC-3" must surely go to msn 4903. Built as C-53 41-20133, it was delivered to the USAAC in March 1942. Declared surplus to requirements in April 1945, it was leased by the Defense Plant Corporation to Transcontinental and Western Air Inc. They removed all the military equipment at their Kansas City base and transformed the aircraft into a standard 21-passenger airliner, which TWA registered as NC44783. Early in 1950 the aircraft underwent another conversion, this time by Remmert-Werner in St. Louis, which refurbished it as an executive transport for the Monsanto Chemical Company. The first of many powerplant changes took place at this time when the Pratt & Whitney R-1830-92 engines were replaced by more powerful -75s. Through a series of subsequent civil owners, the registration eventually became N700CC. Enter Jack Conroy, the Southern California engineer who had developed and built the extraordinary range of *Guppy* jumbo-sized transport aircraft. His Conroy Aircraft Company acquired N700CC in December 1967 and he used it for, among other things, a fishing trip to Mexico.

RMA Claude Johnson (Dakota G-AMDB, msn 26432) in freight service with BEA while equipped with the Rolls-Royce Dart turboprop engines. (McDonnell Douglas)

Unfortunately, one of the piston engines came apart on this trip, necessitating a costly and lengthy replacement before he could get the airplane back to California. Supposedly, this incident convinced Conroy to replace the aging piston engines with more modern and reliable turboprops, and perhaps to develop a global retrofit market for the many DC-3s then flying.

The engines chosen for the conversion were ex-Viscount Rolls Royce Dart 510s, de-rated to 1,350 eshp, fitted in extended nacelles and driving four-bladed Dowty Rotol propellers. Additional fuel was carried in sealed wings, giving the aircraft a total capacity of 1,600 gallons (U.S). The first flight of the *Turbo-Three* was on May 13, 1969, and, following a brief check out, the bright orange and yellow-painted *Zero Zero Charlie Charlie* was ferried over the North Atlantic to the Paris Air Show. Despite a world-wide sales campaign, no other *Turbo-Threes* were built, nor did the FAA ever issue a STC for this first U.S. turboprop-powered DC-3.

While they were designing the DC-1, DC-2, and DC-3 family of aircraft in the 1930s, Douglas engineers were determined to stay away from the three-engine configuration used by the Ford TriMotor and other contemporary airliners. Conroy, however, felt that if two turboprops were good, then three must be better. He and Aircraft Technical Service's Robert Lillibridge went back to the drawing board for yet another derivative of *Zero Zero Charlie Charlie*. This time they came up with a new powerplant, Pratt & Whitney Canada's recently certificated, economical PT6A-45 turboprop driving a five-bladed Hartzell propeller. Three of these 1,120 eshp-rated units would be used, two in streamlined nacelles in the conventional wing positions, and a third mounted in the nose. This center engine could be used for takeoff, climbout, and high-speed cruise, and shut down for economical cruise or loiter over a search area. The actual conversion from the Dart 510s to the new *Tri-Turbo Three* configuration was contracted by Conroy's Specialized Aircraft Company to Aircraft Technical Services Corporation at Van Nuys, California. The first flight of the re-registered N23SA was on November 2, 1977, and once again it was flown to Paris for display at the international air show, this time in the guise of a maritime patrol aircraft. A change in the number of engines required that the whole aircraft be certified as a new type to current FAA standards, an improbable goal for an aircraft designed over 40 years earlier. Conroy applied for an exemption for the *Tri-Turbo Three*, but his application was denied shortly before he died of cancer. The ingenious entrepreneur was never told about the FAA's final decision.

Operating under an experimental airworthiness certificate for the purpose of research and development, N23SA was sold to Santa Barbara Polair, Inc. on February 25, 1979. Fitted with skis, this unique aircraft operated under U.S. Navy research contracts for the next 10 years. Flying mainly in the polar regions, it was used to service the Navy's underwater fixed submarine detection system and to test new INS and GPS navigation systems in the Arctic. In 1986, the center section was damaged by an APU fire

A later effort at refitting turboprops to DC-3s was initiated by Jack Conroy, resulting in the Turbo Three conversion. Conroy initially added ex-Viscount Dart engines to C-53 N4700C (msn 4903) in 1969 and attempted to attain both an FAA Supplemental Type Certificate and a commercial market. Both efforts failed, but Conroy continued development of his Turbo Three concepts. (Larry Smalley via Ed Davies Collection)

The Conroy Tri-Turbo Three on the ramp at Bakersfield, California, in May 1989. This view shows to advantage how the fuselage engine was faired into the nose section. (Ed Davies)

The Tri-Turbo Three (N23SA, msn 4903) at Oxnard, California in September 1981. Because the FAA denied Conroy's application for an STC, this was the only Tri Turbo Three completed. Polair operated the modified aircraft privately under U.S. government contracts, and the aircraft was never issued a standard airworthiness certificate. (Larry Smalley via Ed Davies)

while the aircraft was on the ground. Part of the fuselage was replaced, and the *Tri-Turbo* continued flying the Navy contract. The damaged section was later used in a TV series filmed in Canada. Eventually taken out of service, N23SA languished, first at Santa Barbara airport, but was later moved to Mojave and stripped of its engines.

Incredibly, msn 4903's remarkable career isn't over yet. Basler Turbo Conversions acquired the airframe and, in October 1993, one of their crews stripped off the wings and loaded N32SA on two purpose-built road trailers for the long haul back to their Oshkosh, Wisconsin base. More than likely, this survivor will undergo yet another metamorphosis, eventually emerging as a state-of-the-art Basler *Turbo-67*, ready to fly until well into the 21st century.

Aero Modifications International, Inc. (AMI) was formed in 1985 for the purpose of researching and developing a design for retrofitting Douglas DC-3/C-47 airframes with turboprop engines. AMI selected the proven Pratt & Whitney Canada PT6A-65AR powerplant, and contracted with Schafer Aircraft for the engineering that would lead to a multiple-use FAA-approved STC design. A new production facility was built in Waco, Texas, and DC-3 N887AM (msn 27085) was acquired as the base airframe for the prototype. (This aircraft had been built for the RAF in January 1945 as Dakota IV KN219. It had served with the Belgian and French air forces, and was one of a group of ex-French Navy aircraft that Basler Flight Services had originally imported in 1985.)

The piston engines, landing gear, fuel tanks, wiring and control panels were all removed and the wings demated. The fuselage was fitted into a construction jig and a 40-inch plug inserted forward of the wings. New fuel tanks for 1,030 gallons (U.S.) of useable fuel were built and installed, together with new wiring, instruments and throttle quadrant. The 1,230 eshp flat-rated turbines were fitted in redesigned streamlined cowlings and matched to variable speed Hartzell five-bladed propellers. The prototype flew for the first time in July 1986. Following a year of exhaustive flight and static checks, the FAA presented AMI Chief Executive Officer J.B. Williams with multiple use STC SA3820SW on August 6, 1987. This allowed his company to retrofit DC-3 type aircraft with Pratt and Whitney PT-65-65AR turboprops. AMI began a second conversion in 1986, and noted that potential customers could either have their aircraft refitted at the Waco facility or buy do-it-yourself kits. A June 1988 agreement with Rhoades Aviation saw the prototype *CargoMaster* re-registered as N146JR to operate a Federal Express contract between Houston and Dallas, Texas. The second conversion, N240GB (msn 26713), and two kits went to South Africa via AMI distributor Aeronautical Enterprises of Fort Lauderdale, Florida. This turbo 3 (registered as ZS-KCV) crashed and was destroyed on the November 7, 1993, soon after takeoff from Lokiohogtio, Kenya on a cargo flight to the Sudan.

Another AMI turboprop conversion was completed in Waco during 1987 for the Venezuelan oil company, Corpoven. This corporate aircraft, YV-32CP (msn 13143), was an Oklahoma City-built C-47A and had been featured in the 1985 PBS documentary *Skydive to the Rain Forest*. A prolonged sales tour throughout South and Central America failed to drum up any new orders and, in 1993, the assets of AMI were acquired by the Greenwich Aircraft Corporation of Sausalito, California. Purchased along with the Waco facility was C-47B N376AS (msn 27047), a conversion that is presently being used as a demonstrator by the new company. (N376AS was delivered to the USAAF in January 1945 and, in 1983, was one of the last C-47s to

Looking somewhat worse for wear, the disassembled remains of the Conroy Turbo-Three (msn 4903) at the Mojave, California, airport as prepared for transport to Basler's facility at Oshkosh, Wisconsin, in October 1993. Hopefully, this aircraft will eventually emerge as a Basler Turbo 67 and continue its long and diverse utilization. (Ed Davies)

Greenwich Aircraft's demonstrator, N376AS (msn 27047), showing to good view the AMI modifications including the Pratt & Whitney PT6-65AR engine installation. (via Ed Davies)

be sold from the huge AMARC storage depot alongside Davis-Monthan AFB.) The other aircraft included in the purchase, N33654 (msn 4117, a veteran originally bought by American Airlines in 1941 as NC33654), remains in Waco as a hulk and will probably be scrapped.

The most successful, well known, and lasting company in the field of DC-3 turboprop conversions is Basler Turbo Conversions, Inc. based at Oshkosh, Wisconsin. Well known for refurbishing and converting piston-engined DC-3s, Basler entered the turboprop field by purchasing the prototype aircraft and technology developed by the United States Aircraft Corporation in the early 1980s. USAC, a Van Nuys, California-based company that specialized in major structural conversions, modified ex-RAF Dakota III KK160 (msn 26744), fitting it with Pratt & Whitney Canada PT6A-45R turboprops. A 40-inch plug was inserted in the forward fuselage, and the prototype *DC-3 Turbo Express*, registered as N300TX, made its first flight in July 1982. An STC was issued by the FAA in December 1983. The prototype was later sold to Harold's Air Service, which operated a revenue passenger service in Alaska. Basler bought the plane in 1987 and re-registered it as N300BF.

Two production facilities were set up. The first was located at a leased facility at Van Nuys, managed by Bryan Carmichael, where the first two pre-production aircraft and a number of conversion kits were assembled and tested. This location was phased out in 1990, with the work being moved to the expanded facility that Warren Basler built at Oshkosh. The first Van Nuys DC-3 was N8059P (msn 20875), a Long Beach-built C-47B. Delivered in August 1944, it served

Two of the better-known Basler DC-3 conversions were done for the U.S. Forest Service. This view shows N115Z (msn 33567) at the USFS Missoula, Montana base in July 1992. The Forest Service uses the aircraft for a variety of purposes, including logistical support and smokejumper insertion. (Scott Thompson)

A thoroughly modern cockpit is one of the many modifications to update the DC-3 design to the Basler BT-67. (Nick Veronico)

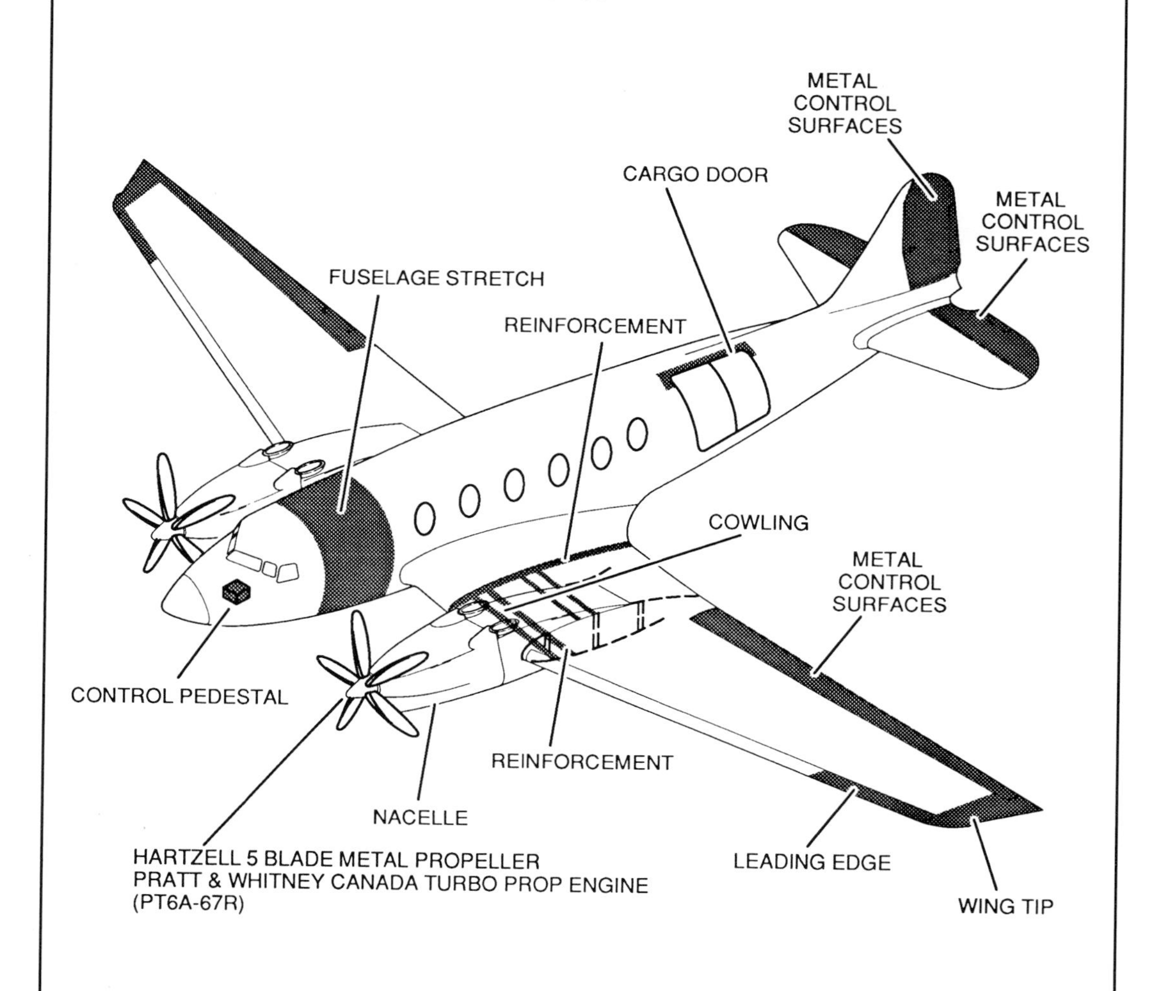

TG-FAG 575 at Oshkosh in July 1992 as airframe modifications were completed.. This aircraft was modified-for the Guatamalan Air Force. (Nick Veronico)

BASLER BT-67 AIRFRAMES IN MODIFICATION OR DELIVERED			
REGISTRATIO	MSN	CUSTOMER	DELIVERED
N72BF	33053	Air Colombia/DEA (#1)	07/30/90
N8059P	20875	Air Colombia/DEA (#2)	07/30/90
FAES 116	unknown	El Salvador (#1)	08/31/90
FAES 118	34238	El Salvador (#2)	08/31/90
N96BF	13321	Demonstrator	12/17/90
N142Z	20494	U.S. Forest Service	04/10/91
N115Z	33567	U.S. Forest Service	06/18/91
TAM 38	20507	Bolivian Air Force	07/03/91
PNC 212	13110	Colombia Police (#1)	09/10/91
N21669	25509	Aero Contractors	05/05/92
A2-ADL	33581	Aerial Surveys	06/29/92
TG-FAG-1	9100	Guatemalan Air Force (#1)	09/05/92
TG-FAG-2	33568	Guatemalan Air Force (#2)	11/06/92
PNC 211	25667	Colombia Police (#2)	02/02/93
TG-FAG-3	unknown	Guatamalan Air Force (#3)	02/16/93
FAES 119	6204	El Salvador (#3)	07/05/93
FAES 117	25409	El Salvador (#4)	08/31/93
N46949	9290	No customer	
TG-FAG-4	34398	Guatamalan Air Force (#4)	02/02/94
TG-FAG-5	33499	Guatamalan Air Force (#5)	Delivered
N29BF	26002	No customer	
TAM-38	unknown	No customer	
FAC-1	unknown	Colombian Air Force (#1)	Delivered
FAC-2	unknown	Colombian Air Force (#2)	Delivered

with Air Transport Command in North Africa, and subsequently went to the French Air Force. The aircraft had several civilian owners in Canada and the U.S. before being acquired by Harold's Air Service, USAC and, eventually, Basler Turbo Conversions in November 1988. The most significant change, of course, involved the replacement of the piston engines with the 1220 eshp continuously-rated PT6A-67R turbines and 5-bladed, 115-inch diameter Hartzell metal props. The maximum cruise speed with this arrangement is 205 knots (236 mph) at 12,500 feet. The 40-inch plug and cabin bulkhead removal enlarges the useful volume of the fuselage from 905 to 1,225 cubic feet. An 8,000-pound winch and new roller cargo floor facilitate handling the 13,000 pound maximum useful load. An optional three-part cargo door can accommodate standard cargo containers.

The first flight of N8059P from Van Nuys was on July 29, 1989. Tests performed by John Mills at nearby Mojave Airport confirmed that the modified DC-3 easily met the FAA Stage 3 noise requirements. This information hardly prepares the veteran DC-3 watcher for the strangely quiet short takeoff and eye-popping climb out of the turbo DC-3! More intriguing were the infrared thermography monitored flights. The cooling within the nacelles and the overwing exhaust stacks resulted in virtually no infrared "rooster tail", and the comforting knowledge that a portable heat-seeking missile would probably fail to lock on to the exhaust of this new stealth transport. Early in the morning of May 7, 1990, the pre-production aircraft, operating at 28,705 pounds gross weight, lifted off from Van Nuys after a short 800-foot roll. Flown by Bob Clark, the 1,600 mile non-stop flight to Oshkosh was scheduled for six and one half hours at a cruising altitude of 25,000 feet.

The second conversion aircraft completed at Van

The ill-fated N96BF (msn 13321) shown here at Goose Bay, Labrador in May 1994. Basler operated this Turbo BT-67 as a factory demonstrator, which explains why it is wearing the markings of a German company. This aircraft crashed in Angola the following December with the loss of the flight crew. (Ed Davies)

DC-3 modification in progress. At left, N46949 (msn 9290) in the Basler shop at Oshkosh, Wisconsin in August 1992. Below, five DC-3 undergoing modifications, with details of the enlarged cargo door shown. (Nick Veronico and Basler)

Nuys, N72BF (msn 33053, ex-RAF Dakota IV KN515), was fitted with much of the optional equipment being offered under the Basler STC. Immediately noticeable are the round windows and metal control surfaces. Less discernible are the leading edge and wing tip modifications, which improve the flight characteristics when compared to the standard DC-3. Also hidden are the additional 800 gallon (U.S.) wing tanks, structural reinforcements to support the higher gross weight, and new electrical system.

The fifth Basler conversion, N96BF (msn 13321), crashed on December 15, 1994, killing pilots Dan Reid and Roland Halter. The turbo DC-3 was chartered to the International Committee of the Red Cross and was flying humanitarian relief supply missions in Angola. The DC-3, carrying five tons of food intended for civilians in the town of Ganda, crashed soon after take off from Lobita airstrip. It is thought that the load of beans, packed in plastic bags, shifted during the climb out.

Basler has enjoyed a great deal of success with their BT-67 conversion. For 1995 the company is working on orders for an additonal 20 conversions for both civil and military customers, with an additional 21 orders for 1996.

The South African Air Force has converted many of its 40 plus Dakota fleet to turboprop power. Designated as C-47TPs, the first modified aircraft were delivered to 35 Squadron at D.F. Malan Air Base in Cape Town for use in the offshore search and rescue role. The conversion is similar to those of AMI and Basler, with the modifications being carried out at Swartkops and Ysterplaat Air Bases using SAAF maintenance personnel. The Strallis Group International, a Pretoria-based company, has also been involved in turboprop Dakota conversions and operation in South Africa.

Turboprop Super DC-3

The post-war "Super" DC-3 derivative, aimed at modernizing the pre-war design, was a commercial disaster for Douglas. Only 105 were produced, these being converted from existing C-47/R4D airframes, with 100 of these being delivered to the U.S. Navy and Marine Corps as R4D-8/C-117Ds.

The only airline sales were three aircraft to Capital Airlines in September 1950. These Super DC-3s were powered by Wright R-1820-C9-HE2 nine-cylinder air-cooled *Cyclones*, rated at 1,450 hp for takeoff. Their scheduled-service careers were short-lived, all three being sold to the U. S. Steel Company in April 1952. Capital Airlines converted them to a corporate transport configuration and continued to operate and maintain them for U.S. Steel. One of the three, N16012 (msn 43193), was later sold to Cook & Company in October 1962 and was re-registered as N542S. The Northwest Refining Company bought it in May 1963 and it was again re-registered, this time as N111SA.

The Western Company of North America, based in Fort Worth, Texas, was the next corporate owner, who registered the Super DC-3 as N156WC. Company President H.E. Chiles later contracted with Jack Conroy's Turbo-Three Corporation to replace the piston engines with more reliable turboprops. The power plant chosen was the Vickers Viscount combination of Rolls Royce Dart 510-65 turbine with Dowty Rotol props. The experimental airworthiness certificate for the commencement of proving flights was requested in April 1974. Western, then under company president John Fanning, had by this time lost interest in the project and the aircraft was sold to Pilgrim Aviation and Aircraft, Inc. of New London, Connecticut.

Contemplating a market for the turboprop Super DC-3s, Jack Conroy's Turbo-Three Corporation acquired 13 other C-117Ds in February 1975 from the surplus storage at Davis-Monthan AFB near Tucson, Arizona. After Conroy's death, Pilgrim bought these aircraft and continued experimenting with the prototype, now registered as N156PM. Dart 532Ls and Rotol R212 props were eventually fitted and an FAA-approved STC was issued in 1978. However, during the protracted development period, newer turboprop aircraft had become available, and N156PM was parked at Groton, Connecticut. During February 1984, a Trans America C-130 slid off the icy runway, its wing slicing through the cockpit of the deteriorating Turbo Super DC-3.

A company named Erickson and Remmert bought the aircraft in 1989 and trucked it to their Roswell, New Mexico base. They advertised it as a "Great Restoration Project" in the July 1992 *Trade-A-Plane* but there were no takers. A company spokesperson recently stated that the company is restoring the airframe and that it will fly again with Rolls-Royce turboprops.

The Navy surplus C-117Ds originally bought by the Turbo Three Corporation and later acquired by Pilgrim were, in turn, sold to Air Power Inc., of Lakeport, California. Sandy Falconer's Air Power consolidated these with other Super DC-3s purchased earlier, refurbishing several of them for resale as piston-powered cargo and express parcel freighters. The remaining Airpower C-117Ds were stored at M.R.I.'s yard adjacent to Davis-Monthan AFB. All were without engines, some had their wings removed, and several had been damaged in a windstorm. During 1994, six were registered to Basler Turbo Conversions, and one, N100BF (msn 43361), was reworked, fitted with piston engines, and flown by Warren Basler and Dan Reid to Oshkosh, Wisconsin. At that time, it was thought that the larger Super DC-3 could more efficiently use the available 1,424 shaft horsepower of the PT6A-67R than the regular DC-3s that were already being fitted with this turboprop engine by Basler. Unfortunately, Pratt & Whitney Canada have since de-rated the engine in several increments down to 1,281 eshp. This precluded its use on the heavier Super DC-3, bringing this latest conversion program to an immediate halt. The C-117Ds registered to Basler Turbo Conversions are:

N100BF (msn 43361)
N102BF (msn 43334)
N105BF (msn 43389)
N106BF (msn 43396)
N107BF (msn 43352)
N110BF (msn 43381)

Finally, perhaps the most radical turbine DC-3 concept was that envisioned by Floyd Snow, chairman of Aircraft Technical Services in Van Nuys, California. Hanging on the wall of his airport office is a painting depicting a pressurized, tri-cycle gear, turboprop-powered DC-3 airliner that was engineered but never built.

Nimble conversions of a plane designed 60 years ago are already sharing the higher altitude airways of the modern airliners. They aren't yet as fast as the Boeing 737s, but who knows? Perhaps before the DC-3 reaches its 100th birthday, another Jack Conroy will come along and hang a big turbofan under each wing. The aviation world would then, at last, have found the long sought-after replacement for the original Douglas DC-3.

The Conroy Super Turbo Three (msn 43193) at Santa Barbara, California in June 1974. This aircraft was fitted with the Dart 510-65 turbines. (Larry Smalley via Ed Davies Collection)

Nick Veronico

Chapter 5

Odds and Ends

One of five DC-3s operated by the U.S. Atomic Energy Commission between 1966 and 1971 is shown here at the FAA's Oklahoma City maintenance base in the mid-1960s. (FAA)

Aerojet's N241AG (msn 19662) at what is now Executive Airport, Sacramento, California, in September 1959. The DC-3 is finished with white upper surfaces, grey lower surfaces, and a dark blue cheat line. The radome on the nose is painted a bright "day-glo" orange. N241AG was built as C-47A 43-15196 and enjoyed a long civil service. (Dusty Carter via Scott Thompson)

One of the more unusual adaptations to the DC-3 occurred in the interest of selling pick-up trucks. These two photos depict N168LG (msn 4089) equipped with the cut-down chassis of a Chevrolet pick-up truck instead of conventional landing gear. Not surprisingly, this was done for a television commercial filmed at Sebring, Florida, in the summer of 1976. N168LG, built for Eastern Air Lines in 1941 and delivered as NC28381, had seen its landing gear assembly replaced by the front end suspension, wheels, tires, brakes, and shock absorbers from a Chevy truck. Mountings for three cameras were installed on and around the landing gear, and more than 14,000 feet of film was shot from those cameras as well as from other air-to-air, ground-to-air, and air-to-ground positions. At the time of the filming N168LG was owned by Florida Airmotive of Lantana, Florida. After the filming was completed, the aircraft returned to its more conventional state and was eventually purchased by Missionair, a group of Christian missionaries which operate the DC-3 as N79MA. No doubt that, as a result of the commercial, Americans were able to go to bed at night secure in the knowledge that yes, in a pinch, they could substitute their Chevy's front end for a DC-3's undercarriage. (Photos courtesey Owen Glassway/Florida Airmotive)

C-53D 42-68834 (msn 11761) was delivered to the USAAF in July 1943 and assigned to the 8th Air Force in England. Surplus to requirements after November 1945, it was flown by Eastern Airlines as NC86562 until 1952. Following a succession of corporate and private owners, the C-53, registered as N130Q, was acquired in 1976 by Dick Folsom and his partners for conversion to a float plane. They had discovered a set of Edo floats in Texas and manufactured the struts and fuselage doublers from the original Douglas drawings. The experimental type certificate for the amphibious DC-3 was awarded in September 1990, and the first flight took place from the Greenville airport that afternoon. This view shows the aircraft at Titusville, Florida, in March 1991. (Kevin Grantham via Ed Davies)

The Fuerza Aerea Ecuatoriana (FAE) operated at least 14 C-47/DC-3s through the years for transportation and logistical support. Though the first few aircraft had FAE serials assigned in a block, aircraft identification reverted to variations of the Douglas msn or the USAAF serial. This view shows FAE 4341 (msn 4341) in August 1974 at Quito, Ecuador. Note that the aircraft also carries the civil registration of HC-AUZ. FAE 4341 was reported withdrawn from service in 1977 and its fate is unknown. (Rene J. Francillon)

A "black" C-47, this being a DC-3 assigned to the federal Drug Enforcement Agency with a somewhat mysterious unattributed registration. As it turns out, N57123 is msn 33170, which had been delivered to the USAAF as C-47B 44-76838, transferred to the U.S. Navy as R4D-7 BuNo 99831, and then to the U.S. Army as 9831. It was evidently mustered out of the Army in the late 1970s and took on a somewhat covert role in the war against drugs. There is no record of its ever officially being assigned a civil registration number, but for the sake of "sales opportunities" to the underbelly of society the DC-3 carries the civil registration of N57123 in this December 1990 view taken at Falcon Field, Arizona. (Scott Thompson)

R4D-8 BuNo 12420 at MCAS El Toro, California in 1961. (msn 43312, built as msn 9442). At this point, Marine transports retained the bright international orange "day-glo" markings on the wings, tail, and fuselage. This aircraft had been delivered as an R4D-5 in 1943 and was later converted by Douglas to the R4D-8/C-117D standard. It was last reported as stored at Davis-Monthan AFB, but its fate is unknown. (Dusty Carter via Scott Thompson)

What if you have a somewhat rare C-53, but your customer wants an example of the plentiful C-47? Though the answer may be obvious, this December 1986 view shows another method. When the Travis Heritage Museum (California) wanted a C-47 for its display, all that could be found (?) was C-53 N1301 (msn 4864). Lacking such attributes as a cargo door and navigator's astrodome, the accomodating Aero Nostalgia of Stockton, California, cut a cargo door opening into the fuselage of the C-53 and inserted the cannibalized door from SC-47D 43-16250 (msn 20716). The airplane never made it to Travis; instead, it languished at Stockton for several years before it was moved to Edwards AFB, where it remains on display. (Scott Thompson)

The DC-3 has long been the aircraft of choice for aerial spraying of insecticide, particularly for mosquito control through the Southeastern U.S. One such aircraft is presently owned by the state of Florida and assigned to the state's Department of Agricultural Consumer Services. Based out of Panama City airport, this aircraft, N843DD (msn 34286), is dedicated to aerial spraying over the beaches of the Emerald Coast during the five-month long summer dogfly season. Fitted with an internal 500-gallon tank, the insecticide is carefully metered and dispensed through a tail-mounted spray boom. These views shows the aircraft at Panama City in April 1994. (Ed Davies)

Ed Davies

Chapter 6

Return to Normandy

More than 10,000 military derivatives of the DC-3 were built in the United States between 1938 and 1945. Designated as C-41, C-47, C-53, R4D and C-117, they were variously called Skytrains, Gooney Birds, Dakotas and Skytroopers. Impressed civilian DC-3s were redesignated as the C-48, C49, C-50, C-51, or C-52, depending upon their original configuration. Available, rugged and reliable transport aircraft, these DC-3s served with distinction in all theaters of operation during World War II. By early 1944, Lend Lease Dakotas had also became the backbone of the transport commands of the Allied Air Forces in Europe and the Pacific.

Perhaps the most significant wartime deployment of this unique plane was during the Allied invasion of Normandy on June 6, 1944. Designed to support the seaborne army that would open the long awaited second front in the European war, a huge aerial armada was assembled in Britain. They were to carry the paratroopers that would spearhead the invasion, and then haul gliders with troops and vehicles to secure strategic targets and protect the flanks of the main force. When the bridgehead was established, these same planes flew hundreds of re-supply missions carrying food, fuel, and ammunition to the Continent. On the return they became angels of mercy, evacuating both wounded soldiers and liberated prisoners of war, many of whom had been incarcerated in Europe since Dunkirk.

Half a century later, two survivors of this famous type crossed the North Atlantic to participate in the commemoration of the 50th anniversary of the D-Day landings. One was a veteran of the original invasion, having hauled a glider to Normandy on the afternoon of June 6, 1944. The other was the historic C-41, the first military transport version of the DC-3, built in 1938 as a V.I.P. transport for the U.S. Army Air Corps. This is the story of these two survivors and their recent pilgrimage to Europe.

The DC-3 revolutionized air transportation when it was introduced into service in early 1936, and by 1940 the big taildragger was carrying 95 percent of the world's airline passengers. While war raged over Europe and the Pacific during the 1940s, the available, rugged, and proven airframe became the basis of the C-47 Skytrain, built in prodigious quantities to meet the transport requirements of the U.S. Armed Forces. The original manufacturing facility was located at the Douglas plant at Santa Monica, California. Overwhelmed by orders for the new transport, the bulk of wartime production took place at new plants located at Long Beach, California, and Oklahoma City, Oklahoma.

Following the passage of the Lend Lease Act in March 1941, many U.S. built aircraft types were made available to the Allied Air Forces. One of these aircraft, C-47A-10-DK 42-92606 (msn 12425), rolled from the Douglas-Oklahoma City plant in January 1944. Assigned to the RAF as Dakota III KG395, it was flown to Dorval in Canada and turned over to Ferry Command for the long ferry flight to the U.K.

Early in the war, aircraft purchased by the Allies in the United States had been shipped to Europe by boat. However, long transit times and unacceptably high losses to German U-Boats prompted the Allies to consider ferrying medium range aircraft from their factories in the United States directly to airfields in Britain. On November 10, 1940, D.C.T "Pathfinder" Bennet led the first flight of Lockheed Hudsons from Gander in Newfoundland. All seven landed safely at Aldergrove in Northern Ireland, initiating what was to become known as the North Atlantic Bridge. Beginning shortly afterwards, airfields approximately 800 nautical miles apart were carved out of the rocks and frozen tundra in Canada, Greenland, and Iceland to support the trans-Atlantic route.

Operation Bolero, the massing of U.S. forces in Britain in preparation for the inevitable invasion of Europe, rapidly increased the number of aircraft being flown across the North Atlantic. On July 14, 1942, two flights of Lockheed P-38 Lightnings, *Tomcat Yellow* and *Tomcat Green,* left BW-8 on the west coast of Greenland bound for Reykjavik in Iceland. The six fighters were accompanied by two B-17 Flying Fortresses whose crews would assist in the overwater navigation for the single-crewed fighters. Deteriorating weather and misinformation broadcast by an enemy radio station caused the squadron to become hopelessly lost. Desperately short of fuel, they successfully crash-landed on the ice cap near the east coast of Greenland. None of the aircrew were seriously injured, and eventually all were picked up by a Coast Guard cutter. The eight fighters and bombers were left to slowly disappear beneath the Arctic ice and snow.

By 1944, the Allies had obtained the right to use landing fields in the Azores as a stepping stone to Europe, providing a preferred alternate route during the Arctic winter. It was via Gander and Lagens (in the Azores) that, in February 1944, Sgt W.F. Symons and his crew ferried Dakota KG395 to war. They flew far south of the snow-covered Lightnings, but years later the Dakota and the fighters would be united in a most unusual way.

On March 1, 1944, the RAF's 48 Squadron commenced its new role with Transport Command while based at the still unfinished airfield at Down Ampney, just north of the village of Cricklade in Gloucestershire. Less than a month earlier they had been flying Lockheed Hudsons from Gibraltar on anti-submarine patrols over the Spanish coastal waters. One of five new squadrons forming Airborne Forces Group 46, they re-equipped with Dakotas and began training for the impending invasion of continental Europe. During the first month at Down Ampney, all of the 48 Squadron crews transitioned to the American-built transport plane, flying more than 1,400 hours of intense training with only two accidents, both of which occurred during taxiing. KG395 was one of the aircraft assigned to the re-formed 48 Squadron.

Through May 1944, 46 Group squadrons trained by day and night, participating in both glider towing and paratroopers dropping. Extensive navigation exercises were conducted, enabling the crews to hone their skills with the GEE equipment, their principal aid in finding the target zone. Escape aids, compasses, magnetic buttons and escape boxes were issued for all future operations. Crews were photographed in civilian clothes to provide passport photographs, useful later to assist in escape if they were unfortunate enough to be taken prisoner. *Consternation* was the last major exercise when, in poor visibility, 75 Horsa gliders were successfully landed at Netherhaven. On May 27, all leave was canceled until further notice and the squadron was notified that further training flying was to cease. They were apparently ready for war.

In England, the first day of June 1944 dawned sunny and warm. At 1400 hours on June 2 the Station Commander, Group Capt. Bradbury, DFC, announced that the camp would be sealed until further notice. Personnel off the base were rounded up with the help of the local police. The following morning, aircrews were given the first preliminary briefing of the part that they would play in the impending D-Day operation. June 4 began with a lecture on security, escape kits were issued, and crews stood by waiting for a final briefing for the operation expected to begin that night. The evening, however, saw the weather turn to rain and the assault on Fortress Europe was postponed for 24 hours.

Early the next day, all crews attended refresher briefings for what was dubbed *Operation Tonga*.

The plan called for the British airborne units to secure the left flank of the Allied bridgehead in Normandy, capture bridges over the River Orme and Caen Canal, and take out the German battery at Merville. Scheduled to commence at 2320 hours, 48 Squadron was slated to provide 30 aircraft carrying 517 paratroopers, their supplies, and 92 containers of arms and ammunition. Tensions heightened as truck after truckload of blackened-faced paratroopers rumbled up to where the Dakotas parked in line. When all the troops had been loaded, a car stopped at each aircraft to hand out a communiqué bearing a Godspeed message from the Allied Supreme Commander, Gen. Dwight Eisenhower. It was quite dark when the large cargo doors were shut and latched on each of the several dozen Dakotas parked across the field. Quickly, the quiet of the English country side was shattered as one by one the Pratt & Whitney radials thundered to life, joining a rising crescendo of noise on the ground and in the air. First off was Squadron Leader C. N. "Mac" McVeigh in KG321. Their course took them over Chedworth, Fairoaks, crossing the English coast at Worthing, then over the channel to their designated drop zone, coded *Victor*, in Normandy. The Down Ampney con-

Horsa gliders with RAF Dakotas from the RAF's 437 Squadron in the background. (via Ed Davies)

RAF Dakotas being used to repatriate Allied POWs in Belgium, date unknown. (via Ed Davies)

tingent were part of a huge armada of 364 aircraft and 98 gliders that delivered troops of the 6th Airborne Division. Several of the squadron's aircraft took hits from flak and small arms fire, but all were able to successfully drop their human cargo on target and return to base. During this operation, and for perhaps the first time in its checkered history, the Douglas transport had also become a bomber. Each plane carried twelve 20 pound bombs to be hurled out of the door as it crossed the French coast and intended to intimidate the waiting German anti-aircraft gunners.

Planned for the late afternoon of June 6 was a second airborne strike to support the main seaborne invasion forces landing at Normandy. *Operation Mallard* was designed to help reinforce the existing airborne bridgehead, with 256 gliders and their tugs taking off from seven airfields in southern England with men and equipment of the 6th Air Landing Brigade. For the first time in the history of airborne warfare, light tanks would be flown into the battle zone aboard giant Hamilcar gliders. The majority of the gliders were to be Airspeed Horsas, high wing monoplanes built almost entirely out of wood and fabric. The wing span was 88 feet, and the Horsa had an overall length of 67 feet. Two pilots from the Glider Pilot Regiment sat side by side in the forward cockpit, while 26 troops and their equipment could be accommodated in the cavernous aft cabin. Alternatively, a jeep and trailer or small artillery piece could be loaded through the hinged nose section. The tow rope was 350 feet long, 3 3/8 inches in circumference, and contained telephone wires used to carry communications between the pilots of the tug and glider. Normal towing speed was 149 to 160 mph, with the gliders setting up for landings at 80 to 91 mph. Large two-piece split flaps allowed a steep angle of descent and a shallow roll out. The ground run was shortened by compressed air-operated brakes.

48 Squadron launched 22 Dakotas from Down Ampney on the afternoon of June 6, and the time had come for KG395 to go to war. High visibility black and white invasion stripes had been crudely painted above and below each wing and around the aft fuselage in an effort to minimize losses from friendly fire. Each aircraft also had the squadron code and individual call sign painted on each side of the aft fuselage, KG395 being identified as 12-AB (Able Baker).

The operational briefing had been held that morning as crews familiarized themselves with the route and aerial photographs of their landing zone, coded *N*. The summer evening was calm and clear as Able Baker, at precisely 1852 hours, became the second aircraft to takeoff. The engines strained at maximum takeoff power, and every foot of the runway was needed to haul the heavily loaded glider into the air. Pilot in command of KG395 was F/L R. R. Keiller, copilot W/O R. T. Barry, navigator F/S S.H. Birch and wireless operator W/O J. I. Parry. Their route took them over the south of England, crossing the coast near Littlehampton. Eureka transponder beacons were set up here and at the landing zone, giving a course to steer when interrogated by the plane's Rebecca transmitter. The channel crossing at 150 mph at an altitude of 500 feet proved uneventful under the watchful eyes of Spitfires and Mustangs flying top cover.

Landfall over the French coast was made near the mouth of the Caen Canal, and visual markers were picked up, identifying their assigned landing zone. KG395's glider was released over the target at 2104 hours. The Dakota made a right turn and flew a reciprocal course at 3,000 feet back to base. Light to heavy flak was encountered but Able Baker returned unscathed from her D-Day combat debut.

Over the next several months, KG395 flew sortie after sortie to continental Europe in support of the advancing ground forces. Reinforcements, supplies, and ammunition were flown into the war zone, while returning aircraft were filled with the wounded and repatriated prisoners of war. In September 1944, the transport role was put aside for another major airborne assault. *Operation Market-Garden* was a planned strike through the Low Countries, crossing the Rhine north of the Siegfried line. *Garden* was the code name for the thrust into Germany by the British 2nd Army. *Market* was essentially a carpet of airborne forces to be laid down ahead of the advancing army to secure the strategic canal and river crossings. At the mid-morning of September 17, 1944, F/L Keiller and his crew again took KG395 to war, this time to the infamous "Bridge Too Far" at Arnhem. Their Horsa glider, chalk number 282, with S/Sgt Dance and Sgt Bird at the controls, carried 26 troops of the King's Own Scottish Borderers. The next day KG395 went back, this time with F/L P. W. "Pete" Smith in command, their towed Horsa carrying elements of the 1st Airborne Division. The Dakota was hit several times by small arms fire but suffered no serious damage. On September 19, braving what was by now an intense flak corridor, KG395 dropped panniers of ammunition to the beleaguered garrison at the bridge at Arnhem.

During this period, 437 Squadron, an all-Canadian unit still under the command of 46 Transport Group RAF, was formed at Blakehill Farm. KG395 was assigned to the new squadron and its first mission was back to Arnhem for yet another re-supply drop on September 21. Emerging once again virtually unscathed from the dangerous airborne missions, the Dakota returned to the more mundane task of supply and medivac operations.

The last major airborne offensive of the war was *Operation Varsity*, which began on March 24, 1945. A day or two earlier, 437 Squadron's aircraft were flown to Birch in Essex to be closer to the target area. KG395's assignment was once again to tow a Horsa glider, this time carrying a jeep, an anti-tank gun, and its crew. Pilot- in-command of the Dakota was F/O J. H. "Sinbad" Philipps, second pilot F/S R. W. Green, navigator F/O W. J. Hughes and wireless operator F/S R. E. Frank. On a clear European afternoon, the British squadrons joined up with USAAF units, arriving from airfields in France, over Wavre in Belgium and proceeded to the target in three massive traffic lanes. After successfully releasing their gliders over the landing zone, 437 Squadron aircraft flew to the advanced landing field B75 near Nivelles in Belgium for debriefing and a possible re-supply mission the following day. They were not needed, however, and instead returned to their base to resume the day-to-day transport role.

After hostilities had ceased in Europe in May 1945, KG395 returned to Canada for post-war service with the RCAF. It was ferried by P/O Jack Wells and his crew, leaving Odiham on June 15, 1946. They flew the north Atlantic route, skirting the southern tip of Greenland, where a group of long-forgotten B-17s and P-38s were already lost from sight beneath the ice and snow. KG395 remained in service with the RCAF/CAF until declared surplus to requirements and sold to Owen Wilson in October 1975. Ferried to Wyoming, it sat in storage for several years until acquired by a Corpus Christi, Texas company in July 1985 and registered as N99FS. Bought next by Basler Flight Services of Oshkosh, Wisconsin, it was converted by them to a freighter configuration and sold to Flite Services Inc., based at Peachtree-Dekalb Airport in Atlanta, Georgia.

During the fall of 1988, the Greenland Expedition Society began planning their 1989 expedition to drill down to one of those forgotten B-17 bombers trapped far beneath Greenland ice, and they were looking for a ski-equipped transport to haul their equipment. A DC-3 seemed the only practical choice, and N99FS was acquired by Don Brooks for use by the group. A new set of skis was found in Yellowknife (Yukon), and the Dakota flew back over the North Atlantic to Kulusuk in Greenland. There were maddening weather delays, but eventually the DC-3 hauled men and materials to the ice cap recovery site. That summer one

N99FS (msn 12425) on the Greenland Ice Cap with the Greenland Expedition Society. The society's efforts eventually led to the recovery of a Lockheed P-38 which is now being restored to flying condition. (via Ed Davies)

of the B-17s was located and a tiny piece of metal from the aircraft recovered, but the efforts to drill a significant hole stalled after 75 feet. The camp was secured, and N99FS, together with the expedition members and equipment, returned to Atlanta. The following summer, two Air Force C-130s were contracted to haul the massive equipment needed at the recovery site. However, before they could land, it was the veteran Dakota that had to taxi up and down on the ice cap, its skis packing the snow on what was to be known as the "Don Brooks International Airport." Towards the end of the summer, the DC-3 lost an engine and had to make an emergency landing at Kulusuk. With winter rapidly approaching, Brooks and Bob Harless flew from Atlanta with a spare engine. Outdoors, in the numbing cold, they replaced the radial and flew the plane back to Atlanta. Their efforts would prove to be an invaluable learning experience for their later "Return to D-Day."

In May 1992 the DC-3 returned to Greenland with a refinanced expedition bent on recovering one of the lost P-38s. On May 30, the first hole bored by the team's *Gopher* drilling rig reached the Lightning at a depth of 257 feet. The veteran aircraft recovery team of Gary Larkins and "Tomcat" Mohr were called in to dismantle the fighter, working in a water-soaked cavern that the team had melted out around the plane. Piece by piece it was hauled to the surface, and major parts were flown to the U.S. for display at the Experimental Aircraft Association's annual air show at Oshkosh, Wisconsin, that August.

Brooks had become aware that his aircraft was a survivor of the invasion of Europe. Several of the British and Canadian crew members who had flown his aircraft during the conflict had been located, and the day-by-day operational history had been well documented. Brooks' connection with the war in Europe was a personal one, as his father had been based in the U.K. during the war, serving as a gunner on B-17s. He decided that he would like to return his Dakota to its 1944, RAF 48 Squadron finish and fly it across the North Atlantic for the forthcoming commemoration of the 50th anniversary of D-Day. However, he needed sponsorship help with the significant expenses involved. A group of Southern California warbird owners had also expressed interest in flying their World War II fighters and bombers to what was being planned as a huge international event. However, efforts to solicit help from the major oil companies, aircraft manufacturers, and airlines came to naught and, one by one, the California warbird owners dropped out of the proposed venture.

Meanwhile in Oakland, California, plans were well underway to fly the historic Douglas C-41 to the D-Day anniversary commemoration in Europe. NC41HQ (msn 2053) is one of two DC-3s owned and operated by Otis Spunkmeyer Air, a subsidiary of the very successful San Leandro cookie manufacturing and distribution company, Otis Spunkmeyer Inc. The aircraft are used as the company's unique flying billboards, operating spectacular sightseeing tours from Oakland's North Field. Founded by Ken and Linda Rawlings as a spinoff of their original cookie retail stores, the company owes its unusual name to their young daughter's imagination. Abandoning the cut-throat retail trade, the Rawlings rapidly expanded the company by producing delicious gourmet cookie dough and distributing it frozen to established retailers. They now have 60 distribution centers throughout the United States, Britain and Mexico, while their San Leandro and Pittsburgh, Pennsylvania, production facilities turn out a staggering 2.5 million

cookies every day.

Victory Lap Inc., another Otis Spunkmeyer company, entered the transportation business in March 1988. Operating out of Oakland's North Terminal, they offered executive jet charters using a Gates Learjet 25. Limousine service throughout the San Francisco Bay Area complemented the jet service. However, after traveling on a DC-3 in Massachusetts, the Rawlings' decided to include a *Sentimental Journey* sky tour venture in their airline package and set about acquiring their own vintage taildragger. The aircraft they bought was N97H (msn 33613), which came complete with an 18-seat executive interior. Originally built by Douglas at their Oklahoma City plant as a C-47B, it was delivered to the U.S. Army Air Forces in July 1945 as serial number 44-77281. Declared surplus to Army requirements less than a year later, it was released for sale by the War Assets Administration. Converted to a DC-3C by Airesearch in 1948, it flew for the Humble Oil & Refining Co. as an executive aircraft until 1967. Passing through several new owners, yet acquiring few flying hours, N97H was

Three views of Otis Spunmkmeyer's rare C-41 (msn 2053). Above is a 1939 view of the aircraft in USAAC service as a transport assigned to Bolling Field in Washington, D.C. (NASM 22406). At right is the aircraft as it arrived at Oakland in March 1989, still in its FAA paint scheme. (Ed Davies) Below is the DC-3 after refurbishing and new paint as it joined the Spunkmeyer fleet in offering "Sentimental Journeys" Bay Tours. (Nick Veronico)

bought by AFS Leasing, fitted with its present interior in Dallas, and began flying sky tours out of Bluefield, West Virginia. The venture was not a huge success, and shortly afterwards the plane was advertised in *Trade-a-Plane* for $160,000 and was bought by Otis Spunkmeyer. The inaugural flight out of Oakland took place on March 3, 1988, with the Rawlings hosting a plane load of guests (including this author) for a delightful champagne flight. Revenue flights began 10 days later with three fully-booked flights on its first day of operation.

Otis Spunkmeyer Air's second DC-3, the one that took part in the Normandy anniversary ceremonies, was registered as N54595 at the time of its acquisition. The only C-41 built, it is historically significant in that it was the first Douglas DC-3-type transport bought by the military, and the forerunner of those thousands built during World War II.

Built by Douglas at Santa Monica, the C-41 was assigned the USAAC serial number 38-502 and delivered to the Army on October 22, 1938. The purchase was authorized as an article in the contract W535 AC11137 for C-39 type airplanes; the sole C-41 has often been confused with this smaller type. It was, in fact, a standard DC-3 fitted with a special VIP interior. Six gray and wine-colored, upholstered swivel chairs occupied each side of the forward fuselage, with a three-seat divan, parachute cabinet, buffet, lavatory and baggage compartment in the rear. Provision was made for two pilots, radio operator and a steward. The aircraft was evaluated at Wright (Ohio) and Bolling (Washington, D.C) Fields before being accepted by Headquarters

Army Air Corps at Bolling in March 1939. The new transport was then assigned to the First Staff Squadron at Bolling Field, whose mission was to provide transport for official Washington. The C-41 was, presumably, used from time to time by Commander of the Air Corps, Gen. "Hap" Arnold. Records seem to indicate that the aircraft never left the continental United States.

Though originally earmarked as one of the aircraft designated by Gen. Arnold for the future Army Air Forces Museum, the C-41 was in fact turned over to the Reconstruction Finance Corporation at Bush Field in Georgia in April 1945, as surplus to requirements. Following an overhaul and removal of military equipment by Southern Airways, the aircraft was registered as NC15473 and leased by the RFC to Alaska Airlines with a mere 2,739 flying hours on its airframe. Returned to the War Assets Administration in early 1948, the C-41 was transferred without reimbursement to the Civil Aeronautics Administration and re-registered as N12. Converted to specific CAA requirements, the unique C-41 became just one of many DC-3 types used by the CAA and, later, Federal Aviation Administration to check navigation aids and communication systems at airports throughout the United States. (See also Chapter 5.) The C-41's registration was later changed to N43 and continued in service through the mid-1970s.

Displaced by more modern types, the DC-3s were phased out as check aircraft and the C-41 was once again put up for disposal, this time consigned to the Missouri State Agency for Surplus Property for use by Southeast Missouri State University. The university registered the aircraft N54595 in April 1978. Converted to a "high density" 26-passenger configuration by William Williams in November 1979, the flying classroom was operated and maintained under a cooperative arrangement with Southern Illinois University and hangared at their facility in Carbondale, Illinois. The C-41, together with two other DC-3s based at Carbondale, was used to transport university students and faculty on scholastic charters and to haul athletic teams to tournaments at other universities.

The university acquired title to the aircraft in June 1985 and subsequently sold it to Red's Aircraft Sales of Jenks, Oklahoma. It quickly passed through Condor Aviation, before being bought and registered to John LaVigne, doing business as Trans Ocean Airways. in McAllen, Texas. LaVigne planned to use the aircraft in the lucrative trade of smuggling audio tapes and equipment into Mexico, thereby avoiding a high import tax. Perhaps fortunately for the aircraft, the demand for this illicit export route evaporated with a change in tariffs and devaluation of the peso. Turning to more legitimate uses, the C-41 was ironically one of the first aircraft to fly relief supplies into Mexico City after their devastating earthquake. Apart from a few TV and movie

A January 1994 view of N97H (msn 33613) at the Oakland Airport after returning from Santa Maria, California, where it had been repainted in the "Art Deco" scheme. (Ed Davies)

Stew Carson (left) and Bill Hartman in the cockpit of N97H at Santa Maria, California on January 31, 1994. More than 61,000 hours of flight time were represented in the cockpit that day, much of it logged in DC-3s (Ed Davies)

appearances, the aircraft was flown very little and, in January 1989, LaVigne called this author saying that he would like to sell the aircraft. He understood its historical significance, and didn't want it to go to another cargo hauler. I suggested that he call Ken Rawlings, and they quickly made a deal. N54595 was ferried from San Diego to Oakland in March 1989, still painted in FAA red, white and black, with its fictitious Southwest International Airways logo on the nose. Refurbishing was started at Oakland with the characteristic FAA-installed rectangular fuselage window being plated over. The C-41 was then flown to Fort Worth, where Langford Aviation installed a luxurious 18-seat interior, very similar to that of her sister ship, N97H. Both aircraft were then made available to operate the nostalgia tours and, in addition, the refurbished C-41 was dispatched on a nationwide promotional tour of cities that were major distribution centers for Otis Spunkmeyer products.

In late 1993, N97H was given a 1930s *art deco* finish, and at this time that the company decided to return the C-41 to its original USAAC finish and to fly it to the U.K. for the commemoration of the 50th anniversary of D-Day. The transformation was to be done by Aeroflair, Inc. at Santa Maria, California, with the aircraft being delivered there on January 31, 1994. The crew returned to Oakland that evening in N97H, flown by Bill Hartman and Stew Carson, probably one of the most experienced crews ever to fly a DC-3. Between them they had amassed more than 61,000 hours of flying time. Resplendent in the red and white eye-catching chevrons on the tail and Bolling Field emblem on the fuselage, the C-41 returned to Oakland late in the evening of March 17, 1994. Seeking a more appropriate registration, the owner had requested *NC41* but it was unfortunately already taken (by the FAA, no less). The next available alternative was NC41HQ, and this mark was reserved for the veteran warbird.

Dale Collier was given the daunting task of preparing the aircraft and arranging the challenging trans-Atlantic schedule. The Otis Spunkmeyer decision to take the plane to Europe reaped an early dividend when the C-41 was invited to take part in the official June 5, 1994 flypast. They were to be the only civilian U.S. registered aircraft in the flyover of Portsmouth Harbor and the Royal Yacht Britannia. Aboard would be the Queen of England and President Clinton. The veteran Douglas twin was to fly in the second squadron, in company with a Lancaster, Hurricane, Firefly, Avenger, B-17, and B-25, and would represent the thousands of military DC-3s that actually took part in the D-Day operation.

The departure for Britain was set for noon on May 9 from the Kaiser FBO at Oakland North Field. The morning was uncharacteristically overcast, but occasional showers did nothing to dampen the enthusiasm of the small crowd of well-wishers. Pilots were Colier and Carson; also aboard were Otis Spunkmeyer Air President Geoff Macfee who was along for the first cross-country segment, and San Francisco *Examiner* reporter Eric Brazil, who would report on the progress of the flight. The first scheduled stop was to have been Colorado Springs, but a snowstorm over the Monarch Pass in the Rocky Mountains caused the plane to spend the first night at Montrose, Colorado. There was more bad news the next day, when the Air Force suddenly withdrew permission for the C-41 to land at the Air Force Academy, saying that the DC-3 was "too heavy"! Far more serious was a worsening flutter on the plane's big flaps. As a diversion was necessary, the DC-3 made another unscheduled stop at Oshkosh, Wisconsin, where Warren Basler and his DC-3 magicians re-rigged the offending flap controls. Next stop was Akron, Ohio, where deicing boots were fitted to the leading edges of the wings and empenage. Unnecessary in California's warm climate, they could be lifesavers in preventing the buildup of ice on the wings while flying over the cold North Atlantic.

Colier's father joined the flight at Rochester and, after the final stop in the United States at Bangor, Maine, the 55-year-old-plane was back on schedule when it arrived late in the evening of Saturday, May 14, at a rain-soaked, overcast, cold, Goose Bay in Labrador. Loaded with survival gear and briefed for the long overwater crossing, the C-41 departed from a gloomy Labrador, climbing through to sunshine at their freezing 8,000 foot cruising altitude.

$4,000 worth of expensive fuel was taken on at Narsaruaq's spectacular airport on the southern tip of Greenland before beginning the second overwater leg to Reykjavic, Iceland, and a well-earned night's rest. On the afternoon of May 18, the jubilant crew made their landfall in the U.K., arriving to a warm welcome at Edinburgh airport. They went on to Duxford, then participated in the Mildenhall Air Show before being swept up in the official D-Day commemorative ceremonies.

Author Nick Veronico and I waved our good-byes to the Otis Spunkmeyer plane over the Northern California hills of Marin County as we followed them for a brief air-to-air photo session before they departed on the first leg of their long journey. I had arranged to meet up with them in the U.K. and perhaps fly with them on the June 6 flypast. When I returned home that evening there was a message from Brooks; he was going to take his KG395 to Britain for the D-Day ceremonies, and would I like to go along?

Departure was scheduled for the early morning of May 24 from Epps Air Service at Atlanta's DeKalb-Peachtree Airport. The schedule would allow us to meet up with the C-41 at Mildenhall and participate with them in the weekend airshow. The Dakota would not take part in the official June 6 flypast, but would drop veteran paratroopers of the U.S. 82nd and 101st Airborne over Normandy. Harless and his crew at the plane's Douglas Georgia base magically restored the exterior finish to the same one worn by the aircraft half a century earlier. An original astrodome was found at California Airframe in Oakland and air-expressed to Atlanta. A static line for the paras was installed in the fuselage, together with a voice communication system between the cockpit and the jump door. The same crew had flown the aircraft to Greenland during the P-38 recovery and knew the capability of the remarkable Global Positioning System navigation receiver.

I left San Francisco on a Markair 737 for Denver, Kansas City, and then Atlanta's sprawling Hartfield International Airport. At the gate a large notice reading "Ed Davies, DC-3 to Normandy" caught my eye (how could it not?), and identified Pierre and my ride over to the other Atlanta airport.

Brooks and his crew had done a magnificent job in a very short time. Bathed in the evening sun, KG395 looked resplendent in her new and barely dry invasion livery. Over supper it was time for the crew and fellow passengers to become acquainted. Pat Epps and Harless were both type-rated DC-3 pilots, and had flown this plane for the past two years. Don Brooks and Joey Hand were multi-engine rated and were to take some of the right seat time. Photo Journalist Todd Huvar would record our experiences, while Dr. Dan Callahan would look after the physical well being of the crew. Dr. Dan and fellow passenger, Ramsey "Bub" Way, were both veterans of the Greenland expeditions. Jorg Hammermeister and Bernd Birkholz had been in the U.S. gathering video and sound for a German documentary on D-Day and were to fly with us to record the event for television. Immersion suits, food, and our personal gear were all loaded and secured along the center of the cabin. Brooks and Epps briefed us on the flight, and at 0140 on a pleasant star-lit morning KG395 thundered into the Georgia sky.

N99FS at Atlanta's DeKalb-Peachtree Airport on the evening of May 23, 1994. At this point, the historic Dakota had just been refinished in the paint and markings it had worn 50 years earlier. (Ed Davies)

The ride was smooth and reasonably quiet as we climbed to our cruising altitude of 9,000 feet. However, the temperature in the unheated cabin dropped very, very quickly and, suitably forewarned, the passengers in the six Boeing 727 economy seats in the rear began putting on their insulated coveralls, boots, gloves, and head gear. In what seemed no time at all the cabin turned from dark to gray to a warm pink as the sun began to climb above the eastern horizon. Barreling along at an indicated 130 knots, sleeping passengers stirred as Quebec City came into sight, and we landed after what proved to be the longest segment, with a recorded flying time of six hours and 53 minutes

The weather remained sunny and warm as we cleared Canadian customs, refueled, and enjoyed a hearty breakfast at the airport restaurant. However, upon return-

N99FS being refueled at Quebec City along the St. Lawrence seaway. The recalcitrant starboard engine gave its first hint of the troubles to come on the leg into Quebec City. (Ed Davies)

Canadian Coast Guard C-FDTH (msm 12591) on the ramp at Quebec City. This C-47 landed shortly after N99FS. (Ed Davies)

ing to the aircraft, tell tale oil stains on the tarmac indicated a potential problem with the starboard engine. A space was found near the Conifair hangar at the rear of the airport, and KG395 was taxied around to where the cowlings could be pulled for a closer look at the oil stained R-1830. Looking across the ramp, it seemed that we had entered a time warp back to the 1940s, when piston engine planes ruled the airways. Two silent rows of Conifair big brother Douglas DC-4s and 6s were off to our left, while ahead were two PBY Catalina flying boats, recently withdrawn from fire-bomber service. The distinctive sound of another DC-3 approached the field, and soon a sparkling aircraft in the red and white colors of the Canadian Coast Guard landed and taxied up to the terminal. The new arrival was C-FDTH (msn 12591), a Dakota built soon after ours, having been given serial number KG479 and having also served with the RCAF. Behind us, the radial engines of a Canadair CL-215 purpose-built firebomber sputtered into life, the rising noise reverberating from the hangars as they ran their magneto checks.

Meanwhile, the suspected Pratt & Whitney was washed down with solvent, and though Harless and Hand went over each oil line and connection, there was no obvious reason found for the ominous oil spill. The engine was ground run for quite a while, exhibiting no apparent oil leaks. Thus assured, the engine was buttoned up, and at 1515 local time we departed Quebec City for our next destination, Goose Bay in Labrador. Heading east along the mighty St. Lawrence River, the pulp mill city of Baie Comeau and the iron ore port of Sept Isles soon passed under the port wing. As the river widened enough to be mistaken for an ocean, we turned north into the forbidding interior of the Labrador plateau. Snow still lay among the stunted trees and frozen lakes in the scarcely inhabited area that Hammond Innis described as "the land that God gave Caine."

The weather had deteriorated to a gray overcast as, 170 miles out of Goose Bay, the starboard engine sputtered and almost stopped. A reduced power setting and the application of carburetor heat revived the powerplant, but not for long. A stream of dark oil poured over the inboard side of the nacelle, and the injured DC-3 crabbed her way through the sky as the power varied on the obviously wounded engine. Quiet passengers took their seats and hitched their seat belts tight as anxious crewmembers came back to look at the growing dark stain on the side of the engine. Goose Bay was informed of the situation, but no emergency was declared as yet. The pilots decided to keep the damaged engine running while it was at least providing some power.

The skilled crew grappled with the sick plane for a very long 20 minutes; then, inexplicably, the oil pressure and temperature settled down, and the Pratt & Whitney Twin Wasp began to growl along at a steady, albeit reduced power. Passenger anxiety eased a few notches, but it was another interminable hour before the welcome sight of the long runway at Goose Bay appeared dead ahead. Conscious of the possibility of a fire as the oil spilled over the hot exhaust manifold, fire trucks raced down the runway alongside the landing aircraft. Fortunately, the drama was over, and their services were not required as the Dakota taxied off the runway and its engines ground to a halt. Oil absorbing mats were thrown under the silent but still bleeding right engine. Too late to do anything that evening, the Dakota was parked on the Woodward Aviation Service's ramp, and we headed for Happy Valley and the Labrador Inn.

A visual check early the following morning revealed one obviously cracked cylinder head and possibly a second one in the same condition. Meeting in Woodward's pilots' lounge, Brooks reviewed the situation and the available options. Despite the previous evening's harrowing experience, the unanimous feeling was that, if possible, we should continue our historic return to Normandy. Pat Epps called Warren Basler, the DC-3 'Guru' in Oshkosh, to inquire about the availability of a replacement engine. Twenty minutes later he called back. Not only did he have a Twin Wasp QEC built up, but one of their amazing turbo DC-3 conversions was leaving for Germany within the hour, scheduled to go via Goose Bay. We were obviously destined to make this journey. They would bring the QEC, prop nut wrench, and special sling needed during the engine replacement.

Goose Bay is a unique Canadian Air Force Base with permanent facilities for NATO forces to practice bombing and defensive sorties. British, German, and Belgian squadrons of Tornados, F-16s, and Phantoms are rotated through this remote base to hone their low-level flying skills. The weather was still cold with occasional snow squalls, so we were fortunate that the RAF agreed to let us use one of their hangars to do the work on KG395. No tow bar was available to fit the ancient warrior. The long trip to the hangar was the first of many improvisations, as we used the plane's good engine to taxi against bitter gale force winds, steering with a bar lashed to the castering tail wheel.

On the ground at Goose Bay in Labrador. It was later determined that the starboard engine had blown two cylinders and lost a massive amount of oil on the way into Goose Bay. (Ed Davies)

That evening, Dan Reid, Basler Turbo Conversion's director of International Operations, arrived at Goose Bay with a Turbo 67, N96BF (msn 13321). Helped by a tail wind at their 23,000-foot cruise altitude, this transformed DC-3 had averaged close to a 300-knot ground speed for the journey from Wisconsin. For this trip, N96BF carried the logos of the potential German customer SL Express. Later, Dan and I discussed meeting up when we arrived in Britain. But it was not to be, and I would never see this skilled pilot and adamant believer in the turbo-DC-3 again. He and his DC-3 "baby" had flown on many mercy missions for relief agencies in Africa but, in December 1994, while taking of from a remote strip in Angola, the cargo load of food shifted and caused N96BF to crash, killing Reid and his co-pilot.

During the morning of May 26th, the replacement engine was off-loaded and the formidable task of changing out the power unit began. Brooks, Hand and Harless were no strangers to the job. Harless had been an engineer with Southern Airlines during the heyday of its DC-3 operations, and two years earlier this crew had installed this same engine, working outdoors in Greenland and racing against the rapidly approaching winter. The damaged engine was soon off and the replacement Pratt & Whitney was swung into position and securely bolted to the firewall. Then problems began with accessories that didn't work, pieces that wouldn't fit, and tools and parts that we had to scrounge. By Friday (May 27) it was apparent that we would not be able to make the Mildenhall Air Show, and we had to call the organizers with the disappointing news.

The following day, however, things really began to come together, and just before noon we were able to test-run the new engine. Spirits were high when later in the day we were able to make a prolonged run to test all the systems and check for leaks. Everything went well, and before dark the cowlings were coaxed over the replacement unit.

QEC to replace the damaged Pratt & Whitney as being unloaded from the N96BF, a Basler Turbo DC-3, at Goose Bay. Basler graciously enabled N99FS and its crew to continue to England by the timely provision of the fresh engine and means of delivery.(Ed Davies)

The next morning the weather was cold, overcast, and windy as we checked out of the Labrador Inn, everyone looking forward to getting the journey underway once more. Unfortunately, our hopes were dashed at the weather briefing: Greenland was reported as "socked in" with little chance of improvement for the rest of the day. The one bright spot was a flawless local flight test, after which we all trekked back to Happy Valley and the Aurora Inn, the town's other hotel. The following morning, we were up at the crack of Labrador's early dawn, sharing the bus to the airport with the Luftwaffe Transvall crews who were also flying to Europe. Again, it was cold, but now we had clear skies that the meteorological office said extended all the way to Iceland and a forecasted 25-knot tailwind that might help us on our way. At 0615 local time, with both engines flawlessly warmed up and checked out, KG395 taxied out for the 674 nautical mile first over water leg of the long North Atlantic crossing. Four uneventful hours later, we approached the southern tip of Greenland and the most spectacular 20 minutes of the flight.

Epps brought the big plane down to 200 feet as we entered the long approach up the fjord to the airfield known as Bluie West One when it was completed in late 1942. Carved out of virgin rock at the only suitable area on the southern part of this inhospitable island, the field and its infamous instrument approach has been solidly engraved in the memory of many wartime ferry pilots. For our trip up the 40-mile fjord, the sun beamed down from a cloudless sky as ice flows and small icebergs drifted under the wings, their underwater sides glowing an iridescent turquoise. Most of the way, the dark walls, occasionally dotted with snow or draped with plunging waterfalls, towered above the air-

Engine runs after the engine change-out. The delay prevented N99FS from participating in the some of the planned activities in commemoration of the 50th anniversery of the D-Day landings. (Ed Davies)

Navigating up the fjord on the approach into the Greenland airfield known as Bluie West One when built in 1942. Now known as Narsarsua, the one-way approach remains the same. Glacial ice and granite await a pilot who misjudges his landing approach. (Ed Davies)

After a successful arrival at Narsarsua, the crew of N99FS hurries to depart in the face of deterioating weather enroute to Iceland. (Ed Davies)

On the ground at Glasgow, Scotland, on May 31, 1994. N99FS was able to participate in many D-Day activities, including the paratrooper drops over France on June 6, 1994 with many veterans who had participated in the D-Day drops 50 years earlier. (Ed Davies)

craft. Up ahead the water widened out, and we had our first glimpse of the single light brown runway, sloping down to the water's edge. A sweeping right turn, and we were headed for the only piece of flat land around. The "overshoot" area was dominated by the black rocks of the coastal range, beyond them a white glacier field and the towering snow-covered mountains. The touchdown was gentle with ample room to spare, and the Dakota taxied over to the pristine terminal. The only other activity was a Gronlandsfly S-61 helicopter being loaded with mail and two passengers. The small fuel truck came alongside and we stretched our legs as the plane's tanks were topped up with expensive gasoline. A pair of small twins, both equipped for aerial photography and being ferried from Africa to Canada, suddenly made the strangely silent airport seem quite busy. The weather ahead was reported as deteriorating, so after exchanging pleasantries with the newly arrived pilots, we taxied out for the trip over the remote ocean from Greenland to Iceland.

The departure was routine as we cut across the southeast corner of the huge island. The original flight plan had called for a more northerly flight over the remaining buried P-38s, with a landing at Kulusuk to meet friends made by the Greenland Expedition members. However, we were now so far behind schedule it was necessary to press for an early evening landfall at Reykjavik. Four hours and 10 minutes later we landed through a cold overcast with light rain. Aviation Services took care of the plane and the crew enjoyed an excellent meal, late night tour of this bustling northern city, and the almost forgotten comforts afforded by the luxurious Hotel Loftleider.

Lulled by the big city comfort and amenities, the departure time from Reykjavik was at a decadent 1030 local time. The route was direct to Glasgow in Scotland, 740 nautical miles away and most of it again over the cold gray ocean. Trip time was four hours 45 minutes, arriving to a warm welcome on another dreary wet, late afternoon. Customs were minimal, landing fees were waived, and Execair had hot coffee for us at their general aviation terminal. The bad news was that our final destination, Duxford, would be closed by the time that we could get there, necessitating another overnight stop. My schedule called for me to arrive in London the following morning, so the good guys at Execair ran me over to the main terminal to catch the British Airways Super Shuttle to Heathrow. It turned out to be anything but super, for after enduring ticket price shock, my 737 flight was canceled due to mechanical, and an hour later I was herded on to the next flight's crowded 757.

Nevertheless, I made it to London. BA hadn't requested that I help them fix or help change the engine on their broken 737, and I'd at last crossed the North Atlantic aboard a very special Dakota. It had taken seven days and just 24 actual flying hours, in the veteran transport with none of the usual experiences of "jet lag." In September 1990, I had also crossed the North Atlantic, that time for the 50th anniversary of the Battle of Britain. The flight time then had been less than four hours aboard a supersonic Concorde.

Meanwhile, the Dakota crew had enjoyed an evening of Scottish hospitality, and the following afternoon we caught up with them at Duxford just before they set off for the commemorative events. Over Normandy, they dropped veterans of the 82nd and 101st Airborne, all of whom had jumped on the actual D-Day in 1944. The plane and its intrepid crew enjoyed a warm welcome wherever they went, except perhaps at Caen, where an irate airport manager told them that they couldn't land. She had obviously never encountered a determined Pat Epps who landed, discharged his appreciative passengers, and then took off again amid the irate ranting of the enraged bureaucrat. The trip back to the U.S. passed uneventfully. Departing Edinburgh on June 7, they called at Kulusuk, stopped at Goose Bay to pick up the damaged engine, and made it to Atlanta safely. Ironically, soon afterwards KG395 suffered considerable damage when it was blown into another aircraft during a near hurricane at its Douglas, Georgia, home base. Undeterred, Brooks had it repaired and finished out 1994 with a flourish at several Southeastern airshows.

Otis Spunkmeyer's immaculate C-41 enjoyed a flawless North Atlantic crossing, participated in the Mildenhall Air Fete, the fly past over the Royal Yacht, and the commemorative events in Normandy. Public relations' flights were made in connection with the Company's U.K. operation, and the strikingly finished aircraft was judged winner of the "FlyPast" best military aircraft award at the Warbirds Air Show at Wroughton. Their return to the U.S. was delayed for a week by weather conditions over the ocean. Departing Glasgow on June 23, bound for Stornaway and Reykjavik, they eventually arrived safely at their Oakland, California base. Sister ship N97H had, meanwhile, been a victim of contaminated gasoline and had to have both engines replaced before this unique fleet could once again be at full strength for its San Francisco Bay nostalgia flights.

There may not be a commemoration ceremony for the 100th anniversary of D-Day but if there is, then there will probably be at least one C-47 or Dakota still flying to remind this future generation of one of the many exploits of an amazing aircraft.

Chapter 7

Anytime...Anywhere: Gooneybirds for hire

Sixty years after the type's first flight, dozens of DC-3s are still earning their keep flying cargo. On the backroads of the airways these DC-3s play a barely visible but still economically viable role in the world's air transport system. Flying diverse cargo on call and around the clock, the veteran DC-3 can still, under some circumstances, economically compete with much newer equipment. Where the requirement for the transport of bulky cargo at modest speeds at low utilization exists, the DC-3 still enjoys a decided advantage over newer turbine-powered cargo transports. As examples of these types of on-call cargo carriers, four DC-3 operators in the United States and four in the Caribbean are noteworthy.

Latin America has numerous DC-3 operators plying freight over the rough terrain, and the type is also returning to carry cargo in Africa. But it is in the Caribbean that the area's island geography has given the DC-3 a new lease on life. Flying freight from one island to the next are Flamenco Airways, Four Star Aviation Inc., Tolair Services Inc., and Borinquen Air. These companies dominate the inter-island freight business and are the only DC-3 cargo operators in the Caribbean. Flamenco and Four Star haul general cargo while Tolair flies UPS packages.

Tolair, Four Star, and Flamenco all fly Pratt & Whitney R-1830-powered DC-3s, but Borinquen Air operates its plane with Wright R-1820s. Borinquen Air Capt. Luis Hernandez recently noted, "It (the DC-3) flies 5 or 6 knots faster with the Wrights. The Wright engines are working engines. You can take a Wright engine, fire it up and go cold, and it will go. The Pratt & Whitney R-1830, unless it's up to temperature, it's not going anywhere. You have to pre-heat it, run it up, and make sure everything is on temp. Sometimes you've got a fast turn-around and you can't bring the airplane up to temperature. The Wrights will go, and it won't hurt the engines. We run our engines at lower power (settings). We're in no hurry to get there. We only use 80 gallons per hour when everybody else is using 100 to 110. This will keep the engines running quite a while."

Borinquen Air's C-47, N86553 (msn 4715), flies about 300 hours per year. What type of cargo does Borinquen's DC-3 carry? Capt. Hernandez replied, "We're

Tol Air Service's N781T (msn 4306) at San Juan, Puerto Rico in 1993. Originally delivered to the U.S. Navy as R4D-1 BuNo 04699 in April 1942, this aircraft joined Tol Air in December 1989. The closely cowled engines indicate that this aircraft was once fitted with a Howard "Maximizer" speed kit. (Ed Davies)

N132FS (msn 25778) is one of Four Star Air Cargo's fleet of five DC-3s that operate from bases at San Juan, Puerto Rico and St. Thomas, U.S. Virgin Islands. Built as R4D-5 BuNo 17275, this aircraft served in the Pacific with the U.S. Navy and, later, with the USMC at MCAS El Toro, California. Sent to storage at Davis Monthan in November 1969, it was sold as surplus in June 1976 and registered as N3029F. Four Star Aviation has operated the DC-3 since June 1988. (Ed Davies)

the *ding-dong* boys. Do you remember 'ding-dong, Avon calling'? Well, we're the *ding-dong* boys. We deliver Avon up and down the Lesser Antilles from San Juan to Saint Vincent. We go port calling every week." The plane departs San Juan with 6,000 pounds of Avon making deliveries all the way to St. Vincent. Then the plane returns empty to San Juan. It also flies a once a week general cargo run between San Juan and St. Kitts.

Turboprop aircraft can not compete with the DC-3 in the Caribbean. The business will not support the operating and maintenance costs of a turboprop. Capt. Hernandez summed up the DC-3's future in the Caribbean by saying, "Can you show me something that's worth its salt money-wise that can carry 6,500 pounds at a reasonable rate? There isn't anything. Turboprops are too expensive. If somebody wants a tax shelter, that's the only way I can see a turboprop hauling cargo here."

Until mid-1995, Business Air Inc., of Bennington, Vermont, operated four Douglas DC-3s. The company sold off three of the aircraft and retains C-47A N57NA (msn 19560) as its largest hauling capacity aircraft. The company's fleet is very diversified, ranging from Cessna Caravans to Piper Navajos, a Mitsubishi MU-2N, and a number of Embraer 110P1 Bandeirantes. Business Air offers freighter aircraft for charter to anyone who has a product to move. This service is used by banks, needing time-sensitive documents transported, to computer-giant IBM, which uses Business Air to haul parts. The DC-3 gets the big jobs, and it is the only high-volume, short-haul freighter in the area. Business Air's Mike Bossert noted, "We generally haul automotive parts with the DC-3—it could be doors, it could be carpet, anything that would be needed to build a car. The auto manufacturers have really patterned themselves around the Japanese with the 'just in time' delivery philosophy. They try to time their deliveries so they're not creating an excess inventory. That's where the DC-3 comes in. The plane is used to haul large quantities of parts from the subcontractor to the auto assembly plant, thereby minimizing costly part's inventories.

"We have carried chickens, missiles, and basically any commodity that will fit in DC-3 that's too bulky for other aircraft. The aircraft is in kind-of-a-niche market. It's not fast, but it will haul 6,000 pounds," Bossert said. "One of the problems with the DC-3 is the winter time. It has a tough effect on the airplane with the engine pre-heating. But the DC-3s are fairly reliable. We have very experienced captains who fly them, so we don't change pilots often. Thus, the planes get the attention they need." Bossert said he does not see the company adding to its DC-3 fleet because "...we have the Bandeirantes, which, although they don't hold 6,000 pounds, are a twin-engine turboprop that will hold 4,000 pounds. They have taken much of the DC-3's market because of their speed, and they can hold the 'automotive baskets' just as well."

In the Southeastern United States, Academy Airlines of Griffin, Georgia, utilizes a pair of DC-3s in its cargo operations. Robert D. McSwiggan founded the company in 1973 and now employs 25 people. The company operates C-47A N130D (msn 19800) and DC-3A-227A N143D (msn 2054). Academy's DC-3s primarily haul automotive freight from vendors to the assembly plants. Company founder McSwiggan notes "Automotive parts hauling is an on-demand business. When they (the parts' manufacturers) want them (DC-3s) they use a lot of them, and when they don't want them, they don't call you."

Will the DC-3 soon end its working days hauling freight in the United States? McSwiggan seems to think so. He stated that "...the DC-3's future in the cargo business is dwindling. There used to be a lot of work for the box companies like Federal Express, UPS, Airborne, and Emery, but they don't use the DC-3s (for feeders). That's kind of a forgotten market."

The Pacific Northwest is home to Salair Inc., of Spokane, Washington. Salair was founded in 1980 by broth-

Typical of Latin American DC-3 operators in the 1970s is this DC-3 operated by Servicos Aereos Nacionales (SAN). This view shows HC-SJI (msn 34394) at Quito, Ecuador in 1974. (Rene Francillon)

One large DC-3 cargo operator was Majestic Airlines which ran an on demand and contract service through the Western U.S. in the 1980s. Majestic ceased service several years ago, but this view shows N305SF (msn 6208) at Billings, Montana in July 1992. (Scott Thompson)

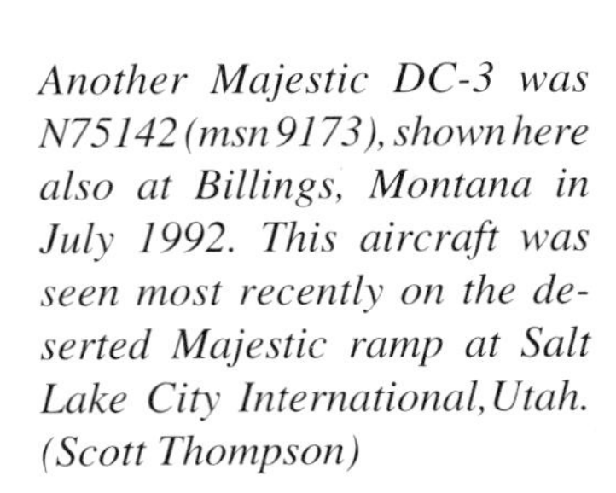

Another Majestic DC-3 was N75142 (msn 9173), shown here also at Billings, Montana in July 1992. This aircraft was seen most recently on the deserted Majestic ramp at Salt Lake City International, Utah. (Scott Thompson)

N31MC (msn 6148) is currently operated by Flamenco Airways in Puerto Rico. This view, taken at Ryan Field near Tucson, Arizona, in November 1982, shows the aircraft as it operated with Air Resorts. Air Resorts, based at the Palomar Airport at Carlsbad, California, sold the aircraft to an Oregon religious cult before it was eventually transferred to the Puerto Rican cargo company. (Scott Thompson)

ers Paul and Bruce Salerno; father Joseph joined the company one year later. The Salerno brothers entered business at the ground floor of the overnight package express boom. Today their operation employs 30 people and has revenues of more than $3 million per year.

During the peak of the package express business in the mid-1980s, Salair was flying nine DC-3s and had an additional three hulks used for parts support. The DC-3 fleet was carrying freight for Emery, Flying Tigers, CF Air Freight, Burlington, UPS, and Federal Express. "That was when the overnight package industry started going crazy with growth. Everyone was trying to capture market share, so they were putting airplanes on these feeder routes, without paying attention to costs. All of the sudden over-capacity existed, yields began to drop, and everybody started losing money. So they gradually started cutting back and we started loosing contracts. We were impacted most by Emery's financial difficulties in 1986. That year Emery canceled all of the feeder contracts nationwide. We had five of those contracts. That really hurt us," said Salerno.

Today Salair is flying overnight package express for UPS, Burlington and, at Christmas, for FedEx. Two DC-3s are used: C-47B N2298C (msn 33201) and C-47A N8061A (msn 6085). N8061A has 40,952 hours on the airframe and N2298C has 24,618 hours total time. "As long as you have the airplane on a maintenance program, you do the 12,000

The Canadian cargo operators are also involved in on-demand charters for the automotive industry. This Millardair C-117D, C-GDOG (msn 43374, built as msn 25446), is shown here at Toronto, Ontario in 1989. (Stewart Bailey)

Chapter 8

On Display: Preserved DC-3s

On display at the Naval Aviation Museum at NAS Pensecola, Florida, is R4D-5 BuNo 12418 (msn 9358). This aircraft is the famous "Que Sera Sera" which landed at the South Pole in 1956 and is on loan from the National Air and Space Museum. (Ed Davies)

The Museum of Flight at Boeing Field, Seattle, Washington has DC-3 NC15748 (msn 6337) on outdoor display. Manufactured as a DC-3-455 at Santa Monica, this aircraft was built for Eastern Airlines but impressed by the USAAF as C-49K 43-2013. It was operated by Delta Airlines as NC15748 after the war, and later went to North Central. Its last civil operator was Salair Air Cargo of Seattle, which donated the airframe to the museum. The museum trucked the airframe from Spokane to SEATAC where Alaska Airlines externally restored the aircraft and marked in in period Alaska Airlines livery before moving to Boeing Field for display. (Ed Davies)

On inside display and hung from the building's superstructure of the Museum of Flight at Boeing Field is DST-318 N138D (msn 2225). This aircraft was delivered to Eastern Airlines as NC25650 in February 1940 but impressed as C-49F 42-56616 in June 1942. It enjoyed three decades of executive transport use after the war before being transferred to the Museum of Flight for permanent display. (Ed Davies)

One of three static display replicas of the Indonesian Airways R1-001 'Seulawah' that made the first commercial flight from Burma to Indonesia during January 1949. This example is spectacularly displayed as mounted on a structure in the main square of the western Sumatra city of Bandar Aceh. The other two 'R1-001' look-alikes in Indonesia are in the capital city of Jakarta, with one at the Tamal Mini theme park (below) and the other in the Satria Mandala Military Museum. The identity of these three preserved Indonesian DC-3s have not been confirmed. (Paul Howard via Ed Davies)

N12907 (msn 27187) owned and operated by the Fleming Corporation. Delivered to the RAF as Dakota V KN258 in February 1945, this aircraft served with the RCAF after World War II and was one of the last Dakotas in service when the RCAF released it in March 1988. This view shows N12907 at Geneseo, New York in August 1994. (Milo Peltzer via Ed Davies)

Because the FAA was one of the largest and last government operators of the DC-3, many ex-FAA aircraft were transferred via the GSA to the USAF Heritage Museum Program. This view shows an ex-FAA airplane as displayed at the Castle AFB Museum in central California. Built as C-47A 43-15997 (msn 20443) and delivered in June 1944, it was transferred after the war to the CAA where it received its first civil registrationof NC812. It continued in CAA and FAA service through 1976 when transferred to the U.S. Department of Agriculture for use as a sprayer. Its last civil registration was N230GB. The GSA finally transferred it to the USAF Museum Program where it was assigned to Castle AFB for display. (Ed Davies)

C-47A 43-15509 (msn 19975) on display in June 1994 at the Imperial War Museum at Duxford in England. This aircraft had a long civil history and last flew as G-BHUB with Aces High at Duxford. This C-47 wears D-Day markings and its assigned serial number. (Ed Davies)

A trio of ex-FAA DC-3s on display: Above is N227GB (msn 33345) which flies with the Confederate Air Force and is shown here at the National Warplane Museum's Geneseo Airshow in August 1989. Flying last with the FAA as N32, the DC-3 retains the characteristic picture windows behind the cockpit. (Scott Thompson)

Another FAA airplane being preserved is shown here at the Anchorage, Alaska airport in April 1983. This ex-Navy R4D operated as N41 (msn 19320) through 1978 when finally retired. The General Services Administration eventually transferred the DC-3 to the Alaskan ANG museum collection in Anchorage. As is evident, the aircraft retains its FAA configuration and paint scheme. (Scott Thompson)

At the aircraft airpark at Dyess AFB near Abilene, Texas, is C-47A 42-108808 (msn 11928). This aircraft was built for the USAAF but operated by the Navy as R4D-5 BuNo 17106 through the mid-1950s when transferred to the CAA. Used for flight inspection through 1975, this aircraft went on to be used as a sprayer by the Department of Agriculture before being transferred in to the USAF Heritage Collection. It is finished in Vietnam-era markings and is shown here in May 1991. (Scott Thompson)

DC-3-277B NC21798 (msn 2202) on display at the C.R. Smith Museum in Fort Worth, Texas. This aircraft was delivered to American Airlines as "Flagship Knoxville" in March 1940 and flew with a number of civil operators in the ensuing five decades. Its last civil owner had operated the DC-3 as N393SW in mosquito control operations through 1989. When an American Airlines pilot group was looking for an original American Airlines DC-3 for the museum, msn 2202 was available. The American Airlines maintenance facility at Dallas-Fort Worth restored the aircraft inside and out, and it now resides in a place of honor at the museum. (Ed Davies)

DC-3-201B (msn 2141) operating as C-GDAK by the Canadian Warplane Heritage at the National Warplane Museum airshow at Geneseo, New York, in August 1989. This aircraft was originally built for Eastern Airlines as a NC21729 and enjoyed a long succession of civil owners. The aircraft remains based at Hamilton, Ontario.

Oklahoma City-built C-47A, s/n 42-92392 (msn 12187) in April 1994 as displayed at Cairns Airport in Queensland, Australia. This aircraft is pylon mounted as a memorial to the many bush pilots who flew the type in Australia. This aircraft had been operated by the RAF as FZ631 as an administrative transport for General Maitland Wilson. Also, King George VI used this Dakota for a trip to Italy to visit Allied troops in 1944. After the war it flew in Australia and New Guinea for Quantas and TAA. Its last civil operator was Air Queensland, which donated the airframe to the city of Cains. (Bernard Deatrick via Ed Davies)

Pylon-mounted C-47A 42-92838 (msn 12683) at the state fairgrounds in Oklahoma City, Oklahoma, in January 1994. This aircraft reportedly served with the 9th Air Force in England during the war and, after being sold surplus, operated as an executive transport for Kerr McGee Oil, carrying the civil registration of N65162. It was donated in 1977 for permanent display at the fairgrounds along with a Boeing B-47, B-52, and an Aero Commander (all mounted on pylons). (Scott Thompson)

Restored to the standard R4D-6 configuration was this ex-FAA DC-3, N229GB (msn 26874). Built as C-47B 43-49613 but transferred to the Navy as R4D-6 BuNo 50819, it went to the CAA in 1958 and operated primarily as N68. When released for disposal in 1976, the GSA transferred the DC-3 to the USDA for use as a sprayer. In 1981 it was transferred to the Mid-Atlantic Air Museum which restored it as an R4D-6. This view shows the aircraft at Geneseo, New York in August 1994. (Milo Peltzer)

On display at MCAS El Toro in southern California is C-117D BuNo 50835 (msn 43321, built as msn 26998). This aircraft's last duty station was at Iwakuni, Japan, which may explain its unusual tail art. (Ed Davies)

C-53D 42-68835 (msn 11762) on display at the McClellan Heritage Musuem at McClellan AFB in Sacramento, California. This C-53 was delivered in July 1943 and later flew under WAA lease with American Airlines as "Flagship Bridgeport," carrying the civil registration of NC19924. The WAA later transferred it to the U.S. Geological Survey. (Ed Davies)

On display at Beale AFB, also in northern California, is C-47A 42-23668 (msn 9530), which last carried the civil registration of N7252N. It primarily served with the U.S. government's Department of Agriculture. (Scott Thompson)

TC-47B 44-76502 (msn 32834) was delivered to the USAAF in March 1945 where it served primarily as a navigation trainer. It was transferred to the South Vietnamese Air Force in 1964 and flew combat operations during the Vietnam War. Consigned to storage at Davis-Monthan AFB in October 1968, it remained inactive until February 1985 when it was disassembled and flown via C-5 to McChord AFB in Washington. Once there, it was reassembled and externally restored to resemble a 4th Troop Carrier Squadron aircraft with invasion stripes. (Ed Davies)

On display at the Pima Air Museum near Tucson, Arizona is C-117D BuNo 50826 (msn 43363, built as msn 26924) which is currently on loan from the Naval Aviation Museum. (Nick Veronico)

Mounted on a tail support at Tinker AFB in Oklahoma City, Oklahoma, is C-47B 43-49012 (msn 26273). This aircraft had last operated with the Department of Agriculture as a pest sprayer and carried the civil registration of N219GB. Its currently is displayed in an airpark along with several other aircraft including a B-52 and B-29. (Scott Thompson)

C-47B 44-76716 (msn 33049) as operated by the Yankee Air Force of Ypsilanti, Michigan. This aircraft, shown here at the National Warplane Museum airshow at Geneseo, New York in August 1989, is maintained in airworthy condition and is flown to a number of east coast airshows each year. It carries the civil registration of N8704. (Scott Thompson)

Built as C-47B 43-48690 (msn 25951) but transferred to the Navy as R4D-6 BuNo 17286, this aircraft eventually went to the FAA for flight inspection. After a long and productive utilization, it was released as excess by the GSA and sold through a number of civil owners. In 1988, registered as N259DC, it was transferred to Brazil's Museu Aerospacial, delivery being accomplished in August 1988. Shortly after arrival, it was used as a ground prop in a Brazilian motion picture where it appeared as FAB 2079. The aircraft retains that paint on the left side of the fuselage, while it wears more appropriate colors on the right in this October 1988 view. (Ron Mak via Ed Davies)

National Warplane Museum's N293WM (msn 13860) at Geneseo, New York in August 1994. Operated by the Navy as R4D-5 BuNo 39091, the museum acquired the DC-3 from Air Manitoba in March 1993. (Milo Peltzer)

A DC-3 under a gradual restoration is C-47A 42-92990 (msn 12852) owned by the American Warbird Company and is shown above in February 1992 with its last civil paint scheme worn when it operated as a sprayer. Below is the same aircraft at the Nut Tree, California, airport in October 1994. This DC-3 reportedly served with the Cambodian Air Force at some time, but no details are available. It now carries the civil registration of N16602. (above-Scott Thompson, below-Ed Davies)

Nick Veronico

Chapter 9

N34 and the DC-3s of the FAA

Ed Davies

The wide concrete expanse of the FAA Aeronautical Center's ramp at Will Rogers World Airport in Oklahoma City, Oklahoma, has played host to a wide variety of CAA and FAA aircraft through the years since 1946. A large and multi-tasked fleet of aircraft, from civil T-33s and Beech 18s to Convairs, Boeing 707s, and more recently, Sabreliner and King Airs, have all but dominated the FAA ramp in their own time. Today, however, this ramp area is a mere shadow of its former self, the victim of a greatly reduced FAA aircraft fleet and a host of modern budgetary restrictions. Only a few active Beech 300s and a Hawker jet occupy the space once home to dozens of busy aircraft.

Tucked in a remote corner of the ramp, however, is a throwback to earlier times. The last example of a great fleet operated by the Civil Aeronautics Administration and its successor organization, today's Federal Aviation Administration, is parked in long-term storage in the corner of an otherwise empty hangar. Resplendent in a 1950s international orange, white, and black paint scheme are the classic lines of a Douglas DC-3, this being a stately veteran of a quarter century of federal airway patrol and flight inspection. Though stripped of its control surfaces and dirty with neglect, the old DC-3 nonetheless juts its distinctive nose above all others on the ramp, seemingly determined to retain a measure of its past dignity.

This last DC-3, carrying the distinctively FAA registration of N34, was one of over 80 DC-3s operated by the FAA between 1941 and 1993, making this United States government agency one of the largest non-military operators of the classic Douglas transports. This fleet of DC-3s was employed for a variety of missions ranging from airway inspection to logistical support and, for many years, a DC-3 in FAA colors was a common sight at airports across the nation and around the globe.

N34 had followed the path of a typical FAA DC-3. It had been built by Douglas at (ironically) Oklahoma City for the Navy as R4D-6 BuNo 99856, being delivered on May 26, 1945. After spending some time in storage, it was sent to a transport unit in England with the Navy, where it was assigned to a unit supporting the Berlin Airlift in 1948. It soldiered along in Navy service through the mid-1950s, when it was deemed excess by the Navy and placed into storage in Arizona. The CAA obtained the use of the aircraft as one of 44 excess R4Ds transferred from the Navy in the late 1950s. N34 was assigned flight inspection duties with the CAA beginning in 1957, a role it continued through the early 1980s when the tired old DC-3, along with dozens of similarly employed DC-3s, was finally removed from FAA service and set aside for disposal.

At this juncture, however, the fate of N34 diverged from that of its brethren. After N34 sat in storage for several years while awaiting an uncertain fate, FAA employees suggested that it be returned to flying status as a symbol of the FAA and its role in aviation. The like-minded FAA Administrator (at the time) Donald Engen agreed, and N34 was refurbished and repainted for its new lease on life, which began in 1986. N34 was used in the FAA's aviation educational programs to promote aviation, the historical aircraft attracting attention wherever it went. The DC-3 retained the same equipment, furnishings, and arrangement

N34 in August 1958, shortly after it joined the CAA fleet. This aircraft went into the CAA shops as a standard R4D-7 and emerged with the distinctive modifications, which included the reworked nose area, air stair door, and picture windows. (L. Smalley via E. Davies)

A later view of N34, this being taken at Oakland in July 1974. The FAA DC-3s were standardized with this paint scheme beginning in the early 1960s. (L. Smalley via E. Davies)

The classic configuration of the FAA DC-3, this being N10 (msn 4661) at the Oakland Flight Inspection District Office (California) in January 1965. N10 had been built for the Navy as an R4D-1 and was transferred from the Reconstruction Finance Corporation to the CAA in October 1946. It served the CAA and FAA for over 30 years, primarily in the flight inspection role. (L. Smalley via Davies Collection)

that had been originally installed in 1957. The public was provided both a close look at a classic aircraft and a perspective on the FAA's historical flight inspection technology, function, and mission. N34 was flown across the country each summer by its volunteer aircrew, showing the public the role of both the FAA and aviation to the general public. For eight years, N34 appeared at Oshkosh, Reno, and Sun'N'Fun, to name but a few of the many public displays it attended.

N34 was visited by hundreds of thousands of aviation enthusiasts and members of the general public in the eight years it flew the show circuit. Visitors included many who had crewed or maintained C-47s during the war. Others recalled being evacuated or transported by them. Former flight attendants and crew members who had flown DC-3s in airline service, and retired FAA personnel who flew on or worked with DC-3s daily for decades also came to pay homage or revisit an old friend. Those from the general public viewed N34 as a DC-3 and thus, the first airplane they had ever seen, or flown on, during an airline trip years ago. N34 also provided the first opportunity for youngsters to go aboard a real airplane, to sit in the cockpit, or to move the controls. The number of aviation careers N34 sparked can never be counted. N34 engendered goodwill and another side of the FAA apart from the "get Bob" mentality seemingly so prevalent in the agency.

With the onset of the 1990s, however, FAA managers gingerly tested the waters of public opinion and came away with the perception that the general public could potentially view N34 as a bit too ostentatious for a government agency. Despite the meager operational costs and valued educational potential of their DC-3 program, the FAA managers decided N34 had no place in the downsized, streamlined, diverse and politically correct image the FAA felt it needed to portray. Though the FAA could reasonably justify the continued operation of N34 as part of its lawful objective to help promote the interests of American aviation, N34 was nonetheless unceremoniously grounded in 1993 and placed in stealth storage at the FAA's Aeronautical Center. In such a whimper did a durable and fruitful utilization of the DC-3 by the FAA finally draw to a close a full 50 years after the first CAA DC-3 had joined its fleet.

To set a perspective, it would be useful to review the history of the United States' aviation regulatory agencies. The first agency specifically created by the federal government to govern air commerce was the Aeronautics Branch, established within the Department of Commerce in 1926. The Aeronautics Branch was derived from the Air Commerce Act and specifically set jurisdiction of both regulation and promotion of air commerce within the scope of the U.S. federal government. In 1934 the Aeronautics Branch was supplanted by the Bureau of Air Commerce, still within the Department of Commerce. The Bureau of Air Commerce gained a larger role in regulating air navigation, pilots, aircraft, and air traffic control. Four years later, in a general reorganization, the Bureau of Air Commerce was replaced by a new agency, the Civil Aeronautics Agency, which was an independent federal agency removed from the Department of Commerce. The CAA's independence was short-lived, as the CAA was re-organized once more into the Civil Aeronautics Administration and placed back within the Department of Commerce in 1940.

The CAA's first DC-3 was purchased as new equipment from the Douglas Aircraft Company at Santa Monica. Built as msn 4080, the CAA accepted delivery on March 21, 1941 and operated the aircraft as NC14. Used primarily for training and equipment tests, the FAA operated NC14 through 1960 when it was sold to a civil owner. Operated as N560R through the early 1970s, its civil registration was finally cancelled in 1975. The fate of N560R remains unknown. This view shows NC14 at the Oakland Airport in 1941, shortly after delivery. (William T. Larkins)

The organizational base for the CAA remained fairly stable for the subsequent two decades as aviation enjoyed unheralded growth through World War II and the post-war years. In 1959, however, the CAA was abolished from within the Department of Commerce, and the Federal Aviation Agency (FAA) was created, once again, as an independent federal agency by the Federal Aviation Act of 1958. The FAA's independence lasted a short seven years, however, as the new Department of Transportation reeled in the FAA as the Federal Aviation Administration in 1967. Though the organization of the FAA has remained generally stable in the ensuing three decades, rumblings are underfoot about major changes in the FAA. The structure of the federal government's aviation agency may be changing once again.

The first DC-3 obtained by the Civil Aeronautics Administration was ordered by the federal government as a new aircraft in August 1940. Built by Douglas as a DC-3A-348 and equipped with Pratt & Whitney R1830-S1C3G engines, it was made available for delivery on March 17, 1941. The new DC-3 was registered as NC14 (msn 4080), in the low block of civil registration numbers reserved for government-operated aircraft. The CAA ordered the airliner primarily to provide its aeronautical inspectors with an aircraft similar in capability and configuration to those they were being asked to inspect. Though aircraft training was its primary use, the purchase of NC14 provided the CAA with its first truly modern airframe. Most aircraft within the CAA fleet at that time remained fabric-covered biplanes, and few had any electrical or other modern instrument systems installed. Thus, NC14 also became an electronics testbed, providing a platform for test installations of a variety of new communication radios, navigation receivers, and instrument configurations. NC14 remained the queen of the CAA fleet through the war years. It was usually based in Houston, Texas, at the CAA's Standardization Center and remained active with the government agency through 1960 when it was finally retired and sold as excess property.

The CAA's DC-3 fleet remained at one aircraft between 1941 and 1945. However, with the vast number of surplus military aircraft becoming available after 1945, the CAA recognized the opportunity to obtain modern aircraft in substantial numbers. The primary need identified for the acquisition of surplus C-47s for the CAA fleet was airway inspection.

Airway inspection, or flight inspection as it is now known, has been an important factor of aviation safety since the advent of radio navigation aids in the late 1920s. Airway inspection is the means used to ensure that the numerous ground-based navigation aids, be they Very High Frequency Omni-directional Ranges (VOR), Instrument Landing Systems (ILS), Low/Medium Frequency Beacons, or any number of other navigation aids, radiate usable radio signals that provide an airborne aircraft with a safe air navigation system. Also, the flight procedures that are developed using the ground-based navigation aids, such as airways, instrument approaches, or instrument departures, are also inspected regularly, both for adequate radio performance and also safe separation from hazardous ground obstacles.

The earliest airway inspections were performed from small biplanes flown by Aeronautics Branch pilots inspecting the lighted airway beacons that preceded the first radio navigation aids. With the development of the early four-course radio ranges, the need for more sophisticated aircraft with adequate electrical systems to support radio receivers became apparent. However, given the constraints of the Depression-era federal budgets, improvements in airway inspection aircraft were slow. The small fleet of airway inspection aircraft of the 1930s consisted of a mixed bag of Bellanca CH-300 Pacemakers, Stearman C-3Bs, and various models of Stinsons.

Even with the development of very precise landing aids such as the ILS, the CAA continued to perform flight inspections with antiquated aircraft lacking the proper equipment to perform an adequate job. With the advent of World War II, the shortcomings of the CAA's inspection fleet quickly became apparent, but the Cessna Bobcats (Bamboo Bombers) purchased as replacements for the older biplanes were themselves woefully inadequate, both for their ability to carry the needed radio receivers and their general performance and reliability. By 1945 the CAA was eager to obtain a number of dependable, modern aircraft with which to conduct flight inspection.

That opportunity came with the gradual release by the various U.S. military services of their enormous fleet of warplanes as surplus property. While a large number of the available surplus aircraft were war-weary combat aircraft, there were also a sizable number of transport-types such as the C-47 and Douglas C-54. Though transport types were needed by domestic air carriers to assist in their transition to a peacetime economy, government agencies were allowed to obtain aircraft on a direct transfer basis prior to their release for sale or lease to civil users.

Between 1945 and 1948, the CAA obtained at least 36 DC-3s as surplus equipment. Most of these aircraft were transferred to the CAA through the Reconstruction Finance Corporation, the government agency charged with allocating the excess property of the U.S. military forces after the war. One aspect of the RFC's authorization was to assist national industries make the transition from a wartime economy.

A number of the CAA DC-3s were first lent by the RFC to U.S. domestic airlines, principally American Airlines and Alaskan Airlines, to supplement their post-war fleets. These aircraft were registered by the air carriers, and included NC15473 (msn 2053), NC15574 (msn 4854), NC15572 (msn 4862), and NC50592 (msn 11703). Also, several of the DC-3s were registered by the War Assets Administration (WAA and successor to the RFC) for civil use and loaned to various civil operators. Among these were NC815 (msn 4438), NC814 (msn 4661), and NC818 (msn 20426).

Those surplus DC-3s transferred directly from the RFC to the CAA were largely ex-USAAF C-47s, though this number also included three C-48s, a C-53, and several C-50s. Also included was one ex-Navy R4D-4 (msn 6355). The three C-48s, which were built as DC-3As and impressed in 1941 by the Army, were transferred to the CAA as administrative transports. The majority of the surplus DC-3s had been stored on RFC lots, such as the one at Bush Field near Atlanta, Georgia, after the USAAF or USN had declared them surplus. The DC-3s, upon acceptance by the CAA, were flown to Oklahoma City for storage or assignment to the CAA flight program.

As an aside, during the same period (1945-1948), the CAA also obtained over 100 AT-6 trainers for aviation inspector currency, over 75 Twin Beeches (many for airway inspection), and numerous examples of various other types such as the Beech Staggerwing, C-54 Skymaster, and even a B-25 bomber for use in their post-war operations.

Reportedly one of the first of the CAA flight inspection DC-3s, this unidentified aircraft is shown at Idylwild Airport in New York in 1950. In the immediate post-war period, each of the CAA's regional offices received at least one war-surplus DC-3 with which to conduct its airway inspections. (FAA History Office)

Unusual paint scheme carried by an early CAA DC-3, this example being N183 (msn 20419) believed taken at the CAA's Experimental Center at Indianapolis, Indiana, in the early 1950s. A variety of new equipment was developed for the airways system at the Expermental Center, including what appears to be early anti-collision lighting installed on the wing-tips of this aircraft. (FAA History Office)

DC-3 NX815 (msn 4438) as assigned to the CAA-Goodyear Landing Wheel Tests. A range of CAA aircraft from Ercoupes and Piper Cubs to this DC-3 was modified with experimental landing gear which castered for crosswind landings. Note that the "C" in the civil registration has been crudely painted over to become an "X." This aircraft was later assigned to the flight inspection fleet and operated as N20. (William T. Larkins via Davies Collection)

Rare photo showing C-47A 42-100857 (msn 19320) on the ramp at Oklahoma City in the late 1940s. The old Army Air Forces markings are still evident and consistent with those of the European Theatre of World War II. This aircraft was stored by the CAA until 1949 when it was rebuilt for flight inspection use. It remained in service with the FAA until 1973. (H.J. Barnett via FAA History Office)

The CAA was organized into nine regions during World War II, and each region operated an airway inspections office. After the war, each office was slated to get a DC-3 and several Beech 18s for airway inspection and other regional work. A number of DC-3s were also assigned to logistics support, particularly in Alaska. The CAA's Experimental Center at Indianapolis, Indiana, was able to obtain several DC-3s to serve their needs. Also, at least six DC-3s were placed into storage to serve future projects and to act as a parts source to support the airworthy aircraft in the ensuing years.

With the addition of the DC-3 and Beech 18s to the regional flight inspection fleets, the airway flight inspectors finally had suitable aircraft with which they could perform their jobs. Each region dispatched its aircraft to provide a scheduled inspection of all the airways, flight procedures, and navigational aids within their jurisdiction. It was left to each regional office, however, to provide for the installation of the necessary equipment and radios on the new aircraft, and diversity in the installations was the rule. Each region operated in a relatively autonomous fashion with little specific or effective direction from the staff levels at the CAA headquarters in Washington.

The work of flight inspection was not without risk. Given the amount of flying required and the diverse operating conditions encountered, the occasional accident occurred. On January 21, 1948, a CAA DC-3 (NC206, msn 4776) departed Denver, Colorado for an inspection of the VHF airway structure in the vicinity of Grand Junction. Less than 30 minutes later, the CAA crew radioed to the Cheyenne Radio Station that they were encountering severe turbulence 50 miles northwest of Denver. No further radio reports were received. Wreckage of the aircraft was located on the north side of Navajo Peak the following May, and the crew of three had perished in the accident. Surprisingly, given the nature of the flight operations and the size of the CAA's flight program, this was the only fatal CAA/FAA DC-3 accident recorded between 1945 and 1963.

The Experimental Center employed a number of DC-3s in a variety of test programs. Among the most unusual was the joint CAA-Goodyear Cross Wind Landing Wheel Test, whereby a number of different aircraft types, including CAA DC-3 NX815 (msn 4438), were fitted with castering landing gear assemblies which could pivot and be aligned to allow better landing control in crosswind conditions. Though later adopted on the Boeing B-52 bomber design, the idea proved generally impractical and was never widely adopted for civil use. NX815 continued in experimental use before being converted to an airway inspection configuration and flown as N20 in later years. Other uses by the Experimental Center for their DC-3s included anti-collision lights testing and radio receiver installations.

Though the CAA had accepted over 30 DC-3s in the immediate post-war period, a number were placed in storage for parts or eventual disposal. One example, msn 4470, was obtained from the RFC in October 1945 and, though assigned a civil registration of N361, disassembled for parts at Oklahoma City. The civil registration was canceled on December 12, 1946. The DC-3's fuselage was sold as scrap to a local aviation dealer in Oklahoma City in September 1947. It was subsequently sold to a number of aviation companies until it was finally reassembled into a DC-3 and re-registered as N361 in October 1951. This DC-3 was eventually exported to Chile, where it reportedly crashed in 1967.

A lack of equipment standardization among the operational DC-3 airway inspection fleet became apparent through the early 1950s, particularly as the use of radio navigation brought on by the advent of the VOR installations became widespread. An early effort to standardize the regional DC-3 aircraft began in 1951, with each aircraft sent through a modification program at the CAA's Aircraft Services Base in Oklahoma City, Oklahoma. One surplus DC-3, being used for training, was pulled into the shop at Oklahoma City as a prototype of the new standardized DC-3. Seats were removed from the cabin and replaced with cus-

One of several CAA/FAA DC-3s to carry the civil registration of N1, this view shows msn 4146 at San Francisco in April 1952. N1 was utilized primarily for the adminstrative transport of the Secretary of Commerce or the CAA Administrator and was based at Washington National Airport. Msn 4146 had been operated by the Army Air Forces as C-48A s/n 41-7682. This aircraft, operating as N6, crashed while still in FAA service in 1975. (Larry Smalley via Davies Collection)

N2 was the second of the three C-48s obtained by the CAA. This aircraft, msn 4147, was lent by the CAA to the Civil Aeronautics Board (CAB) beginning in July 1946 for use as an administrative transport and operated as N424. It became N3 in 1951 and, shortly afterwards, N2. N2 was used actively through 1958 when released for disposal. (Larry Smalley via Davies Collection)

Regional flight inspection DC-3 at Boise, Idaho in August 1953. Each of the regional offices operated at least one DC-3 for airways work. N10 (msn 4661) had been obtained by the CAA from the WAA in June 1947. Its first civil registration, N814, had been obtained by the WAA prior to its transfer. (Larry Smalley via Davies Collection)

Assigned to the U.S. Embassy in London, England, this view shows N17 (msn 4279) in April 1954. A number of CAA aircraft had international assignments, though whether this aircraft was assigned primarily for Commerce or State Department support, or whether it was used by a CAA liason office is not known. (Gradidge via Davies Collection)

Another CAA regional flight inspection aircraft was N15 (msn 25341), shown here at the Oakland Airport in January 1952. The CAA operated a Flight Inspection District Office from Oakland until the early 1970s when it was combined to form the Los Angeles Flight Inspection Field Office. N15 was later operated as N7 and was released from FAA service in 1975. (William T. Larkins via Davies Collection)

tom-designed radio racks, new radio equipment, and a heavier electrical system. An electronic technician's panel and data recorder was installed and the aircraft was generally rewired to accommodate the new systems. The old fuselage cargo door was replaced with an air stair type door, and the engines and airframe received major overhauls. Emerging in late 1951, the prototype DC-3 was re-registered as NC23, and after evaluation, sent to one of the regions for assignment to its airway inspection fleet. As quickly as possible, all the flight inspection DC-3s were rotated through Oklahoma City to receive the standardization modifications. Through the early 1950s the small fleet of these standardized DC-3s, supplemented by Twin Beeches, satisfied the regional flight inspection requirements.

A number of events that occurred in the mid-1950s caused a major expansion in both the airway inspection requirement and the CAA's DC-3 fleet size. Through the early part of the decade, the CAA continued its steady program of installing new ILS and VOR systems across the country. However, increasing air traffic and the advent of the jet airliner began to overload an already creaking airway and air traffic control systems even as budgetary and bureaucratic in-fighting worked against making any substantive improvements. Most of the airway and air traffic systems of 1955 existed much as they had 10 years earlier. The primary navaids remained a mix of four-course low frequency radio ranges and the newer VOR equipment. ILS installations were underway for instrument approaches. Air traffic control remained tied to the airway structure with narrowly defined areas of controlled airspace. In an effort to navigate direct routes, much enroute traffic flew under Visual Flight Rules off-airway with little benefit from the rudimentary air traffic control services. Without enroute radar, air traffic control consisted of fix posting by position reports provided by pilots over a network of radio stations.

Instrument Flight Rules (IFR) separation standards

Below-Between 1956 and 1959 the CAA obtained a group of 44 excess R4Ds. These aircraft were being stored at NAF Litchfield Park, Arizona. This view shows R4D-5 BuNo 17193 (msn 13004) in storage in March 1957. The CAA obtained this aircraft in January 1959 and it was ferried to Oklahoma City as N6517C. Later operated for flight inspection as N55 and N67, this aircraft was operated by the FAA until 1974. (Brian Baker) Inset-NavyR4D-4 BuNo 07003 (msn 6349) in service in the post-war Navy. One R4D-4, BuNo 33820 (msn 6355) was among those Navy transports eventually transferred to the CAA. (NASM 92-8029)

The FAA conversion line at the Aircraft Services Base at Oklahoma City circa 1959. The painted DC-3s, such as N10 (msn 4661) in the foreground, were among those originally transferred in the late 1940s. The unpainted airframes in the background are Navy R4Ds transferred between 1956 and 1959 for use in the CAA's flight inspection mission. The third aircraft on the line from the left is N57 (msn 25775), an R4D-6 obtained in July 1959. These Navy R4Ds were officially on loan from the Navy until their title was transferred in August 1966. (FAA Historical Office)

of at least 10 minutes between aircraft over the same routes at the same altitudes were predicated on the pilot reports filed with air traffic controllers. Pressures of increased air carrier traffic, and the impending arrival of the new jet airliners, were contained only by a patchwork system of airways and air traffic controllers.

Despite the steadily deteriorating situation of the federal airways, budgetary support was not forthcoming from the Congress. Numerous CAA requests for equipment and personnel, sent along with implementation plans, were all whittled down to budgets which only maintained the status quo.

On June 30, 1956, a TWA Constellation and a United DC-6, both operating under Visual Flight Rules off airway at 21,000 feet, collided over the Grand Canyon in Arizona, resulting in the loss of both aircraft and all aboard. The public outcry which followed the accident focused attention on the condition of both the federal airways and the air traffic control system. The net effect was an immediate supplemental appropriation by Congress of $45 million, followed by steadily increasing budgets for the CAA in 1957 and 1958. Within six months of the accident, the CAA had placed before Congress a six-year plan of system improvements with a price tag of more than $450 million which would overhaul the nation's airway and air traffic control systems.

The CAA, responding to a substantial increase in planned facilities and airways, sought to quickly obtain a large number of aircraft with which to supplement its small fleet of DC-3s and Beech 18s remaining in the regional flight inspection programs.

The Navy had available several dozen Navy R4Ds stored at NAF Litchfield Park in Arizona. These Navy aircraft were among over 550 C-47s obtained from the Army Air Forces or procured directly from Douglas during World War II. Most had been in storage in the desert sun of Arizona for at least a year or two. Upon request from the CAA, the Navy Department agreed to loan two surplus R4Ds to the CAA for conversion to a flight inspection configuration. An agreement, Revocable Permit NAER 01782, was negotiated between the Navy's Bureau of Aeronautics and the CAA and signed into effect on September 11, 1956. Its terms provided that the CAA could operate the excess Navy R4Ds on a 30-day notice return basis. (Presumably, if the Ruskies attacked, the Navy wanted its R4Ds back to help clean up the mess.) Title was retained by the Navy; however, the civil registration was held by the CAA.

During the subsequent years, amendments to Permit 01782 authorized an additional 42 R4Ds for transfer to the CAA, as follows: Amendment 1 dated November 1, 1956 for one R4D; Amendment 2 on March 8, 1957 for two R4Ds; Amendment 3 on August 6, 1957 for five aircraft; Amendment 4 on July 31, 1957 for six R4Ds; and Amendment 5 on March 6, 1958 for 18 aircraft; Amendment 7

One of the Navy R4Ds awaiting the conversion process at Oklahoma City in the late 1950s. The FAA quickly became one of the largest civil operators of the DC-3 when it obtained 44 surplus aircraft from the Navy. (FAA Historical Office)

Another later view of N1 at Oklahoma City, probably in 1959 shortly after the transformation of the CAA into the FAA. (FAA)

What would now be considered a "Type I" FAA DC-3, this view shows N12 (msn 2053) at Oakland in February 1959. N12 was the oldest DC-3 operated by the CAA/FAA and was, in fact, the first military DC-3. Built as the sole C-41, USAAC s/n 38-502, this aircraft was used as a VIP transport for many years before going to the CAA in 1948. (Larry Smalley via Davies Collection)

Interim paint scheme worn by several of the newly converted "Type II" DC-3s. Upper surfaces were white with international orange markings on nose, tail, and wings. This view shows N32(msn 33345), probably circa 1960. N32 was retired from FAA service in 1976 and was transferred to the USDA for use as a sprayer. (FAA)

N47 (msn 33155) at the Oakland FIDO in May 1961. N47 enjoyed a short utilization with the FAA, as the aircraft was destroyed in an October 1970 crash at Fire Island, Alaska, with the loss of two FAA flight crewmembers. (Larry Smalley via Davies Collection)

Another "Type II" DC-3 shortly after conversion, this aircraft wearing the carryover paint scheme from CAA days. N30 (msn 33216) had been Navy R4D BuNo 99838 and, after transfer to the CAA, was operated for flight inspection through 1974. It went through several subsequent owners, both government and civil, and is now owned by a museum and carries the civil registration of N2312G. (FAA)

N14 (msn 9526) during an FAA airborne inspection. The purpose of the underwing antenna at right is unknown (FAA)

Evidence suggests that beginning about 1962 the FAA DC-3s were refininshed in this paint scheme, which featured the red fuselage, wing, and tail striping with black trim on the nose Also featured was the FAA seal on the nose below the cockpit. This scheme was standardized for all FAA aircraft, and was the last one worn by the FAA DC-3s. This view shows N32 (msn 33345) in 1966. N32 is now operated by the Confederate Air Force and flies as N227GB. (FAA)

(Amendment 6 was administratively combined with Amendment 5) on January 7, 1959 for six R4Ds; Amendment 8 on July 16, 1959 for three aircraft, and Amendment 9 in 1959 for one additional aircraft. A total of 44 R4Ds were thus transferred to the CAA between 1956 and 1959, and included eight R4D-5s, 22 R4D-6s, and 14 R4D-7s (See also Appendix 1). These aircraft were methodically withdrawn from storage and placed in ferriable condition by CAA and Navy mechanics. Each was issued a temporary ferry registration and flown to the Aircraft Services Base at Oklahoma City. Once there, the aircraft were placed in storage to await the substantial modifications required to bring them to the CAA flight inspection configuration.

This modification program was yet another effort toward standardizing the CAA's flight inspection fleet. The modifications resulted in what became known as the "Type II" CAA DC-3, which became the standard low-altitude flight inspection aircraft for the agency for nearly 20 years. The Pratt & Whitney 1,200 horsepower R-1830-92 engines were replaced by the 1,350 horsepower R-1830-94 versions of the same engine (probably culled from scrapped Navy PB4Y-2 Privateers). The four-piece windshield assembly was replaced by a two-piece windscreen. The interior of the fuselage was stripped out, including the bulkhead between the cockpit and cabin. An airstair-type main door was installed, replacing the old fuselage cargo door. The small external cockpit door and the overhead emergency cockpit escape hatch were removed and skinned over. Large "picture" windows, which would become the hallmark of the FAA DC-3, were added just behind the cockpit to add additional lighting to the electronic technician's position. Radio racks and a technician's work bench were manufactured and installed. The standard C-47 electrical system was replaced by one with heavier capacity, and an auxiliary power unit was installed in the tail of the fuselage. All component parts were overhauled and modified to provide the best possible configuration for the flight inspection mission. (See Appendix 3 for modification listing.)

The prototype Type II DC-3 was registered as N27, and it rolled from the CAA depot in late 1957. Most of the 44 Navy R4Ds were eventually modified to the Type II configuration, and 15 DC-3s already operated by the CAA were eventually brought to the Type II configuration. The flight inspection DC-3s were assigned civil registrations in a block between N14 and N70 (with several gaps for other CAA aircraft). In addition, the CAA and FAA continued to operate a number of the unmodified DC-3s, particularly for logistical support, training, and transportation. As of December 1, 1961 there were 61 DC-3s in the FAA inventory, the majority of which were employed for flight inspection.

Effective August 1, 1966, the Executive Branch, through the Bureau of the Budget, officially transferred

An example of an FAA DC-3 transferred to a foreign government as part of an aid package. TC-KOL (msn 26258) was one of the excess Navy R4Ds that was obtained by the CAA in 1958. Operated by the FAA as N43, this DC-3 was transferred to the Turkish government via the Agency for International Development (AID) in August 1966. TC-KOL continued in the flight inspection role for several years before being transferred to the Turkish Air Force in 1978. (John Wegg)

One of the old CAA DC-3s originally transferred in the mid-1940s is shown here in July 1967 operating in the flight inspection role as N14 (msn 9526). This aircraft reportedly saw service in World War II with the 9th Air Force. Its registration was changed to N24 in 1973, and was slated for disposal shortly afterwards. The FAA changed the registration to N24AH before release to the GSA. (Davies Collection)

The FAA DC-3 often reverted to its military role while in service. This view shows N182 (msn 20560) providing logistical support for FAA operations in 1963. N182 enjoyed a long and fruitful utilization with the FAA. Unfortunately, it was transferred to the Forest Service, surveyed, stripped of parts, and given to the Boise Airport fire department for a practice burn. (FAA)

Flight check DC-3 at work. This view shows an ILS flight inspection, with the DC-3 making a low-level run along the runway to check the alignment of the localizer signal. The survey-type equipment are theololites to provide accurate measurements. The white cross on the nose of the aircraft is to aid the ground technician in precise positioning input into his theodolite. The aircraft is N33 (msn 26583) at Hoquiam, Washington, in 1977. (via John Pearsall)

Another view of an FAA flight inspection in progress. N42 (msn 26268) is checking the ILS glideslope in this view, again utilizing a ground-based theodolite. Though modern flight inspection uses onboard equipment for aircraft positioning, theodolites are still used to obtain the most precise measurements of glide paths. (FAA)

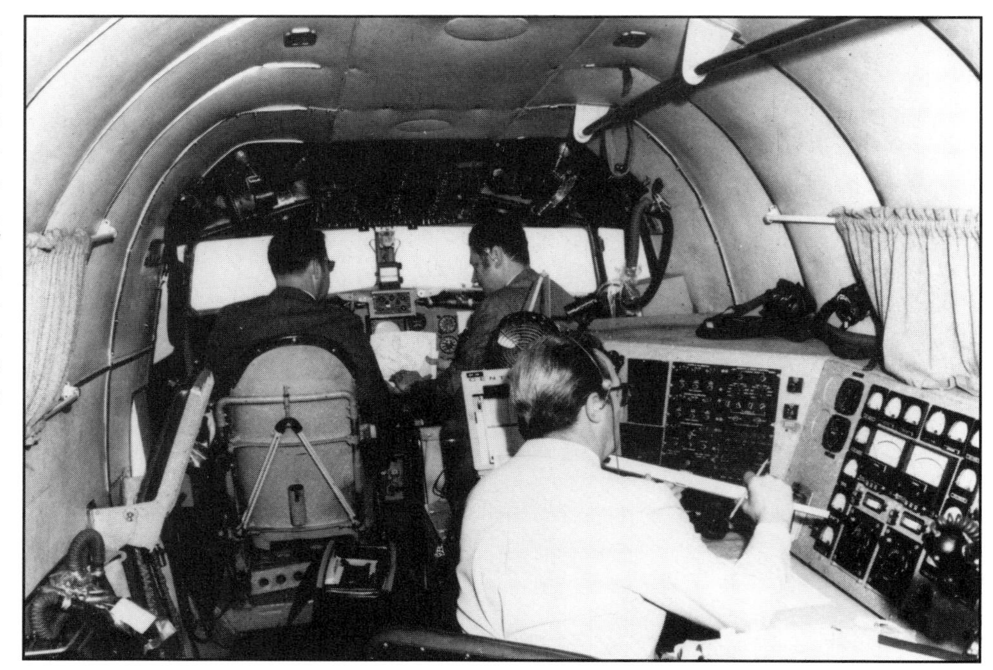

The working end of an FAA flight inspection DC-3. As can be seen, the bulkhead between the cockpit and cabin has been removed, with the pilots sitting forward and the electronics technician at his panel. A curtain covers the "picture" windows on each side of the technician's position. It is apparent the engineering and finishing work which went into the "Type II" DC-3 was set at a high standard. (FAA)

N35 (msn 32794) performing a localizer flight inspection at Ketchikan, Alaska, in September 1980. On the inset, the flight inspection cockpit could be very busy as attention is split between traffic watch, air traffic control, airplane manuvering, and data collection. (Both via FAA History Office)

ownership of 40 of the 44 R4Ds loaned to the FAA by the Department of the Navy to the FAA. The transfer was effected as part of an agreement whereby the FAA would provide the majority of any military flight inspection required. Title documents were executed, and the FAA became both owner and operator of the aircraft. The four R4Ds noted as lent to the CAA in 1959 but not transferred in 1966 (BuNos 17176, 39062, 50776, and 50815) were originally slated for the CAA, but deemed not needed and subsequently returned to the Navy.

Beginning in the early 1960s, the FAA also modified a number of surplus USAF C-47s to a Type II configuration for export to various foreign countries for their flight inspection programs. Of particular interest are three USAF C-47s (43-15958, 43-15288, 43-15550) transferred to the FAA in late 1962. The three aircraft were assigned, respectively, N160, N161, and N162 and were modified for flight inspection. These aircraft were delivered to the Government of Somalia in March 1964. Other recipients of these aircraft included Greece, Kenya, South Vietnam, Mexico, and Columbia. Most of these transfers occurred at the behest of the U.S. State Department to programs under advisement of the FAA. The FAA also transferred an excess flight inspection DC-3, msn 26258, to Turkey in 1966, and lent its expertise in technical matters to a number of nations on a continuing basis over the years.

Through the 1960s and into the 1970s, the FAA DC-3, in its familiar red, white, and black paint scheme, was a common sight as FAA flight crews performed their flight inspection mission. During this period the flight inspection function of the FAA was organized into numerous Flight Inspection District Offices (FIDOs) dotted across the country and responsible to one of the FAA Regional Offices. Each FIDO operated several DC-3s and was responsible for the regular inspection of the enroute low-altitude navigation aids and the instrument approach procedures serving all the airports in the FIDO's district. Mid-altitude and high-altitude flight inspection was performed by, respectively, FAA Convair 580s and Boeing 707s.

In the early 1970s the FIDOs were combined and consolidated into seven domestic Flight Inspection Field Offices (FIFOs). These offices were located at Los Angeles, Seattle, Minneapolis, Battle Creek (Michigan), Atlanta, Atlantic City, and Oklahoma City. Each of the FIFOs retained at least three DC-3s. The FAA also conducted flight inspection from its Anchorage office in Alaska, and provided regional logistical support for far-flung FAA Alaskan operations. Also, two international flight inspection programs were conducted by the FAA from offices at Frankfurt, Germany and Tokyo, Japan. (Though the European office had been assigned several DC-3s in the early 1960s, these had been replaced with Convairs and Sabreliners by the late 1960s. There is no record of an FAA DC-3 being used for Pacific-area flight inspection.). Though generally unheralded, the yeoman DC-3 and the FAA crews worked to ensure that the low-altitude airway system, which served much of the nation's air commerce, performed as advertised.

The FAA lost a total of five DC-3s between 1963 and 1975 in operational accidents. Because the FIDOs were attached to the FAA's regional offices, the DC-3s were often pressed into duty for administrative transport and occasionally piloted by non-current regional administrators with more authority than common sense. At least one of the DC-3s was destroyed when the aircraft got away from its high-ranking pilot in a takeoff accident. The DC-3s were also used for initial and recurrent training of flight crews, and several were assigned to Oklahoma City for just that purpose. Given the demands of the training regimen, it is not surprising that one DC-3 was also lost in training accident.

Caught in the ownership transfer between the Navy and the FAA in August 1966 was one FAA DC-3 (msn 10096, N61). This aircraft was actually returned to the Navy prior to title transfer but was retained on the transfer agreement. Why the FAA decided this aircraft was excess has been lost in the historical record, but the Navy released the DC-3 to the General Services Adminstration (GSA). The GSA subsequently sold it to a Mexican company, which operated the aircraft as XC-DAP through the 1970s.

In the early 1970s, the FAA began pursuing a replacement for its DC-3s. Newer computer technology using inertial navigation systems provided a precise means to accurately position the flight inspection aircraft without re-

Out to pasture. N8QE (msn 4084) in St. Louis, Missouri, in May 1979. At this time the aircraft was operated by Air Indiana but retained virtually all its FAA markings. As noted earlier, this aircraft ended up in Bolivia where it reportedly remains operational. (Heinz Rentmeister via John Wegg)

A post-FAA flight inpsection DC-3. N221GB (msn 11859) at Ryan Field, Arizona, in November 1982. This DC-3 had last operated as N17 with the FAA and had gone to the USDA in August 1976. Note the radome on the nose retains the FAA theodolite mark. This aircraft was last registered in 1983 and its fate is unknown. (Scott Thompson)

Ex-FAA N54595 (msn 2053) at Montgomery Field, San Diego, in August 1987. At this date the aircraft reportedly belonged to Trans Ocean Airways of McAllen, Texas. This aircraft is now operated by Otis Spunkmeyer from the Oakland Airport in California. (John Wegg)

liance on ground checkpoints, as was the method used with the DC-3. Facing another major DC-3 modernization program, combined with the outdated performance of the type and sporadic parts supply difficulties, the FAA began phasing out its DC-3s with replacement North American NA-265 Sabreliners equipped with a new automated flight inspection system. DC-3s continued in the FAA fleet, however, into the early 1980s. The last operational flight inspection FAA DC-3 was retired in 1982 with several DC-3s utilized in the training role at Oklahoma City continuing in service for an additional year.

As the FAA pulled its DC-3s from their active inventory, the aircraft were stripped of their special equipment and registration numbers and released to the GSA for disposal. Though they remained stored at the FAA's Oklahoma City facility, the DC-3s were administered by the GSA. Most of the excess FAA DC-3s were transferred to other government agencies, primarily the Department of Agriculture's U.S. Forest Service for use as agricultural sprayers. These aircraft were assigned to the USDA's U.S.-Mexico Screworm Eradication Program, which sought to eradicate the pest along the border.

The GSA eventually authorized the transfer of eight ex-FAA DC-3s to the USAF Museum Heritage Program for static display at base museums. One aircraft (N7, msn 25341) was transferred by the GSA to Ohio University for use in an avionics test program, where it retained its FAA installed equipment for navigation aids development work. Others went to universities for various flight programs and a number were ultimately transferred by the GSA to local mosquito abatement districts for use as sprayers. A number of FAA DC-3s were also deemed excess to government requirements and released for sale into the civil sector.

By 1985, only one DC-3 remained on the ramp at Oklahoma City. N34, its paint fading and fate sealed, awaited final disposal action. The unexpected reprieve granted in 1985 lasted a short eight years, but the legacy of N34 and, by extension, all the CAA/FAA DC-3s will continue, albeit in a somewhat less dramatic form. N34, the last example of a fleet of more than 80 aircraft operated over a span of 50 years in CAA/FAA service, is fortunately earmarked for permanent loan to Oklahoma City's Kirkpatrick Air and Space Museum.

It would be nice to report that an enlightened and visionary FAA pioneered the effort to preserve this prime example of its classic aviation heritage; however, reality suggests otherwise. FAA management seemed content to let N34 burn for an airport fire demonstration if only to rid itself of its perceived public relations liability. Nonetheless, the continual efforts of a handful of FAA employees with a sharp sense of history apparently have been able to cut the path for N34 to find its way into permanent preservation.

The old and the new in Oklahoma City in 1974. The North American Sabreliners combined automated technology and better performance. (FAA)

Scott Thompson

Chapter 10

Forlorn and Forgotten

Ryan Field, near Tucson, Arizona, was the final resting place for a half dozen surplus C-47s in the early 1980s. This November 1982 view shows three of the doomed aircraft as they await their undignified end. From left to right are C-47B 43-16161 (msn 20627), TC-47D 44-76257 (msn 32589), and C-47B 44-76240 (msn 32572). These C-47s held civil registrations and were owned first by Aero American and, later, Acme Aircraft. (Scott Thompson)

Unidentified wreck at a DC-3 graveyard in February 1993. Located on the coast of Puerto Rico near Naguabo Beach along Highway 3 between San Juan and Humaco, at least four DC-3 carcasses rot away here. (Ed Davies)

N29958 (msn 12357) destroyed by Hurricane Hugo in September 1989. This view shows the DC-3 at St. Thomas (U.S. Virgin Islands) during February 1993. A lend-lease Dakota III, this aircraft carried the RAF serial of KG350 and was delivered to 48 Squadron (RAF) in the U.K. in March 1944. Just before midnight on June 5, 1944, while piloted by Pilot Officer W.R. Pring and his crew, this Dakota was one of many that took off from bases in Britain for the D-Day invasion of Europe. KG350 delivered 14 paratroopers and two containers of supplies and ammunition during the first strike. This veteran warbird took part in other majory airborne assaults in Europe before returning to North American and post-war service with the Royal Canadian Air Force. (Ed Davies)

This unidentified DC-3 fuselage is used by the U.S. Forest Service at their Missoula, Montana air base. Presumably, smokejumpers have used it for practice but it appears abandoned in this July 1993 view. Nearby was a Beech 18 fuselage in a similar condition. (Scott Thompson)

The last C-47 at the Davis-Monthan AFB AMARC facility is C-47D 44-76642 (msn 32974), shown here in July 1993. This Oklahoma City-built aircraft was delivered in March 1945 and reportedly served with the 12th Air Force in Italy. 44-76642 has been in storage at Davis-Monthan since November 1969. Its inventory control number, CB334, can be seen below the nose radome. (Ed Davies)

Looking somewhat odd, this cockpit-less DC-3 is N21713 (msn 2125) at the Arlington, Washington, airport in July 1992. Built as a DC-3A-269 for Northwest and delivered in April 1939, this aircraft retained its initial civil registration throught the entirety of its use. Its last civil operator was Northern Peninsula Fisheries of Alaska. (Scott Thompson)

Another view of one of the Ryan Field C-47s in November 1982. This aircraft, C-47B 43-16161 (msn 20627) has the civil registration of N87649 assigned, but it is doubtful this aircraft used it beyond the short ferry flight from Davis-Monthan to Ryan. Its last civil owner and scrapper was Acme Aircraft. (Scott Thompson)

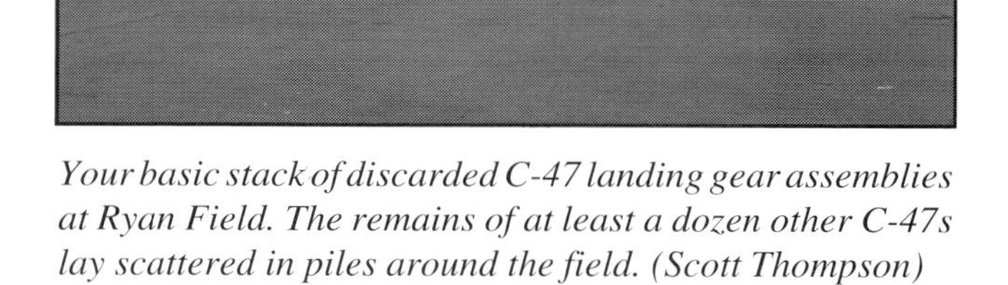

Your basic stack of discarded C-47 landing gear assemblies at Ryan Field. The remains of at least a dozen other C-47s lay scattered in piles around the field. (Scott Thompson)

Ex-FAA DC-3 N78125 (msn 9486) on the Majestic lot at Salt Lake City in April 1994. As can be seen, the DC-3 retains the FAA markings but has lost its engines and wings. This DC-3 has been reassembled and disassembled at least twice by Majestic, but currently remains stored with an uncertain fate. (Scott Thompson)

N100M (msn 19716) photographed on the fire dump at the Oakland Airport in September 1993. Built as C-47A s/n 43-15250, this aircraft was delivered in February 1944 and reportedly served with the Seventh Air Force. After the war it was purchased by the Signal Oil and Gas Company of Los Angeles. Highly modified, it was retrofitted with Wright C9HD engines, a speed kit and "wet wings." Acquired by Trans National Airlines, it was stripped out and re-fitted with a cargo door, but never put into service. Later the airframe was slated to be used as a gate guard at Travis AFB but instead, its wings were removed and the gutted fuselage remains parked at Oakland's North Field. At right is a view of N100M in May 1958. (Both via Ed Davies)

Another C-47 on the Majestic ramp at Salt Lake City in April 1994 was N168Z (msn 20850), an ex-U.S. Forest Service DC-3, which evidently was being used as a parts source. N168Z started as C-47A 43-16384, and after being released by the USAF, remained active with the Forest Service until 1978. (Scott Thompson)

SC-47D 43-16250 (msn 20716) at Aero Nostalgia's Stockton, California yard in July 1989. Aero Nostalgia cannibalized the fuselage for parts to modify and restore a C-53 to a C-47 configuration for the Travis Air Museum. (Scott Thompson)

Ostensibly on display, this view shows DC-3A N600RC (msn 2193) at the Florda Military Museum at Clearwater, Florida, in May 1995. This aircraft enjoyed a long civil career, beginning with Pan Am in 1940, before reverting to use as an instructional airframe in 1983. It has since been placed in the museum collection. (Ed Davies)

Once proud American Airlines NC25629 (msn 2249) photographed on Airport Road at the Santa Monica Airport in June 1988. Retired by American in 1949, it continued in airline service first with Capitol and, later, with Ozark Airlines. Passed through several more owners, it slowly was reduced to a derelict at Chino Airport (in Southern California) before being moved to its birthplace, Santa Monica. The faint tracing of a ficticious civil registration, N137, can be seen on the tail. (Ed Davies)

Continental Express N34PB (msn 2204) at the Barbstable Municipal Airport in Massachussetts in September 1991. Used as a spares ship for the financially strapped Provincetown Boston Airline fleet, it had accumulated further damage during a hurricane. This DC-3 was originally delivered to American Airlines as "Flagship Cleveland" in March 1940 and carried the registration of NC25658. It was impressed into USAAF service in 1942 and then sold in 1949 to Trans Texas Airlines. It joined PBA's fleet in December 1971. This aircraft was subsequently sold to Champlain Enterprises of Plattsburg, New York, in July 1992, and its registration has been changed to N992CA. (Ed Davies)

DC-3-201A N101MX (msn 2102) was delivered to Eastern Airlines as NC21743 in February 1939. By 1950, it was registered to Arthur Godfrey Productions and it was later fitted with R-2000 engines. Recently this aircraft was reportedly sold to the "Arthur Godfrey Memorial Foundation," which has been soliciting funds to restore the aircraft and place it on display at the Leesburg, Virginia, airport. This view was taken at Fort Meyers, Florida, in May 1995. (Ed Davies)

A pair of Navy C-117Ds are stored at the China Lake Naval Weapons Station near Ridgrecrest, California. Both aircraft are tentatively slated for a yet-to-be established base museum. Above is C-117D BuNo 17156 (msn 43342, built as msn 12429), which carried the civil registration of N722 NR while assigned to the Naval Arctic Research Laboratory. It is unusual to see nose art on a Navy aircraft. At left are two views of BuNo 12431 (msn 43395, built as msn 9528), which also was assigned to the Naval Arctic Research Laboratory and carried the civil registration of N31310. The registration of both aircraft was reportedly cancelled in 1982. These photos were taken in May 1994. (Scott Thompson)

Veteran of the Navy, FAA, and Department of Agriculture, this view shows R4D-5 BuNo 17126 (msn 12261) at Fort Meyers, Florida, in May 1995. Operated as N23 with the FAA and used for flight inspection, it was re-registered as N224GB while used as a sprayer for the DOA. In 1976, it was tranferred to the Lee County Mosquito Control District in Florida where it was, evidently, used primarily as a spares source. (Ed Davies)

DC-3A-197B, originally delivered to United Airlines as NC18942 (msn 2008) in April 1938. One of many United DC-3s sold in 1954, this DC-3 flew for a variety of corporate owners. Exported to South Africa in 1976, this DC-3 was registered as ZX-KEX in 1978. This view shows the aircraft in derelict condition at Lanseria, South Africa, in April 1992. (Patrick Vinot Prefontaine via Ed Davies)

N341W (msn 13041) at Buckingham Air Park, Fort Meyers, Florida, in May 1995. Built as C-47A 42-93160 and declared surplus in March 1946, N341W was operated by a series of civil owners in both Canada and the U.S. before being acquired by Lake Wales Air Service in December 1980. (Ed Davies)

Two views of N46950 (msn 32873) at the St. Thomas Airport, U.S. Virgin Islands, in the aftermath of Hurricane Hugo. This DC-3 was last registered to Virgin Air and was damaged beyond repair by the 1989 storm. It now lays at the airport dump, but still retains the RCAF markings of KN443. (Ed Davies)

Another unidentified Puerto Rican DC-3 in a DC-3 graveyard located along a coastal route near San Juan. These aircraft had been slated for display at a park-restaurant complex but are now corroding away in the jungle setting. (Ed Davies)

R4D-8 BuNo 17160 (msn 43331) at Davis-Monthan in July 1993. Almost all the remaining R4D-8s at Davis-Monthan in the mid-1970s were purchased by a civil operator for possible conversion to turboprop power. (Ed Davies)

C-47B-50-DK 45-1074 (msn 34344) at the Pima Air Museum's back lot in March 1990. Delivered in August 1945, this C-47 was used in Europe after the war and continued in service through July 1970, when sent for storage at the vast AMARC facility at Davis-Monthan AFB near Tucson, Arizona. The Pima Air Museum, which adjoins Davis-Monthan, obtained the airframe in the early 1970s. (Scott Thompson)

As if rearing up defiantly against the conquering elements, a stoic DC-3 slowly fades away...

Appendices

Appendix 1
CAA and FAA DC-3s

MSN	USAAF/USAF	S/N	USN	SERIAL	CIVIL	REGISTRATION SEQUENCE
2053	C-41-DO	38-502			DC-3-253	NC15473, NC12, N43, N54595
4080					DC-3A-348	NC14, N14, N560R
4084	C-50D-DO	41-7696			DC-3-313B	NC25698 (NTU), (TO C-50),NC19900 (NTU), NC18669, NC6 (NTU), NC16, N16, N8, N8QE, CP-1941
4146	C-48A-DO	41-7682			DC-3A-368	NC86, N1, N6
4279	C-47-DL	41-7792			DC-3A-360	NC17, N56, N76, N87818 (NTU)
4438			R4D-1	1982	DC-3A-360	NX815, NC815, NX115, N115, N20, N50, N50Q (NTU), N2009J (NTU), N220GB
4470	C-47-DL	41-18408			DC-3A-360	NC361, CHILEAN AF 956
4574	C-47-DL	41-18482			DC-3A-360	NC5, N99, N101Z
4661			R4D-1	5061	DC-3A-360	NC814, N114, N10, N107, N102ZP, N111ST
4776	C-47-DL	41-18615			DC-3A-360	NX206, NC206
4854	C-50-DO	41-20084			DC-3A-405	NC15574, N70B, CF-HXS, CF-QCM
4862	C-50-DO	41-20092			DC-3A-405	NC15572, N83B, N26J, N26S, N2647
6355			R4D-4	33820	DC-3A-447	NC34962 (FOR PAA), (R4D-4), NC226
9005	C-47-DL	42-5698			DC-3A-360	NC181, N71
9486	C-47A-30-DL	42-23624	R4D-5	12429	DC-3A-456	N7632C, N58, N78, N78125
9526	C-47A-30-DL	42-23664			DC-3A-456	NC842, NC342, N21, N14 , N24, N24AH, N238GB
9940	C-47A-40-DL	42-24078	R4D-5	39062	DC-3A-456	N9465Z
10096	C-47A-50-DL	42-24234	R4D-5	39076	DC-3A-456	N6678C, N9053Z, N61, XC-DAP
10243	C-47A-60-DL	42-24381			DC-3A-456	N34988, N28, N25
11703	C-53D-DO	42-68776			DC-3A-457	NC50592, NC18663, NC63
11808	C-47A-DK	42-108796	R4D-5	17094	DC-3A-456	N7232C, N39, N39AH, N239GB, HK-3220
11859	C-47A-1--DK	42-92096			DC-3A-456	NC9, N18, N17, N17715 (NTU), N221GB
11928	C-47A-1-DK	42-108808	R4D-5	17106	DC-3A-456	N9881C, N51, N71, N916 (NTU), N223GB,
12261	C-47A-5-DK	42-92458	R4D-5	17126	DC-3A-456	N3458G, N41, N23, N87788, N2001J, N224GB
12733	C-47A-15-DK	42-92883	R4D-5	17176	DC-3A-456	N9464Z
13004	C-47A-15-DK	42-92127	R4D-5	17193	DC-3A-456	N6517C, N55, N67, N226GB
13447	C-47A-25-DK	42-93526			DC-3A-456	N400, 5Y-ADI (KENYA)
13850	C-47A-DL	43-30699			DC-3A-467	N500, N5009,
19320	C-47A-75-DL	42-100857			DC-3A-456	NC70, N23, N41, N23, N2273K
19754	C-47A-80-DL	43-15288			DC-3A-456	N161, 60S-AAA (SOMALI), 60-SAA, N920, SU-BFY, EI-BSJ, PH-DDZ
20016	C-47A-85-DL	43-15550			DC-3A-360	N162, 60S-AAB (SOMALI), 60-SAB, N925, N512GL(NTU)
20033	C-47A-85-DL	43-15467			DC-3A-456	N202, N22
20400	C-47A-90-DL	43-15934			DC-3A-456	NC200
20403	C-47A-90-DL	43-15937			DC-3A-456	NC109, NC19, N195W
20419	C-47A-90-DL	43-15953			DC-3A-456	NX183, N52
20424	C-47A-90-DL	43-15958			DC-3A-456	N160, 60S-AAC (SOMALI), 60-SAC
20426	C-47A-90-DL	43-15960			DC-3A-456	NC818, NC118, NC3, NC2, N3, N7
20443	C-47A-90-DL	43-15977			DC-3A-456	NC812; NC112; NC24; N14; N21; N24010; N230GB
20494	C-47A-90-DL	43-16028			DC-3A-456	NC100, N8785, N100Z, N142Z

MSN	USAAF/USAF	S/N	USN	SERIAL	CIVIL	REGISTRATION SEQUENCE
20560	C-47A-90-DL	43-16094			DC-3A-456	NC182, N100, N76, N76AB, N102Z
25341	C-47A-30-DK	43-48080			DC-3A-456	NC203, NC15, N7, N7AP
25627	C-47B-1-DK	43-48366	R4D-6	17252	DC-3A-467	N5178V, N57, N77, N77112
25775	C-47B-1-DK	43-48514	R4D-6	17272	DC-3A-467	N7633C, N44, LV-PDJ, LQ-INL, TG-BAC
25824	C-47B-5-DK	43-48563	R4D-6	17278	DC-3A-467	N7634C, N40, N40180
25951	C-47B-5-DK	43-48690	R4D-6	17286	DC-3A-467	N9445Z, N62, N69, N259DC, FAB 2079
25954	C-47B-5-DK	43-48693	R4D-6	17289	DC-3A-467	N6516C, N54, N47, N74, N74Z, N226GB (NTU)
25956	C-47B-5-DK	43-48695	R4D-6	17291	DC-3A-467	N2757A,N9052Z, N67, N25, N51938
26093	C-47B-5-DK	43-48832	R4D-6	50746	DC-3A-467	N9518C, N26, N26AH, N228GB
26108	C-47B-5-DK	43-48847	R4D-6	50749	DC-3A-467	N3455G, N63, N79, N87819, N2002J, N231GB
26133	C-47B-5-DK	43-48872	R4D-6	50754	DC-3A-467	N9118Z, N70, (N70JC, NTU), N211GB
26258	C-47B-10-DK	43-48997	R4D-6	50758	DC-3A-467	N7674C, N43, TC-KOL
26268	C-47B-10-DK	43-49007	R4D-6	50760	DC-3A-467	N7675C, N42, N87815(NTU), N2005J, N232GB
26283	C-47B-10-DK	43-49022	R4D-6	50763	DC-3A-467	N7234C, N11, N13, N47, N473, N207GB, N233GB, N2299Y
26358	C-47B-10-DK	43-49097	R4D-6	50773	DC-3A-467	N7069C, N31, N9049P
26373	C--47B-10-DK	43-49112	R4D-6	50776	DC-3A-476	N9466Z
26558	C-47B-15-DK	43-49297	R4D-6	50788	DC-3A-467	N7678C, N49, N2006J, N235GB, N514AC
26583	C-47B-15-DK	43-49322	R4D-6	50793	DC-3A-467	N7092C, N7072C, N33, N620
26593	C-47B-15-DK	43-49332	R4D-6	50795	DC-3A-467	N3671G, N69, HK-1149G (COLUMBIA)
26713	C-47B-15-DK	43-49452	R4D-6	50813	DC-3A-467	N7489C, N37, N37AH, N240GB, ZS-KCV
26724	C-47B-20-DK	43-49463	R4D-6	50815	DC-3A-467	N9467Z
26733	C-47B-15-DK	43-49472	R4D-6	50816	DC-3A-467	N9508C, N25, N28, N74, 5-YDCA (KENYAI)
26874	C-47B-15-DK	43-49613	R4D-6	50819	DC-3A-467	N9119Z, N60, N68, N68AH, N229GB
26968	C-47B-20-DK	43-49707	R4D-6	50829	DC-3A-467	N7676C, N53, N73, N73AH, N237GB
32794	TC-47B-25-D	44-76462	R4D-7	39098	DC-3A-467	N7478C, N35
33100	TC-47B-30-D	44-76768	R4D-7	99825	DC-3A-467	N7488C, N38, N38114, N208GB, N210GB
33133	TC-47B-30-D	44-76801	R4D-7	99837	DC-3A-467	N7233C, N29
33144	TC-47B-30-D	44-76812	R4D-7	99828	DC-3A-467	N3454G, N66, N49966, N145JR
33155	TC-47B-30-D	44-76823	R4D-7	99829	DC-3A-467	N7677C, N47
33201	TC-47B-35-D	44-76869	R4D-7	99835	DC-3A-467	N7631C, N48, N31179, N211GB, N2298C, N352SA (NTU)
33206	TC-47B-35-D	44-76874	R4D-7	99836	DC-3A-467	N7071C, N29, N17, N73, SX-ECF
33216	TC-47B-35-D	44-76884	R4D-7	99838	DC-3A-467	N7073C, N30, N87814, N2004J (NTU), N212GB, N2312G
33232	TC-47B-35-D	44-76900	R4D-7	99840	DC-3A-467	N5177V, N64, N44, N4405, N2007J (NTU), N213GB
33241	TC-47B-35-D	44-76909	R4D-7	99841	DC-3A-467	N400, N4002
33251	TC-47B-35-D	44-76919	R4D-7	99842	DC-3A-467	NC199, NC300, N46, N87817, N2003J, N225GB
33291	TC-47B-35-D	44-76959	R4D-7	99847	DC-3A-467	N7477C, N36, N87907
33305	TC-47B-35-D	44-76973	R4D-7	99849	DC-3A-467	N27, N21, N21R (NTU), N846MB
33322	TC-47B-35-D	44-76990	R4D-7	99851	DC-3A-467	N7630C, N45
33345	TC-47B-35-D	44-77013	R4D-7	99854	DC-3A-467	N7074C, N32, N32A, N227GB
33359	TC-47B-35-D	44-77027	R4D-7	99856	DC-3A-467	N7091C, N34
34374	C-47B-50-DK	45-1104			DC-3A-467	NC214, N62, N62K, N9947F (PAA), HP-190

Appendix 2
CAA and FAA DC-3 Histories

Abbreviation Key:

D.	delivered	CAA	Civil Aeronautics Adminstration
L.	leased	DPC	Defense Plants Corporation
M.	manufactured	FAA	Federal Aviation Agency (Administration)
msn	manufacturer's serial number	GSA	General Services Adminstration
ntu	not taken up	RFC	Reconstruction Finance Corporation
R.	registered	WAA	War Assets Adminstration
Rr.	re-registered		
S.	sold		

INDIVIDUAL AIRCRAFT HISTORIES

2053 M. as the sole C-41 at the Douglas-Santa Monica plant and d. for service on 22 Oct 1938. Assigned the Air Corps serial of ***38-502***, the C-41 was identical to the civil DC-3A except for some internal furnishing installations for its intended role for assignment with the Firtst Staff Squadron at Bolling Field, Washington, D.C. D. with Pratt & Whitney R-1830-21 engines of 1200 horsepower each, the C-41 was the first DC-3 type to be purchased by the U.S. military services and thus was the forerunner to the more than 10000 examples of the DC-3 which were eventually operated by the U.S. armed forces. Some sources indicate the aircraft may have been used by General H.H. "Hap" Arnold. In early 1945 38-502 was deemed surplus to military needs and transferred to the RFC. On 03 May 1945 it was loaned by the DPC to Alaska Airlines with its initial R. as ***NC15473***. Returned for disposal in 1948, the aircraft was transferred to the CAA on 12 Apr 1948 and Rr. as ***NC12***. In the late 1950s it was configured as a Type II DC-3C and thus fitted with the 1350 horsepower R-1830-94 engines. On 04 Mar 1973 it was Rr. as ***N43***. It continued in FAA service through 1974, primarily as a facility flight inspection aircraft with the FAA's Central Region. Surplus from FAA needs in 1977, it was released on 08 Aug 1977 with 24,811 flight hours to the GSA and R. canceled. Given its historic significance, it was originally slated for the USAF Museum Program upon its withdrawal from FAA service. However, it was instead transferred into the civil fleet through the GSA to the Southern Missouri State University on 15 Feb 1978 for use in university transport. Rr. ***N54595*** on 05 Apr 1978. S. on 10 May 1985 to Red Stevenson, DBA Red (S) Aircraft Sales of Jenks, OK. It was quickly s. again, on 22 May 1985, to Condor Aviation of Tulsa, OK, who again s. it on 27 Jun 1985 to Trans Ocean Airways of McAllen, TX. On 15 Mar 1989 it B. by Bill Celli Leasing Company of Lafayette, CA who, in turn, L. the aircraft to the Otis Spunkmeyer Company for operations with its Sentimental Journeys aviation fleet based at the Oakland, CA airport. Rr as ***NC41HQ*** in April 1994. The aircraft has been refurbished to its 1941 appearance and remains airworthy.

4080 M. as a civil DC-3A-348 for the CAA. Order placed by the CAA as early as Aug 1940 as initial r. application for the aircraft was made in the name of Douglas Aircraft on that date. Bill of sale dated 17 Mar 1941 and d. to the CAA on 21 Mar 1941. R. as ***NC14***. Primary assignment with the CAA was as a flying test-bed to work out instrument installations, navigation-aids testing, and aeronautical inspector qualifications. Wartime maintenance and modifications largely conducted at the United Airlines Modification Center at Cheyenne, Wyoming. Accounts have suggested that this aircraft was operated by the USAAF as a C-50D but nothing in the civil aircraft files would indicate this; rather, the records indicate that this DC-3 was largely based at the CAA's Houston Standardization Center in Texas. NC14 remained in the CAA/FAA inventory through 26 Sep 1960 when s. to the Aircraft Warehouse of Bridgeton, Missouri for $2678.67. The R. of N14 was canceled upon the sale. On 08 Nov 1960 s. again to the Beldex Corporation of St. Louis, Missouri, and the new R. of ***N560R*** was assigned on 14 Dec 1960. On 15 Sep 1966 N560R was s. to Texahoma Airways of Tulsa, OK, and transferred to a part of the same company, Mid America Airlines, also of Tulsa, OK, on 20 Jun 1967. Repossessed by the National Bank of Commerce of Tulsa, OK on 30 Aug 1967. S. on 20 May 1970 to Stan Burnstein, DBA Continental Aviation Company, of Tulsa, OK. A week later, on 28 May 1970, it was s. to W.R. Hall of Grand Junction, Colorado. R. was not issued in the new owner's name, however, and R. was reportedly canceled by 1975. Final disposition of N560R is not known.

4084 M. as civil DC-3-392 for Pennsylvania Central Airlines. Not d., but instead impressed by the USAAC as C-50D s/n 41-7696 on 08 Aug 1941 for use as a military transport. Assigned r. of ***NC25698*** but ntu. Declared surplus to military needs in early 1945 turned over to the RFC for disposal. Initial r. issued as ***NC19900*** but then changed to ***NC18669*** in the name of the DPC on 05 Feb 1945. Loaned to American Airlines to assist in their conversion to peace time operations. Released back to the WAA, in 1947. Subsequently transferred to the CAA on 02 Jun 1947 and Rr. as ***N6***, which was ntu, but changed to ***N16***. Converted to the FAA standard Type II DC-3 configuration in the late 1950s, which included the fitting of the Pratt & Whitney R-1830-94 engines of 1350 horsepower. Operated as N16 in the flight inspection role until 12 Jan 1973 when Rr. as ***N8***. Surplus to FAA needs with 30,076 flight hours and Rr. as ***N8QE*** before transfer to the GSA on 18 Nov 1976 for disposal. S. to Robert Schneider of Topeka, KS on 20 Jun 1977 and operated by Forbes Air, also of Topeka, KS. Subsequently s. to Forbes Air. S. to National Jet of Indianapolis, IN on 20 Mar 1979, and then transferred by repossession to McCorrum Aviation of Danville, IL on 15 Apr 1980. In early 1984 exported to Luwior Limited, San Jose de la Banda, Colhabamba, Bolivia where it was r. as ***CP-1941*** beginning in Apr 1984. Believed still operational.

4146 M. in Sep 1941 as a civil DC-3A-368. Impressed by the USAAC on 30 Jun 1941 at a cost of $95,594 and was the first of three C-48As. Assigned the USAAC serial of ***41-7682***. Beginning on 17 Jul 1941, based at Bolling Field in Washington, D.C. and used as a staff transport. Transferred by the USAAF to the CAA on 30 Apr 1946. R. of ***NC86*** assigned on 01 Aug 1946. Early CAA utilization of this aircraft is not known but in 1953 it was Rr. as ***N1***, indicating assignment in a high-level Department of Commerce/CAA transport role. As of Jul 1956 logged airframe time totaled over 4,606 flight hours. In Jan 1960 the aircraft was re-engined with R-1830-94 engines. It remained assigned to Washington National Airport through the balance of its CAA/FAA service. On 02 Aug 1961 it was Rr. as ***N6*** and continued its administrative role. On 27 Mar 1975 N6 crashed on departure as Dubois, Pennsylvania. The remainder of the airframe was subsequently s. to a local junk dealer in May 1975 for $422.66.

4147 M. in Sep 1941 as a civil DC-3A-368. Impressed by the USAAC on 16 Jul 1941 at a cost of $95,594 and was the second of three C-48As. Assigned the USAAC serial of ***41-7683***. Beginning on 18 Sep 1941, based at Bolling Field in Washington, D.C. and used as a staff transport. Transferred by the USAAF to the CAA on 30 Apr 1946. Transferred by the CAA to the CAB on 19 Jul 1946 and issued the r. of ***N424*** on that date. The CAB utilized the aircraft for adminstrative transport. Rr. ***N3*** on 21 Feb 1951. Shortly thereafter, on 18 Jun 1951, the r. was changed to ***N2***. N2 continued to function as a CAB transport through 1958 and was based at Washington National Airport in Washington D.C along with the CAA's fleet of administrative transports. On 19 Sep 1958 the aircraft was s. to Holloday-Aero, Inc. of Byrd Field, Sandston, VA and was r. as ***N90Q***. It was s. the same day to East Coast Flying Service of Alexandria, VA. On 04 Oct 1965 it was B. by the Charlotte Aircraft Corporation of the Delta Air Base, Charlotte, NC. Charlotte Air Service, an aircraft broker, s. N90Q back to East Coast Flying Service, now of Jacksonville, FL on 11 Jan 1966. On 17 Aug 1967 ownership was transferred to East Coast Leasing of Washington, D.C. On 28 May 1969 N90Q was s. to Coastal West, also of Washington, D.C. In Aug 1970 N90Q was s. via a sheriff's sale to George Lee of Wildwood, New Jersey. It was, in turn, transferred to G.R. Leasing Group which was listed at the same address as Mr. Lee. The airframe was reported destroyed by a fire in Feb 1971 and r. canceled by the FAA in May 1973.

4148 M. in Sep 1941 as a civil DC-3A-368. Impressed by the USAAC on 23 Aug 1941 at a cost of $95,594 and was the third of three C-48As. Assigned the USAAC serial of ***41-7684***. Beginning on 25 Aug 1941, based at Bolling Field in Washington, D.C. and used as a staff transport. Assigned to the Brookley Air Depot, AL as of 15 Jan 1946. Subsequently flown to NAS Jacksonville, FL where it was converted to a civil configuration. Transferred by the USAAF to the CAA on 15 Apr 1946. R. ***NC84*** on 19 Apr 1946. Correspondence relating to the transfer notes that a number of military DC-3s were being transferred to the CAA at the time and all were operating under their military designations and serials. However, for an unspecified reason, the Army would not allow the CAA to fly this particular aircraft until it had its military serial removed a civil r. assigned. NC84 was evidently utilized for airways inspection beginning shortly after acquisition. In 1951 it was standardized for airways inspection with the installation of additional radio equipment, crew positions, and airstair door. On 01 May 1952 Rr. ***NC24***. It continued in airways inspection and was further modified to the FAA standard Type II configuration in Aug 1960, which included the installation of the larger R-1830-94 engines. NC24 was transferred to active storage on 23 Oct 1964 pending assignment to the AID and release to the government of Chile. With its civil r. canceled, the aircraft was flown to Chile in Feb 1965 and assigned to the Fuerza Aerea de Chile (Chilean Air Force). As of Apr 1972 the DC-3 was reportedly operating as ***A1-971*** in Chilean service. Reportedly assigned to the Direccion de Aeronautical Civl during 1974/1975 before reverting to military use in 1975. Withdrawn from service in Feb 1980 and s. by Chile to the Atlas Aircraft Corporation of Miami, FL on 05 Oct 1982. It was s. shortly thereafter, on 05 Nov 1982, to All American Aviation, also of Miami, FL and issued the r. of ***N2782S***. On 12 Jan 1988 N2782S was s. to Aircraft Holdings of Miami, FL, and is believed still active.

4279 M. as C-47-DL s/n ***41-7792*** at Douglas-Long Beach and d. for service to the USAAC on 15 Apr 1942. Reported wartime service includes assignment to the North Atlantic and Alaskan areas with the Air Transport Command. Reported assignement to Penn-Central as of 28 Jun 1944, presumably under contract with ATC. Surplus to military needs and released to the RFC for disposal in 1945. Obtained by the CAA and r. as ***NC17*** 10 Oct 1945. Information is not available from the record but probably assigned to a regional facility flight inspection fleet. Rr. ***N56*** in 1953. Assignment in the early 1960s primarily with the FAA's Eastern and Central Regions and, beginning in 1969, with the Alaskan Region for both flight inspection and logistical support. Rr. ***N76*** on 31 Mar 1973. Reported damaged or destroyed by a hangar fire in Anchorage, AK on 06 Nov 1974. R. subsequently canceled, though the r. of ***N87818*** was assigned on 07 Feb 1975 but ntu. There is no further record of utilization of the aircraft after the 1974 hangar fire and it is probable that the assignment of N87818 was made in error as the FAA removed the aircraft from its inventory records.

4438 M. under a U.S. Navy contract at the Douglas-Long Beach plant and d. as R4D-1 BuNo ***01982*** on 08 Jun 1942. Wartime service with the USMC with several squadrons including VMJ-152 and VMJ-153. Deemed surplus to USN/USMC needs and stricken on 31 Aug 1946. Subsequently transferred to the WAA for disposal, which r. the aircraft as ***NC815***. Obtained by the CAA on 22 Oct 1947. Used in a series of tests in cooperation with the Goodyear Tire Company and fitted with castering main landing gear assemblies, and issue the temporary r. of ***NX815*** during the experimental program. Rr. as ***N20*** on 22 Jan 1951. Joined the facility flight inspection fleet in 1951 and was modified to the DC-3C Type II configuration in 1959 at the FAA's Aircraft Services Base in Oklahoma City. R. again changed to ***N50*** on 01 Feb 1973. Deemed excess to FAA needs and placed into storage on 25 Jul 1975. R. changed to ***N50Q*** on 26 Sep 1975, but ntu and, instead, canceled on 21 Oct 1975. Released to the GSA for disposal on 26 Sep 1975 and transferred to the USDA's U.S.-Mexico Screw Worm Eradication Program being conducted in Mexico. Initially r. ***N2009J***, this also was ntu but rather

r. as ***N220GB*** on 02 Apr 1976. Stored at Douglas-Bisbee Airport, AZ in 1980 and transferred by the GSA to the Monroe County Mosquito Control District at Key West, FL on 23 Sep 1980 for continued use as a sprayer. Aircraft believed still active.

4470 M. as C-47-DL s/n ***41-18408*** at Douglas-Long Beach and d. to the USAAF on 29 Jun 1942. Wartime service reported with the 5th Air Force in the South Pacific. Assigned back within the U.S. in mid-1944 and deemed surplus to military needs and released to the RFC for disposal in 1945. Obtained by the CAA in Oct 1945 and d. from Bush Field, Augusta, GA to the CAA's facility in Oklahoma City on 09 Oct 1945. Assigned the civil r. of ***N361***. Placed in storage and ultimately scrapped for parts to support other CAA DC-3s. R. canceled on 12 Dec 1946. Fuselage s. as scrap on 10 Sep 1947 to Page Aviation Service of Oklahoma City, OK. Subsequently s. to Gordon Hamilton, DBA Aircraft Conversion and Maintenance Company of Tucson, AZ on 20 Apr 1951. S. four days later to International Airports, Inc, of Burbank, CA for $7,000. Actual date of transfer was probably much earlier. Fuselage re-manufactured into a complete aircraft and r. of N361 reassigned on 30 Oct 1951. S. on 25 Oct 1952 to Witbeck Aircraft of Gainsville, TX for $30,000. Aircraft had been s. for export by Witbeck five days earlier to the Government of Chile. Export certificate E-27550 issued. R. of N361 cancelled on 12 Jun 1953. Assigned serial ***A1-956*** by the Fuerza Aereas de Chile (Chilean Air Force) and noted in their inventory as of 27 Apr 1953. Reported crashed and destroyed on 12 May 1967 at El Plumerillo, Chile.

4574 M. as C-47-DL s/n ***41-18482*** at Douglas-Long Beach and d. to the USAAF on 31 Jul 1942. Served domestically during World War II, primarily at Stuttgart, AR and George Field, CA. Records indicate this aircraft was transferred directly from the USAAF to the CAA effective 14 October 1945. CAA issued initial civil r. of ***NC5*** and assignment to CAA Region 6. CAA and FAA utilization for transport and logistical support, primarily in Alaska. R. changed to ***N99*** on 02 Apr 1973. Placed into storage on 03 Dec 1976 in Anchorage and released for disposal on 30 Dec 1976. R. canceled on 03 Jan 1977. Transferred by the GSA to the U.S. Forest Service on 09 Mar 1977 and r. as ***N101Z***. Damaged in 1981 accident and de-registered on 18 Jan 1982. Reportedly transferred by the GSA to the Alaskan Transportation Museum of Palmer, AK on 25 Feb 1982. Fate unknown, though still carried on the civil register as N101Z with the USFS.

4661 M. under a U.S. Navy contract at Douglas-Long Beach and d. as R4D-1 BuNo ***05061*** on 27 Aug 1942. Operations with the Naval Air Transport Service through wartime service. Surplus to Navy needs and released to the WAA for disposal on 15 Aug 1946. Stricken from the Navy inventory on 31 Aug 1946. Presumably stored and assigned initial r. to the WAA as ***N814*** on 15 Oct 1946. Transferred to the CAA on 03 Jun 1947 and Rr. as ***N114*** on 09 Oct 1947. Again Rr. as ***N10*** on 02 Oct 1950. Probably assigned to facility flight inspection beginning on that date. Modified to the standard DC-3 Type II configuration in 1959 or 1960. Subsequent use in flight inspection, primarily with the FAA's Central and Western Regions. Deemed excess to needs and released to the GSA on 01 Sep 1972. R. canceled on 08 Sep 1972. S. via auction on 05 Jun 1973 to Airline Aviation Academy of Griffin, GA and r. as ***N107***. Reserved r. of ***N47791*** ntu. On 28 Jul 1973 s. again to Metro Air Systems of Louisville, KY and reserved r. of ***N107MW*** also ntu. On 31 Dec 1973 s. to Air Freight, also of Louisville, KY. S. to Eagle Aircraft Corp. of Zephyrhills, FL on 14 Nov 1977, and r. was changed to ***N102ZP*** on 24 Jun 1978. On 25 Sep 1978 s. to Aviation Management of Zephyrhills, FS, and on 20 Nov 1978 to Skytrain, Inc., also of Zephyrhills, FL. On 20 Jan 1979 Rr. as ***N111ST***. On 03 Aug 1979 s. to United Aircraft Services of Clear Lake, MN but shortly afterwards seized for suspected drug-running. S. by auction to Aircraft Modifications, Inc., of Miami, FL on 15 Oct 1980, and that same month to Clopine Aircraft Sales of Topeka, KS. Subsequently s. to Gary Hannah of Clear Lake, MN and then, on 14 Apr 1981, again to United Aircraft Services, now of Zephyrhills, FL. Destroyed in take-off accident after an engine failure on 01 Jul 1981 while departing from Pilot Point, Alaska carrying a load of fish to Anchorage. Crew of three, including owner, killed.

4776 M. as C-47-DL s/n ***41-18615*** at the Douglas-Long Beach plant and d. for service to the USAAF on 23 Oct 1942. Reported wartime service assigned to the 5th Air Force in Australia. Reported back in the United States in Jan 1945. Surplus to U.S. military needs and transferred to the RFC. Obtained by the CAA on 08 Oct 1945, reportedly from an unknown AAF or RFC storage yard at Kansas City, Missouri, and assigned the civil r. of ***NC206***. Placed in short-term storage until early 1947 when overhauled and assigned to the CAA's Airways Section and utilized for facility flight inspection beginning in Apr 1947. Crashed 21 Jan 1948 on Navajo Peak, located 7 miles west-southwest of Ward, Colorado, with loss of crew of three. Crash attributed to severe turbulence.

4854 M. as C-53-DO s/n ***41-20084*** at Douglas-Santa Monica and d. for service to the USAAF on 31 Jan 1942. Initial USAAF service within the U.S. Assigned for transport duties in Africa and the Middle East through 1943. Excess to USAAF needs on 29 Jan 1945 and released to the War Aircraft Division, DPC of the RFC for disposal on 08 February 1945. On 16 Feb 1945 civil r. of ***NC15574*** issued in the name of the DPC. Leased in Feb 1945 to Alaska Airlines for civil use. Returned as of 27 Mar 1948 to the War Assets Administration. Transferred by the WAA to the CAA on 16 Apr 1948. CAA use unknown, but probably placed into long term storage and not operated. Excess to CAA needs and s. on 22 Jan 1954 to R.W. Blackwell and D.A. Lanham of Lockheed Air Terminal, Burbank, CA. In establishing a chain of owners dates became mixed up, but reportedly s. on 19 Jan 1954 to Beldex Corporation of Lambert Field, St. Louis, MO. Reported transferred from Blackwell and Lanham to Blackwell alone on 26 Mar 1954, the date inconsistency not being explained. In any event, Beldex Corporation had the aircraft r. changed to ***N70B*** on 30 Mar 1954. S. on 05 Feb 1955 to Shell Aviation Co., Limited of Toronto, Canada. U.S. r. canceled. Canadian r. of ***CF-HXS*** issued on 14 Feb 1955. S. to Quebec Cartier Mining, Limited of Quebec on 30 Jul 1958. r. changed to ***CF-QCM*** on 09 Feb 1959. S. to Fermes Miron Farms, Inc., of Montreal in 1977. S. to British Holdings, Limited of Vancouver, British Columbia on 06 Feb 1979. Civil r. canceled in Mar 1980. Fate unknown.

4862 M. as C-53-DO s/n ***41-20092*** at Douglas-Santa Monica and d. for service to the USAAF on 29 Jan 1942. Operated by Pan American Airways for the Ferry Command, possibly on routes between the U.S. and South America. 1943 service in Africa and, later, Europe. Surplus to USAAF needs on 05 Jan 1945 and released to the DPC. Leased to Alaskan Airlines on 05 Feb 1945 and issued the civil r. of ***NC15572*** on 18 Feb 1945. Returned to the DPC in 1948 and transferred to the CAA on 08 Sep 1948. Retained the r. of NC15572. Though not confirmed, it is probable the aircraft was placed in storage and remained as such through its CAA service, possibly as a spare parts source or as reserve aircraft. In any event, it was Rr. as ***N83B*** on 05 Feb 1954 while still with the CAA. Though the dates are not in agreement, the r. record indicates N83B was s. on 15 Jan 1954 to the Beldex Corporation of St. Louis, MO. Rr. as ***N26B*** on 12 Apr 1954 and s. shortly afterwards to Johnson Motor Lines of Charlotte, NC. S. on 04 Jan 1955 to Sun Oil Company of Philadelphia, PA. Rr. as ***N26S*** on 16 Feb 1955. R. changed to ***N2647*** on 17 Feb 1959 . S. on 01 Jun 1969 to Tri Ville Aviation of Morgan City, LA. S. on 11 Jan 1970 to Gulf Underwriters Management Corp. of Beaumont, TX. S. on 11 Mar 1973 to Flight Dynamics

Corp. of Fort Worth, TX. S. on 30 May 1973 to Ronnie Odom of Lubbock, TX. Transferred on 01 Feb 1976 to Lubbock Aero Services of Lubbock, TX. S. on 19 Feb 1976 to Sky Sales and Service of Oklahoma City, OK. S. on 22 Jun 1976 to Samuel Stewart of Santa Ana, CA. S. on 12 Apr 1973 to Rajneesh Investment Corp. of Rajheeshpuram, OR. Transferred to the Rajneesh Neo Sannyas International Commune on 31 Dec 1984. S. on 24 Oct 1985 to Atorie Air of El Paso, TX. S. on 30 Oct 1985 to Sco Ben Investments of El Paso, TX. S. on 28 Jul 1988 to Godwin Aircraft, Inc. of Memphis, TN. S. on 29 Jul 1988 to Pon Pepin Inc., of Bayamon, Puerto Rico. S. on 30 Apr 1991 to Priv Air Cargo of Bayamon, Puerto Rico. S. on 30 Jul 1990 to Manuel Sanchez of Rio Piedras, Puerto Rico. S. on 29 Oct 1990 to Flamenco Airways of Culebra, Puerto Rico. The last four ownership changes were all submitted and recorded with the FAA on 27 Jul 1991, which may account for some of the dates being out of chronological order. The last r. owner remains on file with the FAA and the aircraft is believed active in Puerto Rico.

6355 M. as a DC-3A-447 by Douglas-Santa Monica for Pan American Airways. Civil r. of ***NC34962*** reserved but ntu. Instead, impressed by the U.S. Navy as R4D-4 BuNo ***33820*** and d. on 30 Jan 1943. Assigned to transport duties at NAS Anacostia beginning in Feb 1943. Excess to military needs and released to the RFC in 1945. Transferred by the WAA to the CAA on 03 Oct 1946 and d. from the WAA storage lot at Bush Field, Atlanta, GA. Civil r. of ***NC226*** issued on 31 Oct 1946. Stored by the CAA and eventually dismantled for parts. R. subsequently canceled. Fuselage s. as scrap to the H and E Distributing Company of Oklahoma City, OK. Undetermined use but probably stored until s. around 1951 to International Airports of Burbank, CA. International Airports reassembled the fuselage with other wings to create a complete aircraft and r. of N226 reissued. S. around 1961 to the Pittsburgh Plate Glass Company of Pittsburgh, PA. S. in Oct 1967 to Ohio University of Athens, OH for use in their Avionics Program. S. in 1972 to W.H. Planigan of Covington, GA. S. in Sep 1977 to Air Kaman, details unknown. S. in Jun 1979 to Mr. F. Reed of Huntington, WV. S. the same month to Doan Helicopters of Daytona Beach, FL. Sale subsequently reported to the FAA but details not known. Reported impounded in Apr 1981 at Grand Truk. Fate unknown.

9005 M. as C-47-DL s/n ***42-5698*** at Douglas-Long Beach and d. to the USAAF on 29 Jan 1943. Served domestically through World War II, primarily at Pope Field, SC and Wright Field, OH. Deemed excess to USAAF needs, released to the RFC for disposal on 08 Nov 1945, and stored at Walnut Ridge, AR. Transferred to the CAA and issued the civil r. of ***NC181***, probably in early 1946. Assigned to the CAA's Experimental Station at Indianapolis, IN and used as a test-bed for a variety of equipment installations. By 1960 in storage at the Aircraft Service Base in Oklahoma City. Scheduled for modifications to the standard FAA Type II configuration, presumably for use in flight inspection. R. changed to ***N71*** in Oct 1962 and in partially disassembled storage as of Jan 1963. Deemed excess to FAA needs and released for disposal in May 1964. R. canceled as of May 1964. S. via auction to Chris Stoltzfus of Coatsville, PA on 27 Aug 1964 for $1686.00. Fuselage removed from ASB storage by the new owner as of Sep 1964, with the remaining parts presumably removed afterwards. No further record of this aircraft's utilization is noted. Presumably scrapped for parts.

9486 M. as C-47A-30-DL s/n ***42-23624*** at the Douglas-Long Beach plant but transferred to the USN as R4D-5 BuNo ***12429*** and d. on 05 May 1943. Service with NATS squadrons including VR-3 and VR-11. Modified to an R4D-5Z configuration in 1948, indicative of VIP transport. Assigned to NAS Anacostia, DC for administrative transports, with several aircraft overhauls performed at NAS Jacksonville, Florida until Feb 1955 when deemed excess to USN needs and placed into storage at NAF Litchfield Park on 12 Sep 1954. Loaned to the CAA for facility flight inspection and issued the ferry r. of ***N7632C*** on 21 Mar 1958 and ferried to Oklahoma City. Rr. as ***N58*** in 1958 and subsequently modified to the standard FAA Type II DC-3 configuration. Re-designated as a VC-47H on 31 Aug 1962 but remaining on loan to the FAA. Ownership transferred from the USN to the FAA on 01 Aug 1966. Rr. as ***N78*** on 22 Jun 1973 and deemed surplus to FAA needs in Dec 1975. Rr. as ***N78125*** and transferred to the GSA for disposal on 06 Jan. On 15 Apr 1975 s. by the GSA to the Northern Peninsula Fisheries of Seattle, WA. It remains r. but as of 1994 stored without engines at the Majestic Aviation ramp at Salt Lake City International Airport, UT.

9526 M. as C-47A-30-DL s/n ***42-23664*** at the Douglas-Long Beach plant and d. to the USAAF on 14 May 1943. Service in Europe with the 9th AF during World War II. Declared surplus and transferred to the WAA for disposal on 01 May 1946. R. to the WAA as ***NC842*** on 13 Jun 1946. (To clarify a note of confusion, the WAA intitially offered up C-47A 43-15736, msn 20202, for the r. of NC842. However, mechanical difficulties apparently precluded the WAA's use of the aircraft and, in a 12 Jun 1946 request, the WAA requested that msn 9526 be assigned as NC842 and that the r. for msn 20202 be canceled.) The CAA obtained msn 9526 on 30 Apr 1947. Rr. as ***NC342*** 22 May 1947. R. was again changed to N21 on 16 May 1951. Assigned specifically to flight inspection training in Aug 1951. Modified to the standard FAA Type II DC-3 configuration in 1959 and subsequently assigned to facility flight inspection, primarily with the Eastern Region of the FAA. R. changed to ***N14*** on 09 Mar 1959 and again to ***N24*** on 02 Apr 1973. Surplus to FAA requirements in Aug 1976 and Rr. as ***N24AH*** prior to transfer to the GSA on 23 Oct 1976 for disposal with 29,426 hours of flight time. Transferred by the GSA to the USDA on 27 Oct 1976 for use in the US-Mexico Screw Worm Eradication Project. Rr. as ***N238GB*** on 17 Jan 1977. Excess to USDA needs and transferred to the USAF Museum Program via the GSA on 26 May 1982. Transferred via trade on 01 Dec 1983 to Bruce Orriss of Inglewood, CA for another C-47 and an AT-6. S. two days later to William Nelson, DBA Rio Leasing, of Loredo, TX. S. on 21 Dec 1983 to Falconaire, Inc, of Wheatley, AR. Aircraft remains r. and is believed active.

9940 M. as C-47A-40-DL s/n ***42-24078*** at the Douglas-Long Beach plant but d. to the USN as R4D-5 BuNo ***39062*** on 24 Jul 1943. Apparently assigned to Marine Air Wings through 1945, with subsequent post-war service with the Pacific Fleet from NAS San Diego. Placed in storage at NAF Litchfield Par, AZ at an unknown date. Transferred by loan to the CAA on 07 Jan 1959 and assigned the civil ferry r. of ***N9465Z***. Probably ferried to Oklahoma City for use as a parts source and subsuquently scrapped. No further record.

10096 M. as C-47A-55-DL s/n ***42-24234*** at Douglas-Long Beach but transferred to the USN as R4D-5 BuNo ***39076*** and d. on 21 Aug 1943. Assigned to the USMC and based at NAS Corpus Christi beginning in May 1944. Modified to the R4D-5R configuration and given post-war assignments at NAS Quonset Pt., RI and NAS Anacostia, DC with the USMC Aviation Division. Deemed excess to USN needs and placed in storage at NAF Litchfield Park in Aug 1954. Loaned to Southwest Airways as of 03 Dec 1956 and operated with the civil r. of ***N6678C***. Returned to Navy jurisdiction and stored at NAF Litchfield Park as of 1958. Loaned to the CAA for flight inspection and issued the initial ferry r. of ***N9053Z*** on 06 Nov 1959. Rr. as ***N61*** in Jul 1961 and subsequently modified to the standard FAA Type II DC-3 configuration. Re-designated by the USN as a TC-47H on 30 Nov 1962 but remaining on loan to the FAA. Primary use for FAA facility flight inspection with the FAA's Eastern region. Excess to FAA needs and placed into storage on 18 Apr 1965. Details not known, but probably released by the FAA back to the Navy, which authorized GSA to dispose of the aircraft. It was s. in May 1966 to Sria de Communicaciones y Teptes of Mexico City. Its U.S. civil r. was canceled and the Mexican r. of ***XC-DAP*** was issued. Mexican service is not known, but XC-DAP reported derelict in Mexico City as of Jan 1979. No further record.

10243 M. as C-47A-50-DL s/n ***42-24381*** at Douglas-Long Beach and d. on 29 Oct 1943. Reported on duty with the Eighth Air Force in England as of 20 Feb 1944. Reported back in the U.S. as of 14 Sep 1945. Deemed excess to military needs and released to the WAA for disposal on 02 Jan 1946. Leased by the WAA to Pegasus Airfreight, Inc. of Philadelphia, PA on 05 Feb 1946 and civil r. of ***NC34988*** assigned. Used to carry U.S. Justice Department deportees on a flight through Central and South America in Oct 1946. As of 03 Jun 1947 L. to Mutual Aviation Company of Buffalo, NY. As of 16 Feb 1948 leased to Continental Charters of Miami, FL. Returned to the jurisdiction of the USAAF in Jul 1948 and civil r. canceled as of 09 Jan 1949. Transferred from the USAF to the CAA on 22 Dec 1948 and ferried from the Middleton Air Depot, PA to Washington National Airport on 28 Dec 1948. New civil r. of ***N28*** issued on 31 Dec 1948. Assigned to the CAA's aircraft control service and based in Washington, D.C. On 10 Oct 1950 assigned to the Aircraft Standardization Project to be modified for flight inspection. Placed in storage on 16 Mar 1954 and r. canceled on 15 Jul 1954. R. of N28 reinstated on 28 Sep 1956 and aircraft dispatched to Frankfurt, Germany for assignment to international flight inspection operations. Returned to Oklahoma City in 1960 for rework; however, to ensure continuity of flight operations in Europe, the aircraft replacing N28 in Frankfurt was Rr. as N28. C/n 10243 was Rr. as ***N25*** on 02 Jun 1960. Modified to the standard FAA Type II configuration in Jan 1961. Assigned to domestic flight inspection through 1971. Crashed on take-off at Lubbock, Texas on 11 Mar 1971. Remains salvaged and disposed on site as of 17 Mar 1971. R. canceled on 23 Mar 1971.

11703 M. as C-53D-DO s/n ***42-68776*** at Douglas-Santa Monica and d. for service to the USAAF on 08 May 1943. Wartime service in domestic U.S. Excess to military needs and transferred to the RFC on 19 Dec 1944. Civil r. of ***NC50592*** assigned in the name of the DPC on 13 Jan 1945 and leased to American Airlines on 01 Feb 1945. R. changed to ***NC18663*** on 12 Feb 1945. Returned by American Airlines to the WAA in 1947 and subsequently transferred to the CAA on 13 May 1947. R. changed to ***NC63*** on 23 May 1947. Operated by CAA Region Six for several months before CAA survey for cannibalization on 01 Dec 1947. Subsequently scrapped for parts and r. canceled on 04 Mar 1948.

11808 M. as C-47A-DK s/n ***42-102796*** at Douglas-Oklahoma City on a USAAF contract but d. to the USN as R4D-5 BuNo ***17094*** on 02 Jun 1943. served primarily as a USMC transport through the war years, with assignment to VMR-352 in Aug 1943, MAW-9 in Mar 1944, NAS Corpus Christi in Dec 1944, and post-war service at NAS Quonset Point, RI and NAS Coco Solo. Assigned to VX-4 in Jan 1947 at Chincoteague, VA through Aug 1948. Re-designated as an R4D-5R indicating use in the transport role. As of Jan 1950 in overhaul at MCAS Cherry Point, NC. Placed into a transportation pool at NAS Memphis, TN in Feb 1950. Stored at NAF Litchfield Park in Aug 1952, and then removed and overhauled at NAS Jacksonville in Feb 1954. Assigned for transport at NAS Anacostia in Aug 1956 and then removed from service and placed into storage at NAF Litchfield Park in Mar 1956. Transferred by loan to the CAA on 24 Oct 1957 and assigned the ferry r. of ***N7232C***. Flown to Oklahoma City and Rr. as ***N39*** on 22 Nov 1957. Subsequently modified to the FAA Type II configuration and assigned to domestic flight inspection duty, primarily with the FAA's Southwest and Eastern Regions. Redesignated by the USN as a TC-47H in 1962. Ownership transferred from the USN to the FAA on 01 Aug 1966. Aircraft's last FAA assignment with the Seattle, WA Flight Inspection District Office. Deemed excess to FAA needs in Sep 1976 with total flight time at 21,874 hours. Rr. as ***N39AH*** and released to the GSA for disposal on 23 Sep 1976. Obtained by the DOA for use as a sprayer in the USDA U.S.-Mexico Screw Worm Eradication Program being carried out in Mexico. Rr. as ***N239GB*** on 17 May 1977. Excess to USDA needs and transferred by the GSA to Southern Illinois University, Carbondale, IL, DBA Air Institute and Service, on 09 Jan 1980 for training and university transport. S. on 02 Jun 1982 to Tembleson Piper of St. Louis, Inc., East Alton, IL. S. on 04 Feb 1983 to Eagle Aircraft of Hammond, Inc., Hammond, IL. S. to Twilight Zone, Inc., of Philipsburg, St. Maarten, in the Netherlands Antilles on 15 Apr 1983. S. on 10 Aug 1983 to Daniel Sneed of Apoka, FL. Aircraft seized in Columbia on 29 Oct 1983. S. by judicial action in Columbia to Aerlineas del Esta, LTD. on 22 Oct 1985 and r. as ***HK-3220***. Noted as active in Apr 1990 at Villavicencio, Columbia and operated by Transoriente.

11859 M. as C-47A-1-DK s/n ***42-92096*** by Douglas-Oklahoma City and d. to the USAAF on 02 Aug 1943. Obtained as surplus by the CAA on 24 Dec 1945 and r. as ***NC9***. Assigned to Region 1, which encompassed the northeast for U.S. airways flight inspection. Rr. as ***N18*** on 22 Jan 1951. Converted to the standard Type II DC-3 configuration in 1960. Primarily assigned to Honolulu, HI for airways inspection through the 1960s. Rr. as ***N17*** on 02 Aug 1973 and deemed excess to FAA needs in Dec 1975. Rr. as ***N17715*** and released to the GSA for disposal on 12 Jan 1976. Transferred to the DOA, USDA U.S.-Mexico Screw Worm Eradication Program for use as a sprayer on 20 Aug 1976 and Rr. as ***N221GB***. Transferred to the USFS on 27 Sep 1979. Excess to USFS needs and turned back to the GSA. Subsequently obtained by the USAF Museum Program and traded on 15 Sep 1982 to Bruce Orriss of Inglewood, CA for another C-47 and various aircraft parts. S. on 11 May 1983 to Westair International, Monument, CO. S. again, on 12 Jun 1983, to Roto Service Enterprises, Shreveport, LA, which neither filed ownership documents nor r. the aircraft with the FAA. Fate unknown but probably exported overseas. No further record.

11928 M. under contract as C-47A-1-DK s/n ***42-108808*** at Douglas-Oklahoma City but d. to the USN as R4D-5 BuNo ***17106*** on 30 Sep 1943. In Aug 1944 assigned to the USMC and active in Pacific units through the end of World War II. Post-war assignments included NAS Quonset Pt., RI, NAS Corpus Christi, TX, and MCAS Cherry Pt., NC., In 1948 it was refitted as an R4D-6S configuration and later was designated as an R4D-5Q. As of May 1950 assigned to the NATTC at NAS Memphis, TN. Overhauled at NAS Jacksonville, FL in Jun 1950 and subseuqently assigned to HEDRON AFRFLANT at MCAS Cherry Point in Jan 1951. Stored at NAF Litchfield after Jul 1953, but then removed from storage and overhauled at NAS Jacksonville, FL in Mar 1954. Assigned to the FAETUPAC at NAS San Diego, CA in Jun 1954. Detached to NAS Alameda, CA in Aug 1954. Placed into storage at NAF Litchfield Park in Sep 1956. Loaned to the CAA in 1958 and assigned the ferry r. of ***N9881C*** on 10 Oct 1958 for its flight to Oklahoma City. Rr. as ***N51*** on 08 Apr 1959 and subsequently modified to the standard FAA Type II configuration for flight inspection. Redesignated by the USN as an EC-47H in 1962. Ownership was transferred to the FAA on 01 Aug 1966. Primary service with the Alaskan Region with later service in various regions. Rr. as ***N71*** on 15 Dec 1973. Surplus to FAA needs and placed in storage on 09 Jul 1975. Rr. as N916 on 11 Dec 1975. Released on 12 Jan 1976 to the GSA for disposal. Transferred to the USDA for use as a pesticide sprayer in the

U.S.-Mexico Screw Worm Eradication Project. R. of ***N2008J*** assigned on 10 Mar 1976 but ntu. R. of ***N223GB*** assigned on 02 Apr 1976. Stored at Douglas-Bisbee Field, AZ as of 1977 and again released to the GSA for disposal. Transferred to the USAF Museum Program in Aug 1971 and sent to Dyess AFB, TX for display with the base collection. It is painted and displayed in USAAF camouflage with its original USAAF serial, 42-108808.

12261 M. as C-47A-5-DK s/n ***42-9245***8 at Douglas-Oklahoma City on a USAAF contract but turned over to the USN and d. as R4D-5 BuNo ***17126*** on 13 Jan 1944. Assigned to various USMC units through the remainder of the year: VMR-352 in Aug 1944; MAW-9 in Dec 1944; MAG-35 in Jun 1945. Further assignment to USN stations through the post-war period, including NAS Corpus Christi, TX in late 1945 and MCAS Cherry Point, NC in 1948. As of Jan 1950 assigned to VR-22 at NAS Norfolk. Reassigned in Jan 1950 to VR-1 at NAS Patuxent River, MD. Reassigned to NAS Corpus Christi, TX and then VR-5 at NAS San Diego, CA in Jul 1950. Overhauled at NAS Jacksonville, FL and redesignated as an R4D-5Q for electronics trainings. Assigned in Feb 1952 to FAETULANT at NAS Norfolk. Excess to USN needs and placed into storage at Litchfield Park, AZ in Aug 1954. Loaned to the CAA in 1958 and issued the civil r. of ***N3458G*** on 03 Jun 1959 for its ferry flight to Oklahoma City, OK. Rr. as ***N41*** on 08 Sep 1959 and subsequently modified to the standard FAA Type II configuration for flight inspection. Redesignated bythe USN as an EC-47H in 1962. Ownership transferred from the USN to the FAA on 01 Aug 1966. Rr. as ***N23*** on 04 Jan 1974 and placed in storage at Oklahoma City shortly afterwards. Deemed excess to FAA needs in Dec 1974. R. of ***N87788*** assigned but ntu. Released to the GSA on 31 Dec 1974 for disposal. Transferred to the USDA for use as a pesticide sprayer in the U.S.-Mexico Screw Worm Eradication Program and Rr. as ***N2001J***. Rr. as ***N224GB*** on 10 May 1976. Excess to USDA needs and turned over to the GSA for disposal in 1980. Transferred by the GSA to Lee County Mosquito Control District, For Meyers, FL on 24 Oct 1980 for continued use as a sprayer. Believed still active.

12733 M. as C-47A-15-DK s/n ***42-92883*** at Douglas-Oklahoma City on a USAAF contract but d. to the USN as R4D-5 BuNo ***17176*** on 17 Mar 1944. Assigned to various domestic Navy transport units including VR-3 and VR-1 from NAS Quonset Pt., RI. Assigned to Patuxent River, MD after 1947. Subsequently stored at NAF Litchfield Park AZ. Transferred by loan to the CAA on 07 Jan 1959 and issued the civil r. of ***N9464Z***. Subsequent service unknown but probably ferried to Oklahoma City for use as a parts source and scrapped. No further record.

13004 M. as C-47A-15-DK s/n ***42-92127*** at Douglas-Oklahoma City on a USAAF contract, but d. to the USN as R4D-5 BuNo ***17193*** on 12 Apr 1944. Service with various NATS units through the war: VR-1 from Aug 1944; VR-9 from 27 Aug 1945. Utilized in Naval Electronics Test Project at Charleston, SC beginning in Mar 1946 and continued at NAS Patuxent River, MD in Mar 1948. Overhauled at NAS Jacksonville, FL in Jan 1950, and returned to the Naval Air Test Center at NAS Patuxent River, MD in Jun 1952. Excess to USN needs and stored at NAF Litchfield Park in Aug 1954. Loaned to the CAA in 1958 and issued the r. of ***N6517C*** on 19 Jan 1959 for a ferry flight to Oklahoma City, OK. Rr. as ***N55*** on 03 Mar 1959 and subsequently modified to the standard FAA Type II configuration. Assigned to facility flight inspection, primarily with the FAA's Central and Eastern Regions. Redesignated by the USN as a C-47H in 1962. Ownership transferred from the USN to the FAA on 01 Aug 1966. Rr. as ***N67*** on 03 Aug 1973. Deemed excess to FAA needs and placed in storage on 14 Jun 1977. Transferred by the GSA to the USDA for use as a sprayer in their U.S.-Mexico Screw Worm Eradication Project. Rr. as ***N226GB*** on 31 May 1978. Deemed excess to USDA requirements and released back to the GSA in 1982. Transferred to the USAF Museum Program on 26 May 1982 and r. subsequently canceled. Aircraft assigned for display to the South Dakota Air and Space Museum, Ellsworth AFB, SD where it remains on static display in the USAAF markings of C-47A s/n 43-93149.

13447 M. as C-47A-25-DK s/n ***42-93526*** at Douglas-Oklahoma City and d. for USAAF service in Jun 1944. Assigned as of Jul 1947 to the USAAF. Transferred to the FAA circa 1963 and issued civil r. of ***N400***. Transferred, probably via U.S. A.I.D. to Kenya in Jan 1966. R. as ***5Y-ADI*** in Kenya service. Reportedly assigned to the Kenya Police Air Wing. Reported crashed on 24 Dec 1968 at Wilson Airport, Nairobi.

13850 M. as C-47A-DL s/n ***43-30699*** at Douglas-Long Beach and d. to the USAAF on 28 Sep 1943. Surplus to USAAF needs and released to the RFC for disposal. Obtained by the CAA on 31 Aug 1946. Probably placed in storage at Oklahoma City for a parts source or spare aircraft. Surveyed in 1950. An internal CAA request to withdraw survey paper dated 20 Sep 1950 also requested that the r. of ***N500*** be assigned. N500 assigned on 04 Oct 1950. Utilized by the CAA and, later, FAA, primarily for training of flight crews. Assigned as of 1961 to the FAA's Technical Center at Atlantic City, NJ. Deemed excess to FAA needs on 12 Mar 1965 and r. changed to ***N5009*** on that date. On 16 Jul 1965 transferred via the GSA to the State of Washington's Surplus Property Section for assignment to the Bend Community College, Moses Lake, WA for use in an aviation program. Transferred via the U.S. Dept. of HEW to the School of the Ozarks, Pt. Lookout, MO on 13 Sep 1976. School of the Ozarks gained title on 26 Apr 1976. S. by the school five days earlier (on 21 Apr 1976) to Two Jacks, Inc. of Olive Branch, MS. S. on 21 Sep 1976 to Basler Flight Service of Oshkosh, WI. S. on 15 Apr 1977 to Alpha Airlines of Deer Park, NY. S. back to Basler Flight Service of Oshkosh, WI on 22 Mar 1983. Exported to the Malawi Army Air Force at the Zomba Air Base, Zomba, Malawi (Africa) on 31 Oct 1990. The record indicates that this aircraft was one of two C-47s (the other was msn 27005 N46938) purchased by the U.S. Government and provided to the Malawi Army Air Force. FAA r. canceled on 20 Dec 1990. No further record.

19320 M. as C-47A-75-DL s/n ***42-100857*** at Douglas-Long Beach and d. for USAAF service on 24 Dec 1943. Assigned for duty with the 8th Air Force in England beginning in Mar 1944 and believed used in D-Day operations on 06 Jun 1944. Deemed excess to USAAF requirements and released to the RFC for disposal in 1945. Transferred from the WAA to CAA on 14 Sep 1948 and issued the initial civil r. of ***NC70***. Placed in storage until 1949 when placed in service as a flight inspection training aircraft for use at Oklahoma City. Used as the prototype for the CAA's standard flight inspection aircraft and modified as such in 1951. Rr. as ***N23*** on 04 May 1951 and joined the flight inspection fleet at Atlanta, Georgia. Continued use in flight inspection but modified again to the standard Type II configuration in 1960. Assigned primarily with the FAA's Western and Eastern regions through the 1960s. Placed in storage in Aug 1973 but removed, overhauled, and Rr. as ***N41*** on 07 Dec 1973. Assigned to the Alaskan Region in Nov 1974. Deemed excess to FAA needs in 1978 and released to the GSA on 05 Jun 1978 with 21,175 flight hours recorded. R. canceled on 12 Jun 1978. ***N2273K*** assigned in Jun 1978 but ntu. Obtained by the USAF Museum Program and placed on display at the Alaskan ANG Museum at Kulis ANG Base, Anchorage, AK. Aircraft is still carried on the civil register as N2273K.

19754 M. as C-47A-80-DL s/n ***43-15288*** at Douglas-Long Beach and d. to the USAAF in Mar 1944. Stored at Davis-Monthan AFB through 1962. Deemed surplus to military needs and earmarked for the Government of Somali by AID in 1962 (along with two other surplus USAF C-47s, msn 20016 and msn 20424). The FAA agreed to perform the necessary modifications and ferry all three aircraft to Somali and they were subsequently transferred to the FAA by the USAF. C/n 19754 assigned the civil r. of ***N161*** on 03 Dec 1962. Subsequent modifications performed by the FAA at Oklahoma City. Aircraft in temporary storage, along with the other two aircraft, as of 21 Nov 1963. D. by the FAA to Somali on 06 Mar 1964 and U.S. r. canceled. Somali r. of ***60S-AAA*** assigned on 22 May 1964. Aircraft possibly utilized by national airline, though details have not been determined. Rr. as ***60-SAA*** in Oct 1970. Somali r. canceled on 09 Jul 1980. Application on 29 Aug 1980 to FAA for r. of ***N920*** on behalf of International Aviation Development Corporation of Danville, CA. Bill of sale dated 29 Sep 1980 for sale from the Somalia government to ATC Inc., of Reno, NV. R. of ***N925*** issued to ATC Leased to the Malta International Aviation Company (MIACO) at Safi, Malta S. in Jun 1982 to Pyramid Airlines and Rr. with the Egyptian r. of ***SU-BFY***. Performed service in Egypt transporting oil field workers. Withdrawn from service in 1985. Reported service in Ireland for Apple Airways while r. as ***EI-BSJ***. S. in Feb 1987 to the Dutch Dakota Association of Amsterdam, the Netherlands. At time of sale airframe had logged 25,887 hours of flight time. Rr. with the Dutch r. of ***PH-DDZ***. The Dutch Dakota Association is committed to the preservation of historic aircraft, particularly the DC-3. PH-DDZ was the second DC-3 to be purchased by the group, the first being msn 19109 (PH-DDA). PH-DDZ is undergoing a restoration program in Amsterdam and is expected to be airworthy again in 1994.

20016 M. as C-47A-85-DL s/n ***43-15550*** at Douglas-Long Beach and d. to the USAAF in Apr 1944. Deemed surplus to military needs and earmarked for the Government of Somali by AID in 1962 (along with two other surplus USAF C-47s, msn 19754 and msn 20424). The FAA agreed to perform the necessary modifications and ferry all three aircraft to Somali and they were subsequently transferred to the FAA by the USAF. C/n 20016 assigned the civil r. of ***N162*** on 04 Dec 1962. Subsequent modifications performed by the FAA at Oklahoma City. Aircraft in temporary storage, along with the other two aircraft, as of 21 Nov 1963. D. by the FAA to Somali in early Mar 1964 and U.S. r. canceled. Somali r. of ***60S-AAB*** assigned in May 1964. Aircraft possibly utilized by national airline, though details have not been determined. Rr. as ***60-SAB*** in Oct 1970. Somali r. canceled on 09 Jul 1980. Application on 29 Aug 1980 to FAA for r. of N925 on behalf of Internationl Aviation Development Corporation of Danville, CA. Bill of sale dated 29 Sep 1980 for sale from the Somalia government to ATC Inc, of Reno, NV. R. of ***N925*** issued to ATC. Leased to the Malta International Aviation Company (MIACO) at Safi, Malta. S. on 01 Apr 1986 to Global Equipment Leasing of Reno, NV. Request for change to a special r. number of ***N512GL*** made on 28 Jan 1987 but never assigned and taken up. S. to Basler/Basler of Oshkosh, WI 23 Feb 1990. Ownership transferred to Basler Airframes, Inc. of Oshkosh on 27 Apr 1990. Current status unknown.

20033 M. as C-47A-85-DL s/n ***43-15467*** at Douglas-Long Beach and d. for service on 11 Apr 1944. Reported service with the Air Transport Command beginning in Apr 1944 and later operated by Pan American crews for ATC. Excess to USAAF needs in 1945 and released to the RFC for disposal. Transferred to the CAA on 12 Dec 1945 and r. as ***NC202***. Rr. as ***N22*** in 1953 and assigned to facility flight inspection. Upgraded to the standard FAA Type II DC-3 configuration in 1960. Service through the 1960s in flight inspection assigned to various FAA regions, particularly the Central Region. Withdrawn from service on 30 Apr 1975 and placed in storage at Oklahoma City. Deemed excess to FAA needs and transferred to the GSA on 07 May 1975. Stripping of usable parts from the airframe by the FAA reported on 13 May 1975 and subsequently s. for scrap.

20400 M. as C-47A-90-DL s/n ***43-15934*** at Douglas-Long Beach and d. for service to the USAAF on 29 May 1944. Reported assigned to Wright Field in Jun 1944. Further service unknown. Surplus to USAAF needs and released to the RFC. Transferred to the CAA on 12 Jan 1947. R. of ***NC200*** assigned on 04 Nov 1947, although records indicate it was unoffically carrying that r. as early as 07 Jan 1947. CAA utilization primarily for training and executive transport and was based both at Oklahoma City, OK and, later, at the FAA Techincal Center at Atlantic City, NJ. Upraded R-1830-94 engines installed in 1959. Crashed and destroyed on 10 May 1963 at Mustang, Oklahoma

20403 M. as C-47A-90-DL s/n ***43-15937*** at Douglas-Long Beach and d. for USAAF service on 29 May 1944. Assigned to the 12th Air Force in Italy on 19 Jul 1944. Returned to the U.S. in Jun 1945 and released to the RFC for disposal. Transferred to the CAA in Sep 1947 and assigned the civil r. of ***NC109*** for use in airways flight inspection with the CAA's Region 7 in Seattle, WA. Assigned to the CAA's Aeronautical Center at Oklahoma City, OK on 16 May 1951 for use in standardization training. Rr. as ***N19*** on 06 Jul 1951. Assigned to Region 8 in Anchorage, AK on 02 Nov 1951 and utilized for logistical support and transport. Deemed excess to FAA needs in Jun 1964 and Rr. as ***N195W*** on 19 Jun 1964. Transferred to the North Carolina Department of Conservation and Development, Raleigh, NC on 13 Oct 1964. Transferred to the Wayne Community College, Goldsboro, NC for use as a non-flying instructional airframe on 10 Mar 1977 and de-registered on 27 Apr 1977. S. on 07 Dec 1982 to Green Ag Aero of Tallula, GA. Carried on the civil register, but possibly used as a source of spare parts. Fate unknown.

20419 M. as C-47A-90-DL s/n ***43-15953*** at Douglas-Long Beach and d. for service to the USAAF on 30 May 1944. Reported assignment to the Air Transport Command on 02 Jun 1944. Balance of wartime service unknown. Surplus to military needs and released to the RFC for disposal in 1945. Obtained by the CAA, possibly as early as Oct 1945. Placed in storage until 1949 when withdrawn, overhauled, and assigned to the CAA's Experimental Center at Indianapolis. Assigned the civil r. of ***NC183*** on 23 Jun 1949. Utilized in a number of test programs through 1958, including experimental wing-tip light pods installed for a test series in 1955. In May 1958 R-1830-94 engines were installed, and the aircraft was Rr. as ***N52***, followed by assignment to a facility flight inspection role. In Feb 1960 the airframe was upgraded to the FAA standard Type II configuration. Assignment to the FAA's Eastern and Southern Regions for flight inspection followed. The aircraft crashed on 09 Nov 1965 near Pittsburgh, PA. By Jul 1966 the remains of the aircraft had been salvaged by the FAA and the remains s. as scrap.

20424 M. as C-47A-90-DL s/n ***43-25958*** at Douglas-Long Beach and d. to the USAAF in May 1944. Deemed surplus to military needs and earmarked for the Government of Somali by AID in 1962 (along with two other surplus USAF C-47s, msn 19754 and msn 20016). The FAA agreed to perform the necessary modifications and ferry all three aircraft to Somali and they were subsequently transferred to the FAA by the USAF. C/n 20424 assigned the civil r. of ***N160*** on 03 Dec 1962. Subsequent modifications performed by the FAA at Oklahoma City. Aircraft in temporary storage, along with the other two aircraft, as of 21 Nov 1963. D. by the FAA to Somali on 06 Mar 1964 and U.S. r. canceled. Somali r. of ***60S-AAC*** assigned on 22 May 1964. Aircraft possibly utilized by national airline, though details have not been determined. Rr. as ***60-SAC*** in 1970. Crashed and destroyed on 16 Aug 1975 at Bosaso, (Somali?).

20426 M. as C-47A-90-DL s/n ***43-15960*** at Douglas-Long Beach and d. to the USAAF on 30 May 1944. Reported assigned to the Air Transport Command in North Atlantic area as of 12 Jun 1944. Deemed excess to USAAF needs and released to the RFC for disposal. The RFC had the civil r. of ***NC818*** assigned on 26 Dec 1945 and probably supplied the aircraft on a lease basis to a civil operator. R. transferred to the War Assets Administration in Sep 1946. Transferred to the CAA on 19 Mar 1948 and r. changed to NC118. R. changed again to ***NC3*** on 01 Dec 1948. Assigned to Washington National Airport for CAA administrative transport. R. changed to NC2 on 30 Jan 1951. R. changed back to ***NC3*** on 13 Jun 1951. Engines upgraded to R-1830-94s in Aug 1959. R. changed to ***N7*** on 13 May 1963. Continued in administrative transport until 04 Jan 1971 when crashed while on approach to La Guardia Airport, NY. Remains of aircraft s. to Brooklyn scrap dealer on 25 Jan 1971. R. canceled on 03 Feb 1971.

20443 M. as C-47A-90-DL s/n ***43-15997*** at Douglas-Long Beach and d. to the USAAF for service on 02 Jun3 1944. Reportedly served with Air Transport Command domestically through World War II. Deemed excess to USAAF needs in 1946 and released to the WAA on 04 Jun 1946. Assigned r. ***NC812*** in the name of the WAA on 08 Jul 1946. Transferred to the CAA on 23 Mar 1948 and Rr. as ***NC118***. Probably utilized for regional flight inspection. Rr. as ***N24*** on 11 Sep 1951. R. changed again to ***N14*** on 15 Apr 1952. R. changed to ***N21*** on 13 Mar 1959. Upgraded to the standard FAA Type II configuration in Jun 1959. Continued utilization for facility flight inspection, primarily with the FAA's Eastern Region, through 1975. Removed from service and released to the GSA for disposal on 06 Jan 1976. Transferred to the USDA Screw Worm Eradication Program on 23 Jan 1976. R. changed to ***N24010*** on 04 Mar 1976. R. changed to ***N230GB*** on 22 Jun 1976. Deemed excess to USDA needs in 1978. Transferred by the GSA to the USAF Museum Program on 05 Dec 1980. Flown to Castle AFB, CA in 1983 and displayed with its USAAF serial number and standard USAAF camouflage with "D-Day" markings.

20494 M. as C-47A-90-DL s/n ***43-16028*** at Douglas-Long Beach and d. for service to the USAAF on 10 Jun 1944. Reportedly assigned to Europe with the 9th Air Force and back in the U.S. in Jul 1945. Deemed excess to USAAF needs and released to the RFC for disposal. Transferred to the CAA and r. as ***NC100*** on 04 Aug 1947. A notation made in a 08 Jun 1947 memo that "this aircraft was reassembled from spare parts covered by survey CAA 3772 dated 5/9/47". Initially assigned to the CAA Standardization Facility in Oklahoma City, OK and believed used for training for its entire utilization with the CAA/FAA. Placed into storage on 09 Jul 1970. Deemed excess to FAA requirements on 06 Aug 1970 and released to the GSA for disposal. R. changed to ***N8785*** on 11 Aug 1970. Transferred to the USDA's Forest Service on 22 Sep and Rr. as ***N100Z*** on 04 Dec 1970. Modified by Basler Airframes of Oshkosh, WI with Garrett turboprop engines, lengthened fuselage, and other changes. Rr. as ***N142Z*** on 15 Mar 1991. Remains active and based at McCall, ID.

20560 M. as C-47A-90-DL s/n ***43-16094*** by Douglas-Long Beach and d. for service to the USAAF on 20 Jun 1944. Deemed excess to USAAF needs and released to the RFC for disposal. Transferred to the CAA and assigned the civil r. of ***NX182*** on 29 Nov 1945. Assigned by the CAA to their Experimental Center at Indianapolis, IN. Beginning in 1950 assigned to cargo and logistics support. Engines upgraded to R-1830-94s in 1960. R. changed to ***N100*** on 12 Jan 1973. R. changed to ***N76*** on 30 Jan 1975. Excess to FAA needs and released to the GSA for disposal in 1977. R. changed to ***N76AB*** on 11 Nov 1977. Transferred by the GSA to the U.S. Forest Service at Ogden, UT on 11 Apr 1978. Rr. as ***N102Z*** on 19 Apr 1978. As of 20 Jun 1980, parts stripped by the USFS and remains given to the fire department at Boise, ID for fire practice.

25341 M. as C-47A-30-DK s/n ***43-48080*** at Douglas-Oklahoma City and d. for service on 13 Jul 1944. Assigned to ATC and served domestically through World War II. Deemed excess by the USAAF and released to the RFC for disposal. Transferred to the CAA with the initial civil r. of ***NC203*** assigned on 31 Oct 1947. Rr. as ***N15*** on 09 Nov 1951. Assigned to perform facility flight inspection. Modified to the standard FAA Type II configuration in 1959. Subsequent assignment in flight inspection with the FAA's Western Region. Rr. as ***N7*** on 02 Aug 1973. Withdrawn from service and placed into storage on 31 Oct 1975. Deemed excess to FAA needs and Rr. as ***N7AP*** on 07 Oct 1976. Released to the GSA for disposal. Transferred by the GSA to the Avionics and Engineering Center at Ohio University, Athens, OH for use in supporting FAA contracted avionics and developmental work. Remains active.

25627 M. as C-47B-1-DK s/n ***43-48366*** at Douglas-Oklahoma City on a USAAF contract but d. to the USN as R4D-6 BuNo ***17252*** on 15 Aug. Assigned to various USN units including: FAW-5 in Sep 1944; FAW-16 in Oct 1944; NAF Rio de Janeiro in Aug 1945, Quonset Point, RI in Dec 1946; Patuxent River, MD in Nov 1947. Assigned to NAS Jacksonville, FL in Mar 1950 for overhaul. Assigned to the 11th Naval District at NAS San Diego in May 1950, and then back to overhaul and modifications to an R4D-6Q configuration in Sep 1952. Assigned to FAETULANT at NAS Norfolk, VA in Mar 1953, and then returned to NAS Jacksonville, FL in Jul 1955 for overhaul. Assigned to FAETUPAC at NAS Whidby Island, WA in Nov 1955. Excess to USN needs and stored at NAF Litchfield Park after Feb 1958. Loaned to the CAA in 1959 and ferried from Litchfield Park to Oklahoma City under the civil r. of ***N5178V***. R. changed to ***N57*** on 15 Jun 1959. Modified to the FAA standard Type II configuration for flight inspection in Feb 1960. Subsequently assigned to FAA facility flight inspection primarily with the FAA's Western and Southwest Regions. Redesignated by the USN as a EC-47J in 1962. Later assignments to other FAA regions. Ownership transferred from the USN to the FAA on 01 Aug 1966. R. changed to ***N77*** on 31 May 1973. Withdrawn from service in 1975 and r. canceled on 22 Dec 1975. Released to the GSA for disposal on 12 Dec 1975 and transferred on 14 Jan 1976 to the Avionics and Engineering Center at Ohio University, Athens, OH for use as a parts source to support both NASA and FAA contracts. R. issued as ***N7712*** on 27 Jan 1976. Reported by Ohio University as scrapped on 14 Sep 1982 and r. canceled.

25775 M. as C-47B-1-DK s/n ***43-48514*** at Douglas-Oklahoma City on a USAAF contract but d. to the USN as R4D-6 BuNo ***17272*** on 02 Sep 1944. Assigned to various USN units including: CFAW-14, NAS San Diego, CA as of Sep 1944; MAG-33 as of Nov 1944; VMC-152 as of Jan 1945; Pearl Harbor as of Sep 1946; NAS Alameda, CA as of Mar 1947. Redesignated as an R4D-6E in Mar 1949. As of May 1950, assigned to the FAETULANT at NAS Norfolk, VA. After overhaul, assigned to the FAETUPAC at NAS San Diego, CA. Assigned to a transportation pool at NAS Memphis, TN in Jun 1955, and then deemed excess to USN needs and stored at NAF Litchfield Park after Oct 1958. Transferred to the CAA in Mar 1958 and ferried to Oklahoma City with the civil r. of ***N7633C***. Rr. as ***N44*** on 06 Jan 1959. Modified to the standard FAA Type II DC-3 configuration for flight inspection in Jan 1959. Primary assignment for facility flight check with the FAA's Western and Central Regions. Redesignated as an SC-47J by the USN in 1962. Excess to FAA needs and transferred via the Navy and the U.S. State Department's Agency for International Relief to the government of Argentina on 12 Mar 1965. U.S. r. canceled on 26 Mar 1965. Assigned Argentinean r. of ***LV-PDJ*** on 08 Apr 1965. Rr. as ***LQ-INL*** on 21 Jun

1965. Argentinean service unknown. S. to Guatemalan civil operator, Aero Express, on 12 Nov 1975 and Rr. as ***TG-BAC***. Reported crashed on 03 Nov 1980 at Yaxchibal, Flores Peten, Guatemala.

25824 M. as C-47B-5-DK a/n ***43-48635*** at Douglas-Oklahoma City on a USAAF contract but d. to the USN as R4D-6 BuNo ***17278*** on 28 Aug 1944. Reported domestic U.S. service included: CFAW-14, NAS San Diego, CA as of Sep 1944; VE-3 as of Dec 1944; Philippine Islands as of Aug 1945; NAS San Diego as of Feb 1946; and NAS Quonset Pt., RI as of Nov 1946. As of Mar 1950 assigned to the 5th Naval District at NAS Norfolk, VA, presumably for transportation. Overhauled an modified at NAS Jacksonville, FL in Nov 1951, afterwhich returned to NAS Norfolk in Jun 1952 and assigned to the FAETULANT as an R4D-6S. Overhauled again in Oct 1954 at NAS Jacksonville, FL and then assigned, in Feb 1955, to the transportation pool at NAS Memphis, TN. Deemed excess to USN needs and stored at NAF Litchfield Park, AZ after Feb 1958. Transferred to the CAA in Mar 1958 and flown to Oklahoma City with the civil r. of ***N7634C***. R. changed to ***N40*** in Feb 1959. Modified to the FAA standard Type II configuration for flight inspection. Early FAA service with the FAA's Eastern and Southwest Regions. Later service with various regions. Redesginated as an SC-47J by the USN in 1962. Ownership transferred from the Navy to the FAA on 01 Aug 1966. Excess to FAA needs in Dec 1975. Rr. as ***N40180*** and released to the GSA for disposal in Dec 1975. Transferred by the GSA to the U.S. Marine Corps Museum at Quantico, VA in Dec 1975. It remains displayed as a USMC R4D-6 with a camouflage paint scheme.

25951 M. as C-47B-5-DK s/n ***43-48690*** at Douglas-Oklahoma City on a USAAF contract but d. to the USN as R4D-6 BuNo ***17286*** on 12 Sep 1944. Served with the Naval Air Transport Service through the war, initally with VR-3 at NAS Olathe, KS beginning in Sep 1944. Assigned to NAS Quonset Pt., RI on 31 Jan 1947. Assigned to NAS Alameda, CA in Jun 1947. Assigned to NAS Anacostia, DC and re-designated as an R4D-6Z, indicating staff transport assignments beginning in Dec 1947. Overhauled at MCAS Cherry Pt., NC in Mar 1950, then returned to NAS Anacostia in Aug 1950. Overhauled in Jul 1952 at NAS Jacksonville, FL, then sent to VR-5 at NAS San Diego, CA in Nov 1952. Assigned to VR-22 at NAS Norfolk, VA in Mar 1953 and then returned to NAS Anacostia in Aug 1953. Deemed excess to USN requirements and stored at NAF Litchfield Park after Dec 1954. Transferred via loan to the CAA in Jul 1959 and flown to Oklahoma City with the ferry r. of ***N9445Z*** on 09 May 1960. R. changed to ***N62*** on 16 Aug 1960. Subsequently modified to the standard FAA Type II configuration for flight inspection. Primary assignment with the Alaska Region through the early 1960s, then rotated through the various FAA regions. Designation changed from R4D-6Z to VC-47J in USN records in 1962. Ownership transferred from the USN to the FAA on 01 Aug 1966. R. changed to ***N69*** on 26 Jun 1973. Deemed excess to requirements on 15 Jul 1981 and de-registered. Reactivated by the FAA in Anchorage, AK and again r. as ***N69*** on 02 Nov 1981. Transferred to Oklahoma City for use in a flight training program. Finally retired and de-registered on 24 Mar 1982, and subsequently released to the GSA for disposal. Transferred to the Naval Aviation Museum, Pensecola, FL. S. on 04 Sep 1985 to Airplane Sales International Corporation, Beverly Hills, CA and r. as ***N259DC*** on 11 Sep 1985. Ownership formally transferred on on 31 May 1988 to the Brazilian Aeronautical Commission operating on behalf of the Museu Aerospacial in Brazil.After undergoing extensive mechanical work in the spring of 1988 at Chino, CA, it was ferried in Aug 1988 to Campo dos Afonsos, located about 25 miles from Rio de Janeiro. Airframe was partially repainted for a role in Brazilian motion picture, with the bogus Brazilian Air Force serial of ***FAB 2079*** also applied for the filming. Much of the former FAA paint remained on the airframe, however. After the filming was completed, the DC-3 reportedly remained at Campos dos Afonsos on static display. However, the Brazilian Ministry of Aeronautics noted in correspondence with the FAA that the aircraft had been s. back to Airplane Sales International Corporation on 29 Mar 1991. Disposition of the aircraft is unknown but believed to remain with the Museum Aerospacial collection in Brazil.

(25953) M. as C-47B-5-DK s/n ***43-48692*** by Douglas-Oklahoma City on a USAAF contract but d. for service to the USN as R4D-6 BuNo ***17288*** on 12 Sep 1944. Though some accounts show this aircraft going to the CAA, transfer records between the USN and CAA in 1958 clearly indicate BuNo ***17289*** was transferred and a transcription error occurred which erroneously gave BuNo ***17289*** the msn of ***25953*** in aircraft paperwork. This error was carried forth in all subsequent aircraft documents. (See also msn 25954.)

25954 M. as C-47B-5-DK s/n ***43-48693*** by Douglas-Oklahoma City on a USAAF contract but d. for service to the USN as R4D-6 BuNo ***17289*** on 12 Sep 1944. (See also msn 25953.) Initial USN service with VR-3 at NAS Jacksonville, FL through Jun 1946. Later service with: COMNAV Europe in Dec 1946, VRU-4 and VR-24 in the United Kingdom in 1947 and 1948. Redesignated as an R4D-6Z, indicative of staff transport, in 1949. As of May 1950 assigned to NAS Anacostia. Overhauled at NAS Jacksonville, FL in Apr 1951, afterwhich returned to NAS Anacostia, DC in Nov 1951. Excess to USN needs and stored at NAF Litchfield Park after Aug 1954. Transferred to the CAA in Mar 1958 and ferried to Oklahoma City with the civil r. of ***N6516C***. R. changed to ***N54*** on 22 May 1959. Modified to the FAA standard Type II configuration for flight inspection in 1959. Initial service with the FAA's Eastern and Central Regions performing facility flight inspection. Redesignated in Navy records as a VC-47J in 1962. Ownership transferred from the USN to the FAA on 01Aug 1966. R. changed to ***N47*** on 26 Jun 1973. R. changed to ***N74*** on 02 Aug 1973. Suffered a left engine fire on 26 Jan 1976 at Oxnard, CA while performing flight inspection work, with damage to nacelle. Stored at Oxnard. Deemed excess to FAA needs and released to the GSA for disposal on 22 Mar 1976 while still stored at Oxnard awaiting repairs. Transferred to the USDA's U.S.-Mexico Screw Worm Eradication Program on 02 Apr 1976. Rr. as ***N74Z*** on 28 Apr 1976. Also, on 28 Apr 1976 assigned r. of ***N226GB*** which was ntu. As of Jan 1977 aircraft remained stored at Oxnard with estimated repair costs of $75,000. USDA decided not to utilize the aircraft, no doubt due to the extensive repairs needed, and instead s. by the GSA to A.D. Mallard of Shelly, Idaho on 08 Apr 1977. S. on 10 Apr 1977 to International Air Limited of Fresno, CA. S. on 26 May 1977 to Nevada Airlines of Las Vegas, NV. S. on 09 Jun 1977 to Evergreen Air of Montana, Missoula, MT. S. on 20 Aug 1978 to James Maher of North White Plains, NY. No further record of the aircraft with the FAA. Last owner did not register the aircraft, and on 21 May 1982 the FAA revoked the r. in the name of Evergreen Air. Fate remains unknown.

25956 M. as C-47B-10-DK s/n ***43-49007*** at Douglas-Oklahoma City on a USAAF contract but d. to the USN as R4D-6 BuNo ***17291*** on 12 Sep 1944. Operated with VR-3 of the Naval Air Transport Service through Jun 1946 when assigned to NAS Jacksonville, FL. Additional service in Brazil in Feb 1947 and at MCAS Cherry Pt., NC in Aug 1948 when re-designated as an R4D-5R. Placed in overhaul at NAS Jacksonville, FL in Jan 1951. Assigned to the 10th Naval District at NAS San Juan, PR in May 1952. Excess to USN needs and stored at NAF Litchfield Park after May 1954. Loaned to Wien Alaska Airlines on 13 Jul 1956 and r. as ***N2757A***. Returned to USN jurisdiction on unknown date. Stored at NAF Litchfield Park, AZ. Transferred via loan to the CAA in 1959. Issued ferry r. of ***N9052Z*** on 06 Nov 1959 and brought to Oklahoma City. R. changed to ***N67*** on 30 Sep 1960. Subsequently modified to the standard FAA Type II configuration for flight inspection. Initially assigned to the FAA's Southwest Region and, then, in 1963 to the Aeronautical Center for training. Redesignated in USN records as a TC-47J in 1962. Ownership transferred from the USN to the FAA on 01 Aug

1966. R. changed to ***N25*** on 09 Jan 1973. Deemed excess to FAA needs in Sep 1977 with 21,255 flight hours. R. canceled on 30 Sep 1977 and subsequently transferred to the GSA for disposal. Transferred by the GSA to the Linn Technical College, Linn, MO on 14 Feb 1978 and r. issued as ***N51938*** on 09 May 1978. S. on 26 Aug 1980 to Maples Aviation of Vichy, MO and again, on 04 Aug 1982, to Baron Aviation Services of Vichy, MO. Aircraft remains r. and is believed active.

26093 M. as C-47B-5-DK s/n ***43-48832*** at Douglas-Oklahoma City on a USAAF contract but d. to the USN as R4D-6 BuNo ***50746*** on 27 Sep 1944. Wartime service at NAS San Diego, CA. Post-war assignments at Pearl Harbor through 1946 and then with Marine Air Groups at NAS Quonset Pt., RI. Redesignated as an R4D-6R. As of May 1950 in overhaul at MCAS Cherry Point, NC. Assigned to a transportation pool at MCAS Cherry Point in Sep 1950. Placed into overhaul at NAS Jacksonville, FL in Feb 1953. Assigned to NAS Anacostia, DC for transportation in Nov 1953. Excess to USN needs and stored at NAF Litchfield Park after Feb 1956. Transferred via loan to the CAA in Sep 1956 and issued the r. of ***N9518C*** for a ferry flight to Oklahoma City. R. changed to ***N26*** on 12 Dec 1956. Subsequently modified to the standard Type II configuration for facility flight inspection. Designation changed to TC-47 in USN records in 1962. Ownership transferred from USN to the FAA on 01 Aug 1966. Service as flight inspection aircraft with various regions until 23 Sep 1976 when deemed excess to FAA requirements and transferred to the GSA for disposal. Rr. as ***N26AH*** on 07 Oct 1976. Transferred by GSA to the USDA's U.S.-Mexico Screw Worm Eradication Program being conducted in Mexico. R. changed to ***N228GB*** on 20 Apr 1977. Excess to USDA needs and transferred by the GSA to the Texas State Guard at Corsicana, TX on 17 Jan 1980. Aircraft de-registered on 25 Apr 1983 by Tradewinds Aircraft Supply of San Antonio, TX. Fate unknown, but presumably scrapped for parts.

26108 M. as C-47B-5-DK s/n ***43-48847*** at Douglas-Oklahoma City on a USAAF contract but d. to the USN as R4D-6 BuNo ***50749*** on 26 Sep 1944. Served domestically in the U.S. during World War II primarily with the Naval Air Transport Service. Re-designated as an R4D-6E in Mar 1947 indicating use in an electronics program. As of May 1950 assigned the FAETULANT at NAS Norfolk. Overhauled at NAS Jacksonville, FL in Nov 1951. Reassigned to NAS Norfolk in Nov 1951 and then returned to NAS Jacksonville, FL in Sep 1952. Assigned to the FAETUPAC at NAS San Diego in Dec 1952. Overhauled at San Diego in Jul 1955, afterwhich assigned to a transportation pool at NAS Memphis in Aug 1955. Deemed excess to USN needs and stored at NAF Litchfield Park in Feb 1958. Transferred via loan to the CAA in 1959. Ferry r. of ***N3455G*** assigned on 03 Jun 1959. R. changed to ***N63*** on 22 Dec 1959. Subsequently modified to the FAA standard Type II flight inspection configuration. Redesignated in USN records as an SC-47J in 1962. Ownership transferred from the USN to the FAA on 01 Aug 1966. R. changed to ***N79*** on 02 Apr 1973. Deemed excess to FAA needs on 31 Dec 1974 and released to the GSA for disposal. R. changed to ***N87819*** on 06 Feb 1975. Transferred by the GSA to the USDA for the U.S.-Mexico Screw Worm Eradication Program on 18 Feb 1975. R. changed to ***N2002J*** on 02 Oct 1976. R. changed again to ***N231GB*** on 10 Mar 1977. Excess to USDA needs and transferred by the GSA on 18 Sep 1980 to the Monroe County Mosquito Control District at Key West, FL. Aircraft believed still active as a sprayer.

26133 M. as C-47B-5-DK s/n ***43-48872*** at Douglas-Oklahoma City on a USAAF contract but d. to the USN as R4D-6 BuNo ***50754*** on 30 Sep 1944. Initial assignment ot the Fleet Air Wing at NAS San Diego, CA in Oct 1944. Subsequent wartime assignment to Commander, Air Force 7th Fleet in Dec 1944, Commander, Air Forces, Philippines in Aug 1945, and assigned to Pearl Harbor in 1946. Reassigned to NAS San Diego in Sep 1946 and overhauled at Columbus, OH in early 1947. Reassigned to NAS San Diego in Oct 1947. Assigned to VRU-3 at NAS Seattle, WA in Jan 1948. Redesignated as an R4D-6Q. Assigned to a VRU-3 Detachment at NAS San Diego in late 1948, and then to NAS Whidbey Island, WA in Jan 1950 with VR-23. Assigned back to NAS San Diego, for overhaul in Apr 1950, and then modified to an R4D-6S configuration at NAS Jacksonville, FL in May 1951. Assigned to the FAETUPAC at NAS San Diego, CA in Jun 1953. Overhauled again at NAS Jacksonville, in Oct 1954. Assigned to the FAETULANT at NAS Norfolk, VA in Apr 1955, and then deemed excess to USN needs and stored at NAF Litchfield Park after Feb 1958. Loaned to the FAA and issued the initial civil r. of ***N9118Z*** on 19 Jan 1960. Ferried to Oklahoma City and Rr. as ***N70*** on 30 Aug 1960. Subsequently modified to the FAA's standard Type II flight inspection configuration. Initial assignment to the FAA's Central Region, with subsequent assignment to various regions. Redesignated in USN records as an SC-47J in 1962. Ownership transferred from the USN to the FAA on 01 Aug 1966. Deemed excess to FAA needs on 24 Mar 1977 with 20,206 hours of recorded flight time. ***N70JC*** reserved on 29 Mar 1977 but ntu. Instead, r. canceled and released to the GSA for disposal. Transferred on 29 Jun 1977 to the USDA for use in its U.S.-Mexico Screw Worm Eradication program and used as a pesticide sprayer. R. changed to ***N211GB*** on 23 Jun 1978. Excess to USDA needs and transferred to the Lee County Mosquito Control District at Fort Meyers, FL for continued use as a sprayer. Active and based at Buckingham Airpark, FL.

26258 M. as C-47B-10-DK s/n ***43-48997*** at Douglas-Oklahoma City on a USAAF contract but d. to the USN as R4D-6 BuNo ***50758*** on 17 Oct 1944. Initial service assigned to the FAW at San Diego, CA. Additional assignments to Com Air 7th Fleet, Com Air Philippines, NAF Tatuila in Oct 1945, and Pearl Harbor in Jun 1946. Post-war service including NAS San Diego in Sep 1947, NAS Jacksonville, FL in Mar 1948, and back to NAS San Diego in Jul 1948. Re-designated as an R4D-6E. Assogmed to the FAETUPAC at NAS San Diego in 1052. Overhauled at NAS Jacksonville in Apr 1955 and then reassigned to the FAETUPAC at NAS San Diego in Sep 1955. Excess to USN needs and stored at NAF Litchfield Park, AZ after 27 Jun 1957. Loaned to the CAA in May 1958 and flown to Oklahoma City under the ferry r. of ***N7674C***. Rr. as ***N43*** in late 1958. Modified to the Standard Type II configuration for flight inspection in 1959. Assigned to various FAA regions for flight inspection, including the FAA's Western and Southwest Regions. Re-designated as a SC-47J in 1962. Deemed excess to FAA needs on 02 Mar 1965 and placed into storage at the Oklahoma City ASB. As of 08 Jul 1966, slated for transfer to Turkey via the Agency for International Development. Ownership transferred from the USN to the FAA on 01 Aug 1966. Departed the U.S. for Turkey on 17 Aug 1966. De-r. from the U.S. register in Sep 1966. As of Mar 1968 R. with Turkey as ***TC-KOL*** and employed by Devlet Hava Meydaniari Isletmesine (radio aid check). Transferred to the Turkish Air Force as of 1978. Fate unknown.

26268 M. as C-47B-10-DK s/n ***43-49007*** at Douglas-Oklahoma City on a USAAF contract but d. for service to the USN as R4D-6 BuNo ***50760*** on 13 Oct 1944. Initial USN service with VRS-1 at NAS New York. Later service at MCAS Quantico, VA, NAS Quonset Pt., RI, and NAS Jacksonville, FL. Redesignated as an R4D-6E in 1948. As of Jun 1948 assigned to FAETUPAC at NAS San Diego. Overhauled at NAS San Diego in Sep 1951 and redesignated as an R4D-6S. Assigned to the FAETULANT at NAS Norfolk, VA in Feb 1952. Overhauled at NAS Jacksonville, FL in May 1954 and then returned to the FAETUPAC at NAS San Diego in Oct 1954. Excess to USN needs and stored at NAF Litchfield Park after Feb 1958. Loaned to the CAA and issued the civil r. of ***N7675C*** on 20

May 1958 for its ferry flight to Oklahoma City. R. changed to ***N42*** on 12 Jan 1959. Subsequently modified to the standard FAA Type II flight inspection configuration. Initial FAA service primarily with the FAA's Central and Eastern Regions for flight inspection. Designation changed to SC-47J in USN records in 1962. Ownership transferred from the USN to the FAA on 01 Aug 1966. Excess to FAA needs on 31 Dec 1974. Stricken from the FAA inventory and released to the GSA for disposal on 22 Jan 1975. R. canceled. For disposal purposes, r. changed to ***N87815*** but r. ntu. Transferred to the USDA for use a sprayer with their U.S.-Mexico Screw Worm Eradication Program being conducted in Mexico. r. of ***N2005J*** assigned on 10 Oct 1975. R. changed to ***N232GB*** on 10 May 1976. Excess to USDA needs and released to the GSA for disposal. Transferred to the Georgia Historic Aviation Museum at Lawrenceville, GA on 09 Jan 1980. Remains r. and on static display.

26283 M. as C-47B-10-DK s/n ***43-49022*** at Douglas-Oklahoma City on a USAAF contract but d. to the USN as R4D-6 BuNo ***50763*** on 14 Oct 1944. Initial USN service with VR-3 at Olathe, KS. Later service with various NATS units including VR-1 (Apr 1946) and again with VR-3 at Patuxent River in 1947. As of May 1950 designated as an R4D-6R and assigned to NAS Anacostia, DC for transport. Overhauled at NAS Jacksonville, FL in Aug 1951 and then returned to NAS Anacostia in Feb 1954. Excess to USN needs and stored at NAF Litchfield Park after Apr 1954. Loaned to the CAA in 1957 and r. as ***N7234C*** on 21 Oct 1957 for a ferry flight to Oklahoma City. R. changed to ***N11*** on 03 Jan 1958. Subsequently modified to the standard FAA Type II configuration for facility flight inspection. Assigned to regional flight inspection programs. Designation changed from R4D-6R to TC-47J in Navy records in 1962. Ownership changed from the USN to the FAA on 01 Aug 1966. R. changed to ***N13*** on 26 Jun 1973. (R. of N39 never assigned to this aircraft.) R. changed to ***N47*** on 17 Apr 1973. Deemed excess to FAA needs and released to the GSA on 12 Dec 1975 for disposal. R. changed to ***N473*** for disposal. GSA reported the aircraft was transferred to the USMC on 22 Jan 1976. Instead, transferred to the USDA in 1976 and assigned to the U.S.-Mexico Screw Worm Eradication Program. R. changed to ***N207GB*** in 1976. Deemed excess to USDA needs and released to the GSA for disposal. R. changed to ***N2299Y*** in Oct 1978. S. to Way Mac Enterprises of Jackson, MI on 02 Aug 1978. Fate unknown.

26358 M. as C-47B-10-DK s/n ***43-49097*** at Douglas-Oklahoma City on a USAAF contract but d. for service to the USN as R4D-6 BuNo ***50773*** on 06 Nov 1944. USN assignment with various transport units as part of the Naval Air Transport Service. Assigned to a transportation pool at NAS Quonset Point, RI in 1948. Redesignated as an R4D-6R on 03 Mar 1949, indicating use as a staff transport. Assigned as of May 1950 to a transportation pool at NAS Corpus Christi, TX. Overhauled at NAS Jacksonville, FL in Dec 1950. Assigned to the 12th Naval District at NAS Alameda, CA in Jul 1951 and returned to NAS Jacksonville in Sep 1953 for overhaul. Assigned to MCAS Cherry Point, NC in Dec 1953. Excess to USN needs and stored at NAF Litchfield Park after May 1954. Transferred via loan from the USN to the CAA on 08 Mar 1957. Assigned ***N7069C*** on 15 Mar 1957 for its ferry flight to Oklahoma City. R. changed to ***N31*** on 03 May 1957 and subsequently modified to the standard Type II configuration for facility flight inspection. Operated as ***NX31*** for developmental work for the testing of a new autopilot installation. Reverted to the standard certificate on 12 Feb 1958. Initial flight inspection assignment with the FAA's Western Region. Designation changed from R4D-6R to TC-47J by the USN in 1962. Ownership transferred from the USN to the FAA on 01 Aug 1966. Deemed excess to FAA needs and released to the GSA for disposal on 14 Aug 1978. De-r. on 21 Aug 1978. Transferred by the GSA to the Collier Mosquito Control District of Naples, FL for use as a pesticide sprayer on 19 Feb 1979. R. as ***N9049P*** on 12 Mar 1979. Reverted to a spares source in 1981 and r. canceled on 09 Jun 1983. Presumably scrapped.

26373 M. as C-47B-10-DK s/n ***43-49112*** at Douglas-Oklahoma City on a USAAF contract but d. for service to the USN as R4D-6 BuNo ***50776*** on 21 Oct 1944. Service with Pacific fleet transport units through World War II, continuing with post-war service. Assigned to NAS Quonset Pt., RI in Mar 1948 and Norfolk, VA in Jun 48. Subsequent Navy service unknown, but placed in storage at NAF Litchfield Park, AZ. Earmarked via loan to the CAA on 07 January 1959 and assigned the civil ferry r. of ***N9466Z***. Subsequently returned to the Navy as unneeded by the CAA. Subsequent Navy service was possibly with the Arctic Research Lab in 1970. No further record.

26558 M. as C-47B-15-DK s/n ***43-49297*** at Douglas-Oklahoma City on a USAAF contract but d. to the USN as R4D-6 BuNo ***50788*** on 09 Nov 1944. Initial assignment to VR-3 at NAS Olathe, KS in Nov 1944. Assigned to MCAS Cherry Point in Apr 1946. Subsequent post-war assignments to various bases including NAS Jacksonville, FL and NAS Columbus, OH. Assigned to the FAETUPAC at NAS San Diego in Aug 1948 as an R4D-6E. Overhauled at NAS San Diego in Sep 1951 and redesignated as an R4D-6S. Assigned back to the FAETUPAC at NAS San Diego in Jul 1952, and then to NAS Whidbey Island, WA in Oct 1952. Assigned NAS Jacksonville, FL for overhaul in Dec 1954 and then to the FAETULANT at NAS Norfolk, VA in Apr 1955.I Excess to USN needs and stored at NAF Litchfield Park after Feb 1958. Transferred to the CAA on 20 May 1958. Assigned the ferry r. of ***N7678C*** on 20 May 1958. Ferried to Oklahoma City and r. changed to ***N49***. Subsequently modified to the FAA standard Type II configuration for flight inspection. Assigned to the various FAA regions for flight inspection including the Eastern, Central, and Western Regions. Designatio changed from R4D-6S to SC-47J in USN records in 1962. Ownership transferred from the USN to the FAA on 01 Aug 1966. Excess to FAA needs and released to the GSA for disposal on 19 May 1975. Transferred by the GSA to the USDA for use in the U.S. Screw Worm Eradication Program as a pesticide sprayer. R. changed to ***N2006J*** in Jul 1975. R. changed to ***N235GB*** in May 1976. Excess to USDA needs and released again to the GSA for disposal. Transferred to the Texas State Guard at Corsicana, TX on 07 Feb 1980. S. in Dec 1984 to Atkins Aviation and r. changed to ***N514AC***. S. in Sep 1991 to IFL Group. Current status unknown.

26583 M. as C-47B-15-DK s/n ***43-49322*** at the Douglas-Oklahoma City plant on a USAAF contract but transferred to the USN as R4D-6 BuNo ***50793*** and d. on 14 Nov 1944. Initial USN assignment to VR-3 at NAS Olathe, Kansas. Additional assignments to NAS Jacksonville, FL and re-designated as an R4D-6R in Apr 1949. As of May 1950 assigned to the 17th Naval District at Kodiak, AK. Assigned to NAS Jacksonville for overhaul in May 1952, then placed in storage at NAF Litchfield Park in Nov 1952. Removed from storage and assigned to NAS Anacostia, DC for transport in Sep 1953. Excess to USN needs and stored at NAF Litchfield Park after Dec 1955. Transferred via loan to the CAA in May 1957. Initial civil r. of ***N7092C*** assigned on 08 May 1957. Due to a mix-up, r. changed to ***N7072C*** on 09 May 1957. Ferried to Oklahoma City. R. changed to ***N33*** on 22 Aug 1957 and subsequently modified to the standard Type II configuration in Dec 1957. Assignment to the various FAA regions for flight inspection. Type designation changed in USN records from an R4D-6R to a TC-47J in 1962. Ownership changed from the USN to the FAA on 01 Aug 1966. Withdrawn from FAA service and r. canceled on 24 Mar 1982. Placed into storage at Oklahoma City. Transferred by the GSA to the USAF Museum Heritage program and assigned to the Minnesota ANG Museum in Minneapolis for display. Assigned the ferry r. of ***N620*** in Dec 1982.

Upon arrival, its engines were removed and replaced by run-out R-1830s. The good engines were sent back to Oklahoma City and installed on msn 32794 (N35) for its ferry flight to Pope AFB, NC for display, also with the USAF Heritage Program. Meanwhile, msn 26583 remains on display outdoors in its last FAA paint scheme with much of its FAA equipment intact.

26593 M. as C-47B-15-DK s/n ***43-49332*** at Douglas-Oklahoma City on a USAAF contract but d. to the USN as R4D-6 BuNo ***50795*** on 15 Nov 1944. Initial USN service with VR-3 at NAS Olathe, KS. Assigned to NACA at Langley Field, VA in Aug 1946, and then to the NACA Research Laboratory at Cleveland, OH in Oct 1946. Redesignated as an R4D-6R and assigned to NAS Oakland in May 1950. Assigned to a transportation pool at NAS Memphis, TN in Jun 1952. Excess to USN needs and stored at NAF Litchfield Park after Jun 1957. Transferred via loan to the CAA in May 1959. Civil r. of ***N3761G*** issued on 14 Aug 1959 for a ferry flight to Oklahoma City. R. changed to ***N69*** in late 1959 and subsequently modified to the standard FAA Type II configuration for flight inspection. Assigned to the various FAA regions, initially with the Eastern and Central Regions, for facility flight inspection. Designation changed in USN records from an R4D-6R to an SC-47J in 1962. Deemed excess to FAA needs and placed into storage on 08 Apr 1965. Transferred by the Navy via the FAA to the Government of Columbia and turned over to a Colombian ferry crew on 01 Oct 1965. U.S. r. canceled in Sep 1965. Colombian r. of ***HK-1149G*** issued. Operated by Dept. Admin de Aeron Civil, El Dorado, Columbia as of Dec 1965. Fate unknown.

26713 M. as C-47B-15-DK s/n ***43-49452*** at Douglas-Oklahoma City on a USAAF contract but d. to the USN as R4D-6 BuNo ***50813*** on 25 Nov 1944. Served domestically through it USN service. Re-designated as an R4D-6R. in Apr 1947 As of May 1950 assigned to the 12th Naval District at NAS Alameda, CA. Assigned to NAS Jacksonville, FL for overhaul in Jul 1951. Assigned to a transportation pool at NAS Memphis, TN in Mar 1952. Overhauled again at NAS Jacksonville in Apr 1954. Assigned to the 15th Naval District at NAS Coco Solo in Nov 1954. Assigned to a transportation pool at NAS Anacostia, DC in Apr 1055. Excess to USN needs and stored at NAF Litchfield Park after Oct 1956. Transferred via loan to the CAA in Oct 1957. Civil r. of ***N7489C*** issued on 10 Oct 1957. Ferried to Oklahoma City. R. changed to ***N37*** and subsequently modified to the standard FAA Type II configuration for flight inspection. Assigned to the various FAA regions to perform facility flight inspection. Designation changed by USN to TC-47J in 1962. Transferred from the USN to the FAA on 01 Aug 1966. Excess to FAA needs and placed into storage on 23 Sep 1976. R. changed to ***N37AH*** and released to the GSA for disposal. Transferred by the GSA to the USDA for use in the U.S.-Mexico Screw Worm Eradication Program as a pesticide sprayer. R. changed to ***N240GB*** in May 1977. Excess to USDA needs and transferred to the Wisconsin State Department of Natural Resources, Madison, WI on 05 Jun 1981. Excess to department needs in Dec 1981 and r. canceled. S. in May 1983 to Basler Flight Service of Oshkosh, WI and r. re-instated at that time. Sold to AMI which fitted airframe with Pratt & Whitney PT-6A-65AR turboprop engines and with other modifications including an extended fuselage. S. in 1987 to Aeronautical Enterprises of Fort Lauderdale, FL.Exported to South Africa for cargo use and r. as ***ZS-KCV***. Crashed and destroyed on 07 November 1993 in Kenya.

26724 M. as C-47B-20-DK s/n ***43-49463*** at Douglas-Oklahoma City on a USAAF contract but d. to the USN as R4D-6 BuNo ***50815*** on 28 Nov 1944. Initial service at Norfolk, VA, with subsequent service with FAW-5, FAW-16, and VX-2. Post-war service with transports squadrons at Quonset Pt., RI and Alameda, CA. Assigned to VR-22 as of Jul 1948. Subsequent service unknown but stored at NAF Litchfield Park, AZ in the mid-1950s. Earmarked via loan to the CAA as of 06 Mar 1958 and assigned the civil ferry r. of ***N9467Z***. Remained in storage at NAF Litchfield and not transferred. Returned to Navy jurisdiction in January 1962. No further record. (The civil registration of N9467Z was later assigned to R4D-7 BuNo 39102 (msn 32810) for export to South Korea and service with Far East Airways Corporation as HL-2010.)

26733 M. as C-47B-15-DK s/n ***43-49472*** at Douglas-Oklahoma City on a USAAF contract but d. to the USN as R4D-6 BuNo ***50816*** on 26 Nov 1944. Initial USN assignment to NAS Norfolk with further assignment to VRU-2 in Aug 1946. Subsequently assigned to NAS Quonset Pt. in May 1948. Re-designated as an R4D-6R on 04 Apr 1949. Assigned to a transportation pool at NAS Anacostia, DC as of May 1950. Overhauled at MCAS Cherry Point, NC in Jan 1952, and then assigned to the 10th Naval District at NAS San Juan, PR in May 1954. Excess to USN needs and stored at NAF Litchfield Park after Jun 1956. Transferred via loan to the CAA in Sep 1956. Civil r. of ***N9508C*** assigned on 21 Sep 1956. Ferried to Oklahoma City. R. changed to ***N25*** on 08 Nov 1956. Subsequently modified to the standard Type II configuration for FAA flight inspection. Assigned to the FAA's Frankfurt flight inspection office in 1960 and r. changed to ***N28*** on 10 Jun 1960. R. changed to ***N74*** on 11 Jan 1963. Designation changed from R4D-6R to TC-47J in USN records in 1962. Deemed excess to FAA needs and in storage at Frankfurt as of Jun 1963. As of Sep 1964 earmarked for the U.S. State Department's Agency for International Development. On 13 Dec 1964, transferred from the Navy to the Government of Kenya via the FAA and AID. U.S. r. canceled on 13 Jan 1965. Kenya r. of ***5Y-DCA*** issued and operated by the Kenyan Department of Civil Aviation. Reported crashed and destroyed in Nairobi in Apr 1973.

26874 M. as C-47B-15-DK s/n ***43-49613*** at Douglas-Oklahoma City on a USAAF contract but d. to the USN as R4D-6 BuNo ***50819*** on 13 Dec 1944. Served domestically with the Naval Air Transport Service through most of its wartime service. As of May 1948 assigned to NAS Norfolk, VA. Overhauled at NAS Jacksonville, FL in Mar 1950. Assigned to Fleet Air Squadron 8 at NAS Alameda, CA in Apr 1950. Assigned to the 14th Naval District at NAS Barbers Point, HI in Jun 1950. Assigned to NAS San Diego, CA for overhaul in Jul 1952. Modified at NAS Jacksonville and designated as an R4D-6S in Oct 1952. Assigned to a transportation pool at NAS Memphis in Dec 1952. Overhauled again at NAS Jacksonville in Mar 1955 and then returned to NAS Memphis in Jul 1955. Excess to USN needs and placed in storage at NAF Litchfield Park after Nov 1957. Transferred via loan to the CAA in Jul 1959 and issued the ferry r. of ***N9119Z*** on 19 Jan 1960 for its ferry flight to Oklahoma City. R. changed to ***N60*** on 30 Aug 1960 and subsequently modified to the standard FAA Type II flight inspection configuration. Initial assignment to the FAA's Central Region. Designation changed from R4D-6S to SC-47J in USN records in 1962. Ownership transferred from the USN to the FAA on 01 Aug 1966. R. changed to ***N68*** on 02 Jun 1973. Excess to FAA needs and placed into storage in 1976 with 21,990 logged flight hours. Released to the GSA for disposal on 23 Sep 1976 and r. changed to ***N68AH*** on 29 Nov 1976. Transferred by the GSA to the USDA for use in their U.S.-Mexico Screw Worm Eradication Program. R. changed to ***N229GB*** on 02 Jun 1977. Excess to USDA needs in 1979 and released back to the GSA for disposal. Stored at Douglas-Bisbee Airport in Arizona. Transferred by the GSA to the Confederate Air Force's Mid-Atlantic Wing at Harrisburg, PA on 20 Oct 1980. Difficulties in obtaining sponsorship by the CAF caused the original transfer agreement to be terminated on 19 May 1981. Request by the newly formed Mid-Atlantic Air Museum was made two days later on 21 May 1981. Transferred by the GSA to the new museum, which began a long-term restoration to an accurate R4D-6 configuration. Ownership transferred from the GSA to the Mid-Atlantic Air Museum on 29 Aug 1990. Aircraft remains airworthy.

26968 M. as C-47B-20-DK s/n ***43-49707*** at Douglas-Oklahoma City on a USAAF contract but d. to the USN as R4D-6 BuNo ***50829*** on 23 Dec 1944. Assigned to Special Project Unit CAST at NAS Squantum, MA where it was utilized in the development of radio and radar equipment. It was later overhauled at NAS Jacksonville, FL. As of May 1950 assigned to a transportation pool at NAS Memphis, TN as an R4D-6E. Overhauled again at NAS Jacksonville in Jun 1950, and then assigned to the FAETUPAC at NAS San Diego, CA in Dec 1950. Overhauled and modified at NAS Jacksonville in Mar 1953 and redesignated as an R4D-6S. Stored at NAF Litchfield Park in Oct 1953, and then reassigned to the FAETUPAC at NAS San Diego in Sep 1954. Excess to USN needs and stored at NAF Litchfield Park after Nov 1957. Loaned to the CAA in Mar 1958 and issued the ferry r. of ***N7676C*** on 20 May 1958. R. changed to ***N53*** on 25 Sep 1959 and subsequently modified to the standard FAA Type II configuration. Initial flight inspection assignments with the FAA's Eastern Region and, later, the various FAA regions. Designation changed from R4D-6S to SC-47J in USN records in 1962. Ownership transferred from the USN to the FAA on 01 Aug 1966. R. changed to ***N73*** on 02 Aug 1973. Surplus to FAA needs and placed into storage in 1976. Transferred to the GSA for disposal on 23 Sep 1976 with 18,994 logged flight hours. R. changed to ***N73AH*** on 07 Oct 1976 for disposal. Transferred by the GSA to the USDA for use as a pesticide sprayer in the U.S.-Mexico Screw Worm Eradication Program. R. changed to ***N237GB*** on 17 May 1977. Excess to USDA needs and released to the GSA for disposal. Transferred to the USAF Museum Program on 26 May 1982. Placed on display with the North Dakota Air National Guard Fargo, ND and de-registered on 02 Jul 1985. Currently painted in the markings of its original USAAF identity, s/n 43-49707.

32794 M. as TC-47B-25-DK s/n ***44-76462*** at Douglas-Oklahoma City and d. to the USAAF on 19 Mar 1945. Transferred to the USN as R4D-7 BuNo ***39098***. Initial USN service in the Philippines with an aircraft service unit. As of Apr 1948 assigned to a transportation pool at NAS San Diego, CA. Redesignated as an R4D-6R and assigned to NAS Pensecola, FL as of May 1950. Overhauled at NAS Jacksonville, FL and then assigned to the 11th Naval District at NAS San Diego in May 1952. Returned to NAS Jacksonville for overhaul in Jul 1954 and then placed into storage at NAF Litchfield Park in Aug 1954. Removed from storage and assigned to MCAS El Toro, CA in Jun 1955. Assigned to NAS Anacostia, DC in Dec 1955. Excess to USN needs and stored at NAF Litchfield Park after early 1957. Transferred by loan to the CAA in 1957, and issued the ferry r. of ***N7487C*** on 29 Jul 1957. R. changed to ***N35*** on 06 Dec 1957. Modified to the standard FAA Type II configuration in Feb 1958.. Initial FAA service with the various FAA regions performing facility flight inspection. Re-designated as an TC-47J by the USN in its inventory records in 1962. Ownership transferred from the USN to the FAA on 01 Aug 1966. Assigned to the Anchorage Flight Inspection Office around 1978. Returned to Oklahoma City in Nov 1981 for use in training. Excess to FAA needs and released to the GSA for disposal in Apr 1982. Transferred to the USAF Museum Program and assigned for display at Pope AFB, NC. Currently painted and marked as TC-47B s/n 44-76462.

33100 M. as TC-47B-30-DK s/n ***44-76768*** at Douglas-Oklahoma City on a USAAF contract but d. to the USN as R4D-7 BuNo ***99825*** on 20 Apr 1945. USN service beginning at NAS Jacksonville, FL, and followed by service at various USN facilities including: VB-2 at Lake City in Dec 1945; NAS Hutchinson in Feb 1946; Pensecola in Sep 1947; NAS Quonset Point, RI in Mar 1948. Re-designated as an R4D-6R on 31 Oct 1948. As of May 1950 assigned to MCAS El Toro, CA. Overhauled at NAS Jacksonville, FL in Aug 1951 and then assigned to the 1st Naval District at NAS Quonset Pt., RI in Feb 1952. Assigned to a transportation pool at NAS Memphis in Mar 1954. Excess to USN needs and stored at NAF Litchfield Park after May 1956. Transferred via loan to the CAA in Oct 1957 and assigned the ferry civil r. of ***N7488C*** on 10 Oct 1957. R. changed to ***N38*** on 26 Nov 1957 and modified to an FAA Type II configuration for FAA flight inspection in Apr 1958. Subsequently assigned to FAA flight inspection. Designation changed from R4D-6R to TC-47J in Navy inventory records in 1962. Ownership transferred from the USN to the FAA on 01 Aug 1966. Deemed excess to FAA needs in Dec 1975. R. changed to ***N38114*** on 23 Dec 1975 and transferred to the GSA for disposal on 30 Dec 1975. Transferred by the GSA to the USDA for assignment to their U.S.-Mexico Screw Worm Eradication Program as a pesticide sprayer. R. changed to ***N208GB*** on 15 Jan 1976. R. changed to ***N210GB*** on 17 Jun 1976. Deemed excess by the USDA to their needs and released back to the GSA for disposal. Transferred on 26 Sep 1979 to the USAF and assigned to the Inter-American Air Force Academy at Howard AFB, Panama. USAF records indicate it was re-designated as a GC-117D and issued the serial number of ***45-33100***. (This is particularly unusual, for though the C-117 designation is valid for the DC-3 type, the serial number is bogus and based upon the Douglas constructor's number. Why this was done by the USAF is unknown, as the aircraft had been assigned a valid designation and serial number by the USAAF in 1945.) The r. record notes that the USAF planned to use the aircraft as a ground trainer. Fate unknown.

33133 M. as TC-47B-30-DK s/n ***44-76801*** at Douglas-Oklahoma City and on a USAAF contract but d. to the USN as R4D-7 BuNo ***99837*** on 05 May 1945. Assigned to VRS-1 at NAS New York, with subsequent duty with various USN units including: NAS Quonset Pt., RI in Jun 1946; NAS Memphis in Sep 1946; NAS San Diego, CA in Jun 1948. Re-designated as an R4D-6R in 1948. As of May 1950 assigned to NAS Anacostia, DC. Placed into storage at NAF Litchfield Park in Jun 1953. Withdrawn from storage and overhauled at NAS Jacksonville, FL in Jan 1954. Assigned to the 11th Naval District at NAS San Diego in Jul 1954. Excess to USN needs and stored at NAF Litchfield Park after Jun 1957. Transferred via loan to the CAA in Oct 1957 and issued the ferry r. of ***N7233C*** on 21 Oct 1957. R. changed to ***N29*** in late 1957. Modified to the Type II flight inspection configuration in May 1958. Subsequently assigned to FAA flight inspection, primarily with the FAA's Central Region. USN changed designation from R4D-6R to TC-47J in 1962. Ownership transferred from the USN to the FAA on 01 Aug 1966. Excess to FAA needs in Jan 1975. R. canceled on 15 Jan 1975 and transferred to the GSA on 18 Jan 1975. Utilized for fire demonstration by the FAA at Oklahoma City on 07 May 1975 and remains presumably scrapped shortly thereafter.

33144 M. as TC-47B-30-DK s/n ***44-76812*** at Douglas-Oklahoma City on a USAAF contract but d. to the USN as R4D-7 BuNo ***99828*** on 04 May 1945. Placed into storage by the USN at Clinton, OK until late 1945 when activated and placed into use at Corry Field. Assigned to NAS Quonset Pt., RI in Oct 1947. Assigned to the FAETULANT at NAS Norfolk, VA in Feb 1948. Overhauled at NAS Jacksonville, FL in Mar 1951 and redesignated as an R4D-6Q in Jul 1951. Assigned to the FAETUPAC at NAS San Diego, CA in Feb 1952. Overhauled at NAS San Diego in Jul 1954 and then assigned back to the FAETULANT at NAS Norfolk in Apr 1955. Assigned to FASRON 101 at NAS Quonset Pt. in Jul 1957. Surplus to USN needs and placed into storage at NAF Litchfield Park after Feb 1958. Loaned to the CAA and r. as ***N3454G*** on 03 Jun 1959 for its ferry flight to Oklahoma City. R. changed to ***N66*** on 02 May 1960 and subsequently modified to the FAA Type II configuration in Jul 1960. Initial assignments for flight inspection with the FAA's Central and Western regions. Designation changed from R4D-6Q to EC-47J in USN inventory records in 1962. Ownership transferred from the USN to the FAA on 01 Aug 1966. Deemed excess to FAA needs in 1978 and transferred to the GSA for disposal on 02 Mar 1978 with 20,566 logged flight hours. De-r. on 09 Mar 1978 and transferred by the GSA to the Georgia Historical Aviation Museum of Stone Mountain, GA on 05 Jul 1978. R. as ***N49666*** on 22 Aug 1978. Title transferred from the GSA to the museum on 16 Apr 1984. S. on 22 May 1984 to National Aero Sales of Zephyr Cove, NV. S. on 05 Aug 1985 to KDD Aviation Leasing of Upper Saddle River, NJ. S. back to National Aero Sales on 01 Oct 1985. S. on 11 Oct 1985 to Ron Farish Aircraft, Inc., of Tyler, TX, and to Jack Rhodes Aircraft Sales, Columbus, IN on 06 Feb 1987. Transferred to Rhodes International of Columbus, IN on 12 Aug 1987 and r. changed to ***N145JR*** on 22 Sep 1987. Aircraft embroiled in legal ownership disputes with several prior owners and the matter has been turned over to the courts for decision. It believed the aircraft remains based at Columbus, IN.

33155 M. as TC-47B-30-DK s/n ***44-76823*** at Douglas-Oklahoma City on a USAAF contract but d. to the USN as R4D-7 BuNo ***99829*** on 05 May 1945. Placed into storage by the USN at Clinton, OK until Dec 1945. Assigned to NAS Corpus Christi, TX in Dec 1945 and NAS Jacksonville, FL in Mar 1947 for overhaul. Assigned to NAS Quonset Pt., RI in May 1948 and re-designated as an R4D-6E. As of May 1950 assigned tothe FAETUPAC at NAS San Diego, CA. Detached with that unit to NAS Whidbey Island, WA in Jun 1950, and then returned to NAS San Diego in Jul 1951. Overhauled at NAS Jacksonville in Jul 1951 and redeisgnated as an R4D-6SX. Assigned to the FAETULANT at NAS Norfolk and redesignated as an R4D-6S in Mar 1952. Returned to NAS Jacksonville for overhaul in Jun 1954 and then assigned to VX-1 at Key West, FL in Dec 1954. Excess to USN needs and placed into storage at NAF Litchfield Park after Feb 1958. Transferred via loan to the CAA in Mar 1958. Civil r. of ***N7677C*** assigned on 15 Jul 1958. R. changed to ***N47*** on 30 Jan 1959. Modified to the FAA standard Type II configuration in Feb 1959 and subsequently assigned to facility flight inspection. Designation changed from R4D-6S to SC-47J in USN inventory records in 1962. Assigned to the Alaskan Region in 1965. Ownership transferred from the USN to the FAA on 01 Aug 1966. Crashed and destroyed at Fire Island, AK on 02 Oct 1970 with the loss of two FAA crewmembers. R. canceled on 06 Oct 1970.

33201 M. as TC-47B-30-DK s/n ***44-76869*** at Douglas-Oklahoma City on a USAAF contract but d. to the USN as R4D-7 BuNo ***99835*** on 08 May 1945. Immediately placed into storage at Clinton, OK but removed in Dec 1945 and assigned to VRS-1 at NAS New York. Served in various domestic squadrons including VRJ-2 at NAS Quonset Pt., RI and at NAS Alameda, CA. As of Feb 1950 in overhaul at MCAS Cherry Point, NC and designated as an R4D-6Z. Assigned to a VR-5 detachment at NAS San Diego in Sep 1950. Overhauled at NAS Jacksonville, FL in Nov 1952. Assigned for transportation at NAS Anacostia, DC in Aug 1953. Excess to USN needs and placed into storage at NAF Litchfield Park after May 1954. Obtained on loan by the CAA in Mar 1958 and issued the ferry r. of ***N7631C*** on 21 Mar 1958 for its ferry flight to Oklahoma City. R. changed to ***N48*** on 01 Jul 1958 and subsequently converted to a standard Type II configuration for FAA flight inspection. Initial assignments to the FAA's Eastern and Western Regions. Designation changed from R4D-6Z to VC-47J in USN records in 1962. Ownership changed from the USN to the FAA on 01 Aug 1966. Excess to the FAA needs and placed into storage on 17 Jul 1975. R. changed to ***N31179*** for disposal purposes on 20 Oct 1975 and released to the GSA on the same date. Transferred to the USDA for use in their U.S.-Mexico Screw Worm Eradication Program for use as a pesticide sprayer. R. changed to ***N211GB*** on 02 Jun 1977. Excess to USDA needs and released back to the GSA on 08 Jan 1978. S. on 01 Jun 1978 to R.D. McSwiggan of Griffin, GA and again on 19 Jun 1978 to WayMac Enterprises of Jackson, MS. R. changed to ***N2298C*** also on 19 Jun 1978. S. on 21 Nov 1979 to Air Taxi of Haiti, based at Port Au Prince, Haiti. S. on 17 Feb 1981 to Robert Hedrix of Lakewood, CO, who had the aircraft re-engined with the conventional R-1820-75 engines. S. on 20 May 1983 to Accelerated Charter Express of Broomfield, CO. Finally, on 01 May 1984, s. to Sal-Air, Incorporated, a northwest regional cargo carrier based in Seattle, WA. R. of ***N352SA*** reserved but ntu. Aircraft believed still active and re-equipped with R-1830-90D engines in 1985.

33206 M. as TC-47B-35-DK s/n ***44-76874*** at Douglas-Oklahoma City on a USAAF contract but d. to the USN as R4D-7 BuNo ***99836*** on 08 May 1945. Immediately placed into storage at Clinton, OK but removed in Dec 1945 and assigned to VRS-1 at NAS New York. Served in various domestic squadrons including: NAS Quonset Pt., RI as of Jun 1946; MAG-21 in Sep 1946, and the Fleet Air Electronic Test Unit, Atlantic at NAS Norfolk, VA in Mar 1947. Redesignated as an R4D-6R in 1948. As of May 1950 assigned to MCAS Cherry Pt., NC. Assigned to NAS Jacksonville, FL for overhaul in Mar 1951. Assigned to VR-1 at NAS Quonset Pt. in Aug 1951, then transferred to VR-25 at Naples, Italy in Nov 1951. Assigned to VR-25 at London, England in Jun 1952, then returned to NAS Jacksonville, FL for overhaul in Jun 1953. Assigned to the 1st Naval District at NAS Quonset Pt. in Dec 1953 and then the 5th Naval District at NAS Norfolk in Dec 1954. Excess to USN needs and placed into storage at NAF Litchfield Park after Jun 1956. Obtained on loan by the CAA in Mar 1957 and issued the ferry r. of ***N7071C*** on 15 Mar 1957 for its ferry flight to Oklahoma City. R. changed to ***N28*** in Apr 1957. R. changed to ***N17*** on 14 Oct 1957 and assigned to international flight inspection in Europe. As of 1961 based at the FAA's flight inspection office in Beirut, Lebanon. Designation changed from R4D-6R to TC-47J in USN inventory records in 1962. Assigned to the international office in Frankfurt, Germany in 1963 and r. changed to ***N73***. (R. exchanged with an FAA DC-4 also based in Frankfurt.) Excess to FAA needs and as of 02 Sep 1964, being held in storage at Frankfurt for disposal by the USN via the U.S. State Department's Agency for International Development. As of Mar 1965 earmarked for the government of Greece for airways inspection. Accepted by a Greek flight crew in Frankfurt on 12 Mar 1965. U.S. r. canceled and Greek r. of ***SX-ECF*** assigned. Utilized for airways inspection by the Ypiresia Politikis Aeroporias (Civil Aviation Service) and based at Athens, Greece until 1983 when withdrawn from service. Subsequently placed on static display at the Athens Airport.

33216 M. as TC-47B-35-DK s/n ***44-76884*** at Douglas-Oklahoma City on a USAAF contract but d. for service as R4D-7 BuNo ***99838*** on 15 May 1945. Placed in storage upon delivery at Clinton, OK. Placed into service in Dec 1945 at NAS Norfolk, VA. Assigned to VPB-2 , location unknown, and then overhauled at NAS Jacksonville, FL in Jun 1946. Assigned to NAS Quonset Pt., RI in Jul 1947 and then MCAS El Toro, CA in Aug 1948. Redesignated as an R4D-6R in 1948. Overhauled at MCAS Cherry Pt., NC in Sep 1950 and then assigned to NAS Anacostia, DC in Aug 1951. Overhauled again at NAS Jacksonville in Oct 1953 and then assigned to NAS Glenview, IL in Jan 1954. Excess to USN needs and placed into storage at NAF Litchfield Park after Apr 1956. Transferred via loan to the CAA in early 1959 and issued the ferry r. of ***N7073C*** on 25 Mar 1959. R. changed to ***N30*** on 15 Aug 1959 and modified to the FAA standard Type II DC-3C configuration. Initial assignment to the FAA's Western Region. Designation changed from R4D-6R to TC-47J in USN inventory records in 1962. Ownership transferred from the USN to the FAA on 01 Aug 1966. Continued in flight inspection service through Jun 1974 when placed in storage at Oklahoma City, OK. R. canceled on 25 Nov 1974. Declared excess and released to the GSA for disposal on 08 Jan 1975. Transferred to the USDA for use as a pesticide sprayer with the U.S.-Mexico Screw Worm Eradication Program on 18 Feb 1975. Assigned r. of ***N2004J*** but apparently ntu. Assigned r. of ***N212GB*** on 10 May 1976. Excess to USDA needs and released back to the GSA on 08 Jan 1978. S. to R.D. McSwiggan of Griffin, GA on 01 Jun 1978.

S. to WayMac Enterprises of Jackson, MS on 19 Jun 1978. R. changed to ***N2312G*** also on 19 Jun 1978. S. on 23 Feb 1982 to Specialty Restaurants of Anaheim, CA, one of aircraft collector David C. Tallichet's companies. (Tallichet also operates the Military Aircraft Restoration Corporation of Chino, CA.) Current status unknown.

33232 M. as TC-47B-35-DK s/n ***44-76900*** at Douglas-Oklahoma City on a USAAF contract but d. to the USN as R4D-7 BuNo ***99840*** on 09 May 1945. Immediately placed into storage at Clinton, OK but pulled and placed into service in Dec 1945, initially at NAS Corpus Christi. Assigned to NAS Jacksonville, FL in Jun 1946, possibly for overhaul. Assigned to the NATC at NAS Patuxent River, MD in Jun 1947. Ovehauled again at NAS Jacksonville in Nov 1947 and then modified at MCAS Cherry Point, NC and redesignated as an R4D-6E in May 1948. As of May 1950 assigned to VX-1 and based at NAS Key West, FL. Overhauled at NAS Jacksonville and redesignated as an R4D-6S in Feb 1952. Assigned to NAS Memphis, TN in Oct 1952 and then overhauled again at NAS Jacksonville. Returned to VX-1 at NAS Key West in Oct 1955. Excess to USN needs and placed into storage at NAF Litchfield Park after Oct 1956. Transferred to the CAA in 1958 and issued the ferry r. of ***N5177V*** on 09 Dec 1958. R. changed to ***N64*** on 16 Apr 1959 and modified to the standard FAA Type II configuration for FAA facility flight inspection. Initial FAA service with the FAA's Eastern Region. Designation changed from R4D-6S to SC-47J in USN inventory records in 1962. Ownership transferred from the USN to the FAA on 01 Aug 1966. R. changed to ***N44*** on 02 Apr 1973. Damaged at Fulton County Airport, GA on 17 Apr 1974 after a ground collision with a Beech 18. Repaired and placed back into service. Excess to FAA needs in 1976 and r. changed to ***N4405*** for disposal purposes. Released to the GSA for disposal in Jan 1976. Transferred to the USDA for use as a sprayer in the U.S.-Mexico Screw Worm Eradication Program on 03 Feb 1976. R. of ***N2007J*** assigned but apparently ntu. R. changed to ***N213GB*** on 09 Jun 1977. Deemed excess to USDA needs and released to the GSA for disposal on 02 Mar 1978. Transferred by the GSA to the Monroe County Mosquito Control District at Key West, FL for continued use as a sprayer. Current status unknown.

33241 M. as TC-47B-35-DK s/n ***44-76909*** at Douglas-Oklahoma City on a USAAF contract but d. to the USN as R4D-7 BuNo ***99841*** on 07 May 1945. Immediately placed into storage at Clinton, OK. Excess to USN needs and released to the RFC for disposal . Transferred to the CAA as of 16 Feb 1948 when civil r. of ***NC400*** issued. As of May 1961 in use at the Technical Center located at Atlantic City, New Jersey. Excess to FAA needs and placed into storage on 01 Jul 1965. R. changed to ***N4002*** on 13 Aug 1965. Released to the GSA for disposal. Transferred by the GSA on 18 Aug 1965 to Ohio University, Athens, OH for use in contracted FAA research programs. S. by Ohio University to Jilco Industries of Kidron, OH on 09 Dec 1982. S. on 07 Jul 1983 to Westair Intl. of Monument, CO. Fate unknown.

33251 M. as TC-47B-35-DK s/n ***44-76919*** at Douglas-Oklahoma City on a USAAF contract but d. to the USN as R4D-7 BuNo ***99842*** on 14 May 1945. Immediately placed into storage at Clinton, OK. Deemed excess to USN needs and turned over to the RFC for disposal. Transferred to the CAA in early 1948 and assigned r. of ***NC199*** on 25 Feb 1948. R. changed three days later, on 28 Feb, to ***NC300***. Placed in long-term storage, believed at Oklahoma City, shortly thereafter. Removed from storage on 07 Sep 1954 and probably assigned to a flight inspection role with one of the CAA's regions. R. changed to ***N46*** on 07 May 1958 and re-configured to the standard FAA Type II configuration shortly thereafter. Service through the 1960s primarily with the FAA's Southwest and Eastern Regions. Deemed excess to FAA needs and r. changed to ***N87817*** in late 1974 for disposal purposes. Released to the GSA for disposal on 07 Jan 1975. Transferred to the USDA on 18 Feb 1975 for use as a pesticide sprayer with the U.S.-Mexico Screw Worm Eradication Program. R. changed to ***N2003J*** on 02 Oct 1975. R. changed to ***N225GB*** on 20 Aug 1976. Excess to USDA needs and released to the GSA for disposal. Transferred by the GSA to the Lee County Mosquito Control District at Fort Meyers, FL for continued use as a sprayer. GSA released ownership to Lee County on 03 Jan 1985 with subsequent sale on 17 Jan 1985 to Mark Three Productions of North Miami, FL. S. on 02 Feb 1987 to Aero Specialists, Coolidge, AZ. Current status unknown.

33291 M. as TC-47B-30-DK s/n ***44-76959*** at Douglas-Oklahoma City on a USAAF contract but d. to the USN as R4D-7 BuNo ***99847*** on 31 May 1945. Immediately placed into storage at Clinton, OK. Assigned to NAS Quonset Pt., RI in Oct 1945 and then to a transportation pool at NAS Anacostia, DC in Jul 1946. Returned to NAS Quonset Pt. in May 1948 and redesignated as an R4D-6R. As of May 1950 assigned to the 15th Naval District at NAS Coco Solo. Assigned to FASRON 102 at NAS Norfolk, VA in Jun 1950. Overhauled at MCAS Cherry Pt., NC in Sep 1950. Assigned to a transportation pool at Curry Field in May 1952, then sent NAS Jacksonville, FL for overhaul in Apr 1954. Returned to Curry Field in Sep 1954. Assigned to at transportation pool at NAS Pensecola, FL in Sep 1955. Deemed excess to USN needs and stored at NAF Litchfield Park after Jan 1957. Transferred via loan to the CAA in 1957, with the ferry r. of ***N7477C*** assigned on 29 Jul 1957. R. changed to ***N36*** on 22 Aug 1957 and modified to the FAA standard Type II configuration in Mar 1958. Initial service with the Eastern Region through 1962, then various regions afterwards. Designation changed from R4D-6R to TC-47J in USN inventory records i 1962. Ownership transferred from the USN to the FAA on 01 Aug 1966. Surplus to FAA needs on 04 Aug 1977 with 20,800 logged flight hours. R. changed to ***N87907*** on 04 Aug 1977 for disposal and subsequently released to the GSA. De-R. on 12 Sep 1977. Utilization of the aircraft between 1977 and 1990 is unknown. However, a request by a new owner, Genavco Corporation of Honolulu, HI, was made on 18 Apr 1990 to reinstate the r. of ***N87907*** for the aircraft. Lacking aircraft title or other documentation the matter remains pending. Location of the aircraft and its current status unknown.

33305 M. as TC-47B-35-DK s/n ***44-76973*** at Douglas-Oklahoma City on a USAAF contract but d. to the USN as R4D-7 BuNo ***99849*** on 21 May 1945. Immediately placed into storage at Clinton, OK. Activated in Dec 1945 and assigned to NAS Norfolk with VRS-1. Assigned to NAS Quonset Pt. RI in Jun 1946, and then to NAS Corpus Christi in Mar 1947. Assigned to NAS Pensecola in Jun 1947 and then assigned transport duties at NAS Anacostia, DC in Sep 1947. Subsequently redesignated as an R4D-6R. As of Feb 1950 in overhaul at MCAS Cherry Pt., NC. Assigned to a transportation pool at NAS Glenview, IL in Mar 1950. Ovehauled at NAS Jacksonville, FL in Feb 1953 and then assigned to NAS Miami, FL in Mar 1954. Assigned to the 15th Naval District at NAS Coco Solo in Jun 1954. Excess to USN needs and placed into storage at NAF Litchfield Park after Nov 1954. Loaned to the CAA in Nov 1956. Ferry r., if any, unknown. R. as ***N27*** on 19 Dec 1956 and subsequently modified to the standard Type II flight inspection configuration. Initial assignment to the Alaskan Region at Anchorage. Subsequent assignments to the various FAA regions. USN designation changed from R4D-6R to TC-47J in 1962. Ownership changed from the USN to the FAA on 01 Aug 1966. R. changed to ***N21*** on 16 Nov 1976. Excess to FAA needs and released to the GSA for disposal on 16 Aug 1978. R. canceled on 21 Aug 1978. Reserved r. of ***N21R*** ntu. Transferred by the GSA to the Collier Mosquito Control District of Naples, FL for use as a sprayer on 22 Sep 1978. R. of ***N846MB*** assigned on 26 Feb 1979. Apparently left for derelict by 1983 and obtained by the Provincetown-Boston Airlines for a spares source shortly thereafter. Presumably scrapped for parts.

33322 M. as TC-47B-35-DK s/n ***44-76990*** at Douglas-Oklahoma City on a USAAF contract but d. to the USN as R4D-7 BuNo ***99851*** oı 21 May 1945. Assigned to duty at NAS Norfolk, VA as of May 1945. Other USN duty included: NAS Anacostia, DC as of Oct 1946 NAS Quonset Pt., RI as of Apr 1948; and back to NAS Anacostia as of Jun 1948. Re-designated as an R4D-6Z in 1948. Overhaulec at NAS Jacksonville, FL in Jun 1950 and then returned to NAS Anacostia. Overhauled again at NAS Jacksonville in Dec 1952 and then assigned to VR-5, location unknown. in Apr 1953. Assigned to VR-22 at NAS Atsugi, Japan in Jun 1953, and then returned to NAS San Diego, CA in May 1955. Excess to USN needs and placed into storage at NAF Litchfield Park after Sep 1955. Transferred via loan to the CAA in 1958. Assigned r. of ***N7630C*** for ferry flight on 21 Mar 1958. R. changed to ***N45*** on 05 Jun 1958 and subsequently modified to the FAA Type II standard flight inspection configuration in Sep 1958. Initial flight inspection assignment with the FAA's Eastern Region, with duty with the various FAA regions following. Designation changed from R4D-6Z to VC-47J in USN inventory records in 1962. Ownership transferred from the USN to the FAA on 01 Aug 1966. Deemed excess to FAA needs on 20 Oct 1977 and placed into storage at Atlantic City, NJ. R. canceled on 20 Dec 1977 and assigned to the GSA for disposal. Reported assigned to the National Airways Facilities Experimental Center (NAFEC) as of late 1977 for use as a static display. Reported in an airfield storage yard at Atlantic City in Mar 1982 with a cracked wing spar. Subsequent fate unknown but believed scrapped at Atlantic City, NJ.

33345 M. as TC-47B-35-DK s/n ***44-77013*** at Douglas-Oklahoma City on a USAAF contract but d. to the USN as R4D-7 BuNo ***99854*** on 25 May 1945. Immediately placed into storage at Clinton, OK but activated in Sep 1945 and assigned to NAS Quonset Pt. RI. Assigned to NAS Corpus Christi, TX in Jan 1946 and returned to NAS Quonset Pt. in Jan 1947. Assigned to NAS Anacostia, DC in May 1947 and redesignated as an R4D-6R. Overhauled at MCAS Cherry Pt., NC in Apr 1950 and then assigned to transport at Rio de Janiero, Brazil, possibly in support of the the U.S. embassy. Returned to NAS Jacksonville, FL fo overhaul inMay 1952 and then assigned to the 12th Naval District at NAS Alameda, CA in Nov 1954. Excess to USN needs and placed into storage at NAF Litchfield Park after Jun 1954. Transferred via loan to the CAA in early 1957. Assigned the ferry r. of ***N7074C*** on 25 Mar 1957 and flown to Oklahoma City. R. changed to ***N32*** on 22 Aug 1957 and subsequently modified to the standard Type II configuration for flight inspection. Designation changed from R4D-6R to TC-47J in USN inventory records in 1962. Ownership transferred from the USN to the FAA on 01 Aug 1966. Deemed excess to FAA needs and placed into storage on 26 Jul 1976 at Oklahoma City. R. changed to ***N32A*** on 06 Aug 1976 for disposal. Released to the GSA on the same date. Transferred by the GSA to the USDA for use as a pesticide sprayer with the U.S.-Mexico Screw Worm Eradication Program. R. changed to ***N227GB*** on 21 Dec 1976. Deemed excess to USDA needs and transferred to the GSA for disposal. Transferred by the GSA to the Confederate Air Force's Toledo Wing on 22 Aug 1980. Ownership transferred from the GSA to the American Air Power Heritage Flying Museum, Midlands, TX on 14 Aug 1991. Believed still operational and based at the Toledo, OH CAF wing.

33359 M. as TC-47B-35-DK s/n ***44-77027*** at Douglas-Oklahoma City on a USAAF contract but d. to the USN as R4D-7 BuNo ***99856*** on 26 May 1945. Placed into storage at Clinton, OK until Dec 1945 when activated and assigned to NAS Norfolk, VA. Subsequently assigned to NAS Quonset Point in Jun 1946 and then tc VR-24 in London, England in Feb 1948. Redesignated as an R4D-6R in 1948. As of May 1950 assigned to MCAS Cherry Pt., NC for overhaul, followed by assignment to a transportation pool at NAS Glenview, IL in Sep 1950. Overhauled at NAS Jacksonville, FL in Mar 1953 and subsequently assigned to the 5th Naval District at NAS Norfolk in Sep 1953. Excess to USN needs and placed into storage at NAF Litchfield Park after Feb 1956. Transferred via loan to the CAA in early 1957. R. of ***N7091C*** assigned on 07 May 1957 for ferry flight to Oklahoma City, OK. R. changed to ***N34*** on 22 Aug 1957. Subsequently modified to the FAA standard Type II configuration. Initial assignment to the FAA's Southwest region and, subsequently, to the FAA's various regions for flight inspection. USN designation changed from R4D-6R to TC-47J in 1962. Ownership transferred from the USN to the FAA on 01 Aug 1966. Withdrawn from flight inspection in 1981 and assigned to training at the FAA's Aeronautical Center in Oklahoma City. Deemed excess to FAA needs and dropped form the FAA inventory on 31 Dec 1982. Slated to the GSA for disposal in Oct 1983 but, instead, placed into storage at Oklahoma City. Reinstated to the FAA inventory on 01 Jun 1985 with the intention of operating N34 as an example of aviation heritage. Repainted in the pre-1958 paint scheme (not accurate for N34) and overhauled as necessary. Utilized for airshow displays and remained in airworthy condition through 1993 when withdrawn from service for budgetary reasons. Slated for display in Oklahoma City.

34374 M. as C-47B-50-DK s/n ***45-1104*** at Douglas-Oklahoma City and d. for service to the USAAF on 11 Oct 1945. Placed directly into storage and released to the RFC for disposal on 02 Mar 1946. Transferred on an unknown date, probably early 1946, to the CAA. R. issued as ***NC214***. R. change to ***NC62*** in 1947. CAA use unknown. Deemed excess to CAA needs and r. changed to ***N62K*** in Oct 1952. S. to Spokane Aero Supply, Mountain View, AR in Oct 1952. S. in Apr 1953 to Allied Aircraft Company, North Hollywood, CA. S. in Dec 1953 to Florida Trading Company, location unknown. Reportedly S. to Pan American Airways and r. changed to ***N9947F*** in 1954. U.S. r. subsequently canceled and reportedly issued the Panamanian r. of ***HP-190*** and operated by COPA as "Puerto Armuelles". R. reportedly canceled in 1968. Fate unknown.

Appendix 3
Type II Modifications to the FAA DC-3

The following listing indicates the general modifications undertaken to convert a CAA DC-3 or Navy R4D to the FAA Type II configuration. These modifications were undertaken at the FAA's Aircraft Services Base at Oklahoma City, OK between 1957 and 1961 and performed on approximately 60 FAA DC-3s to create a standardized FAA Flight Inspection Fleet. This listing is compiled primarily from FAA registration records for N40 but edited to reflect the standardized modifications.

Aircraft given a major inspection and standardized as listed below

As per Supplemental Type Certificate #SA2-197:
1. Radio racks manufactured and installed.
2. Radio console manufactured and installed.
3. Work bench manufactured and installed.
4. Left and right picture windows installed.
5. A driftmeter and driftmeter seat installed.
6. Inverter racks manufactured and installed.
7. Two conduits installed through cockpit area.
8. 300 amp generator system installed and electrical system was rewired throughout.
9. Electrical load analysis was made, and it was determined that the maximum probably continuous load was 200 amps and the maximum total generator output is 600 amps, therefore the load did not exceed 80% of continuous output.
10. Adjustable recorder rack manufactured and installed.
11. Hydraulic system modified by relocating reservoir and accumulator, removal of handpump and engine selector, and installation of electrical auxiliary pump.
12. Alcohol system consisting of one tank in each wing fillet, two pumps, flow meter to props and controls to windshield and carburetors.
13. Windshield defroster system manufactured and installed.
14. Instrument panel, overhead switch panel manufactured and installed.
15. Sperry SP-20 autopilot system installed.
16. Beacon lights installed on vertical stabilizer and bottom of fuselage.
17. Engine blower actuator motor brackets installed.
18. Access holes installed in firewall aft of starter.
19. Cowl flap positive closing mechanism manufactured and installed.

Other modifications:
1. Lavatory area standardized by installation of wash basin, stool, urinal, and upholstery
2. Standard APU and related systems installed with electrical discharge for fire extinguisher.
3. Standard clothes closet, parachute rack, APU compartment, and control lock stowage drawer installed.
4. Airstair door installed with hydraulic snubber.
5. Low pressure oxygen system installed to incorporate six each type G1 bottles, full flow outlets to passengers, demand system to crew with controls mounted forward of main door. Original Douglas bottle installation retained.
6. Four each Navy type passenger seats and mounting retained.
7. Standard floor and upholstery installed in cabin area.
8. Flat upholstered ceiling panel installed in cabin.
9. Standard Douglas cabin heat ducts retained at floor level.
10. Heater system modified with two spill valve controls located on left side at Station # -37, Open-closed control aft of copilot seat, automatic thermostat controlling the right and left mixing valves with manual override.
11. Bulkhead removed at Station # -106.5. Removal considered non-structural.
12. Old baggage door and cockpit overhead emergency escape were removed, stringers and circumferential stiffener, and skin installed as per C.A.M. 18 and typical to Douglas installation.
13. Two ice detection and two service lights installed.

14. Main electrical junction box ventilated.
15. All electrical circuits on trip free circuit breakers.
16. Standardized reinforcements installed at gear rear brace strut fittings.
17. Fluxgate transmitter and doubler installed in right wing. CAA Dwg. D10, D85.
18. Standard Douglas type cockpit seats retained.
19. Two jump seats manufactured and installed at Station # -30 and at Station #-80.5.
20. One piece windshields installed as per Executive Aircraft Service Dwg 352544.
21. Pitot system installed as per Pan American World Airways, Inc. Dwg B1536
22. Radome manufactured under Pan American Airways and installed as per Remmert-Werner, Inc. 23. Engineering Supplemental Type Certificate #SA-3-78.
24. Cold air duct installed in clothes closet.
25. Left and right engines overhauled. (R-1830-94)
26. Left and right props overhauled.
27. All control surfaces recovered.
28. Douglas fuel-oil-hydraulic emergency manual shut-off was retained with controls aft of engine fire extinguisher controls.
29. All instruments were overhauled by an approved repairs station in accordance with C.A.M. 18.
30. Main and tail gear assemblies overhauled.
31. Main wheel assemblies overhauled, new brake blocks and expander tubes installed.
32. All de-icer boots replaced new.
33. New main and tail tires installed.
34. All seats reupholstered.
35. Vertical and horizontal stabilizers and wings removed for inspection.
36. Control column removed for inspection and overhaul.
37. All primary control cables were replaced new.
38. Fuel tanks removed, repaired, and airchecked.
39. Oil tanks removed, cleaned, and modified as per Douglas Service Bulletin C47B #21.
40. All hydraulic units overhauled.
41. Vent for recorder installed.
42. Plastic covers installed at cabin emergency exit handles.
43. Cockpit cold air vents installed.
44. Gear retraction accomplished.
45. Special wing attach bolts installed and torqued as per Douglas Service Bulletin 249.
46. All antennas installed as per C.A.M. 18.
47. Aircraft was stripped, brightened and repainted with Switzer Day-Glo Fluorescent.

Type II FAA Flight Inspection DC-3s

MSN	REGN	MSN	REGN	MSN	REGN	MSN	REGN
2053	N12	13004	N55	26133	N70	33133	N29
4084	N16	19320	N23	26258	N43	33144	N66
4148	N24	20033	N22	26268	N42	33155	N47
4279	N56	20419	N52	26283	N11	33201	N48
4438	N20	20443	N21	26358	N31	33216	N30
4661	N10	25341	N15	26558	N49	33232	N64
9486	N58	25627	N57	26583	N33	33251	N46
9526	N14	25775	N44	26593	N69	33291	N36
10096	N61	25824	N40	26713	N37	33305	N27
10243	N25	25951	N62	26733	N28	33322	N45
11808	N39	25954	N54	26874	N60	33345	N32
11859	N18	25956	N67	26968	N53	33359	N34
11928	N51	26093	N26	32794	N35		
12261	N41	26108	N63	33100	N38		

Appendix 4
Preserved DC-3s: A World-Wide Listing

DC-3 types listed in this catch-all category are dominated by the many aircraft on display at aviation museums throughout the world. Gate guards and planes on poles are included, as well as those refurbished by dedicated preservation groups. Excluded are the wrecks that still litter the fire training areas and dumps of airports, those that are used on regular freight or passenger revenue services, and the few in the hands of private individuals that are not available for public viewing.

Aircraft are sorted by country, and then by ascending order of manufacturer's serial number (msn), a term often used interchangeably with constructor's number (c/n). As a bit of background, the Davis-Douglas Company assigned the fuselage number 100 to the Cloudster, the first aircraft that they built. Thereafter, Douglas companies have given sequential serial numbers to each of the planes they have built. This unique number stays with the aircraft throughout its life. Mistakes were made with this system, the most significant being during WWII when two plants both manufacturing C-47s used the same numbers starting with 13779. Oklahoma City production aircraft were later given a corrected and higher number series that is used throughout this book.

Registrations quoted are those that were actually used by the aircraft at some time during it's operational career. Beware that many museum DC-3s have been marked with fictitious or wrong registrations and military serials. A few have unlisted registrations, used by law agencies and for covert operations. N57123 (msn 33170), owned by Marsh Aviation and displayed at the CAF hanger at Falcon Field in Mesa, Arizona, is typical example.

USAAC/USAAF serial numbers begin with the last two digits of the fiscal year in which the contract was placed. The serials do not indicate when the aircraft was actually built. The Army was the procurement agency for all DC-3 type aircraft during WWII, with each plane initially assigned an Army Air Forces serial number. Those that were delivered to the U.S. Navy or Marine Corps also assumed Bureau Numbers (BuNo). Lend-lease Dakotas for the RAF and Commonwealth Air Arms were marked with the RAF's two letter, three number serial (e.g. KG436). Commonwealth Air Forces went on to use their own numbering systems after the war. (For example, the Royal Australian Air Force used A65-1 through A65-124 for their post war Dakotas).

A brief museum name or location is given, together with the nearest city. For exact locations, opening times etc., consult one of the several country-wide museum guides published in the U.K. and the United States.

MSN	IDENT	LOCATION	CITY	COUNTRY	STATUS	REMARKS
4365	CTA-15	Naval Aviation Museum	Buenos Aires	Argentina	Static	
27131	A65-71	War Memorial	Canberrra, ACT	Austrailia	Static	
2029	VH-ABR	Ansett Historical Aircraft	Melbounre, VIC	Australia	Flying	
4120	VH-ANH	Moorabiin Air Museum	Moorabiin, VIC	Australia	Static	
6007	VH-AER	McDonalds, West Beach	Adelaide, SA	Australia	Static	
6021	VH-AES	"Hawdon"	Tullamarine, VIC	Australia	Flying	
6024	VH-AEQ	Car Dealer	Melbourne, VIC	Australia	Static	
6051	VH-DAS	Heritage Homestead	Kuranda, QLD	Australia	Static	
12187	VH-SBD	Bush Pilot Memorial	Cairns, QLD	Australia	Static	Mounted on pylon
12542	N2-43	Naval Aviation Museum	Nowra, NSW	Australia	Static	
13084	VH-BAA	Warbirds Air Museum	Mildura, VIC	Australia	Static	
13624	VH-ANW	McDonalds, Midlands	Midland, WA	Australia	Static	
20041	PK-GDC	Western Aust. Museum of Aviation	Jandakot, WA	Australia	Static	
25367	VH-EDD	Hotel	Cairns, QLD	Australia	Static	Cockpit only
25495	VH-BAB	Air World	Wangaratta, VIC	Australia	Static	
26638	VH-PTE	Amaroo Tavern	Moree, NSW	Australia	Static	
32671	A65-73	Sid Beck's Air Museum	Mareeba, QLD	Australia	Static	
32883	N2-90	RAN Historical Flight	Nowra, NW	Australia	Flying	
33099	VH-RRA	Fire Dump	Mascot, QLD	Australia	Static	
33297	A65-108	RAAF Museum	Point Cook, VIC	Australia	Static	
33301	VH-MMD	Power House Museum	Ultimo, NSW	Australia	Static	
33304	A65-111	David Anderson	Wastonia, VIC	Australia	Static	Nose Only
33460	A65-114	S. Aust. Hist. Aviation Museum	Port Adelaide, SA	Australia	Static	
34220	A65-124	Air Force Association	Bull Creek, WA	Australia	Static	
20823	OT-CWG	Musee Royal de L'Armee	Brussels	Belgium	Static	
26501	OT-CWA	Dakota Unlimited	Gits	Belgium	Static	
33119	F-BAIF	Victoria Memorial Museum	Hondelage	Belgium	Static	

MSN	IDENT	LOCATION	CITY	COUNTRY	STATUS	REMARKS
1934	TAM-01	TAM Base Museum	La Paz	Bolivia	Static	Ex TWA NC17319
1545	PP-SQH	Varig Museum	Porto Alegre	Brazil	Static	
4969	PP-CBT	Park	Manaus	Brazil	Static	Preserved in a park
25588	PP-VBT	Bar	Garibaldi	Brazil	Static	Fuselage used as a bar
25685	FAB-07	Museu Aerospacial de FAB	Rio de Janeiro	Brazil	Static	
25951	N259DC	Museu Aerospacial de FAB	Rio de Janiero	Brazil	Static	
26823	PP-VBK	Armase Vehiculas	Sao Paulo	Brazil	Static	
34287	PP-VAZ	Bar	Porte Alegre	Brazil	Static	
2141	C-GDAK	Canadian Warplane Heritage	Hamilton, Ontario	Canada	Flying	
2198	CF-PWH	Friends of the DC-3, Canada	Burnaby, BC	Canada	Static	
4563	CF-IAE	Reynolds Aviation Museum	Edmonton, Alberta	Canada	Static	
4665	CF-CPY	Pole	Whitehorse, Yukon	Canada	Static	Wind direction indicator
6179	CF-QBI	Airport display	Harbour Grace, NF	Canada	Static	
6261	CF-TDJ	National Aviation Museum	Ottawa, Ontario	Canada	Static	
7340	CF-BFV	Western Canada Aviation Museum	Winnipeg, Manitoba	Canada	Static	
9041	CF-FST	Antique & Military Aviation Museum	St. Chrystome, Quebec	Canada	Static	
11780	CF-GHX	Atlantic Canada Aviation Museum	Halifax, Nova Scotia	Canada	Static	
11906	CF-TES	Western Canada	Winnipeg, Manitoba	Canada	Static	
12217	12963	RCAF Memorial Museum	CFB Trenton, Ontario	Canada	Static	
12490	KG455	Airborne Forces Museum	Petawawa, Ontario	Canada	Static	
13448	CF-BZI	Calgary Airport	Calgary, Alberta	Canada	Static	
26248	KJ956	Memorial Park	Winnipeg, Manitoba	Canada	Static	Ex-RAF & RCAF Dakota III
32922	KN451	National Aviation Museum	Ottawa, Ontario	Canada	Static	
unknown	XT-115	Air Force Museum	Datangshan	China	Static	
1995	N142JR	Kbely Museum	Prague	Czechoslovakia	Static	
9664	OY-DDA	Danish Aviation Museum	Billund	Denmark	Flying	
19200	K-687	Danish Aviation Museum	Billund	Denmark	Static	
20019	OY-BPB	Danish Aviation Museum	Billund	Denmark	Static	Ex-SAS "Terje Viking"
33496	HC-AUT	Ecuadorian Air Force Museum	Quito	Ecaudor	Static	
11747	HC-AUY	Ecuadorian Air Force Museum	Quito	Ecuador	Static	
1975	OH-VKB	Suomen Ilnailumuseo	Helsinki	Finland	Flying	
6346	OH-LCH	Airveteran OY	Helsinki-Malmi Airport	Finland	Flying	
19309	OH-LCD	Airveteran OY	Helsinki-Malmi Airport	Finland	Flying	
25515	OH-LCF	Keski-Suomen Museum	Tikkakoski	Finland	Static	On the E4 Highway
12251	F-BEFB	Musee de L'Air	Paris	France	Static	
13142	F-SEBD	Jean Salis	Ferte Alais	France	Flying	
13590	F-GBOL	Ailes Anciennes	Toulouse	France	Static	
19288	42-100825	Airborne Troop	St. Mere L'Englise	France	Static	
26445	F-OGFI	Musee de L'Air	Paris	France	Static	Nose only
26717	G-AMSU	Euro Disney World	Marne la Vallee	France	Static	
32935	F-GILV	Gilbert Villa	Marguerittes	France	Flying	
33448	KP229	Aeronautique Naval	Rochefort	France	Static	
32752	KN379	Aeronautique	Nancy-Essey	France	Static	
4828	N65371	Air Classic	Frankfurt	Germany	Static	
10100	N569R	Airport	Frankfurt	Germany	Static	Airport Observation Area
19460	42-100997	Hermeskeil Aviation Collection	Hermeskeil	Germany	Static	
25450	D-CORA	Auto & Technik Museum	Sinsheim	Germany	Static	
26432	N1350M	Rhein Main AB	Frankfurt	Germany	Static	
26989	14+01	Deutsches Museum	Munich	Germany	Static	
27108	G-41-2-67	Auto & Technik Museum	Sinsheim	Germany	Static	
27127	A65-69	Templehof	Berlin	Germany	Static	RAF Gatow, Berlin
34214	45-951	USAF Museum	Berlin	Germany	Static	Tempelhof AB
33206	SX-ECF	Athens Airport	Athens	Greece	Static	CAA Headquarters
4423	VR-HDB	Hong Kong Science Museum	Kowloon	Hong Kong	Static	Cathay-Pacific "Betsey"
9860	TF-ISB	Aviation Historical Society	Reykjavik	Iceland	Static	
43379	17191	Gate Guard	Keflavik Airport	Iceland	Static	Pylon-mounted C-117D
9858	PK-JJM	Kebon Jeruk	Jarkata	Indonesia	Static	Atop KFC restaurant

MSN	IDENT	LOCATION	CITY	COUNTRY	STATUS	REMARKS
12719	PK-GDT	Akedemi Angkatan Museum	Jawa/Tengah	Indonesia	Static	
13639	PK-GDH	Aviation training school	Jakarta	Indonesia	Static	
25489	T-482	Pusat TNI-AU	Yogyakarta	Indonesia	Static	
unknown	R1-001	Satria Mandala Military Museum	Jakarta	Indonesia	Static	
unknown	R1-001	Tamal Mini theme Park	Jakarta	Indonesia	Static	
unknown	R1-001	Downtown square	Bandar Aceh	Indonesia	Static	Pylon-mounted
19420	42-100957	Haifa AFB	Tel Aviv	Israel	Static	
unknown	4X-FNL	Israeli Air Force	Beersheba	Israel	Static	
unknown	4X-FNZ	Israeli Air Force	Beersheba	Israel	Static	
33095	99824	NAS Kanoya	Kagoshima	Japan	Static	
4282	XC-CTM	Technical Museum	Mexico City	Mexico	Static	
19109	PH-DDA	Dutch Dakota Association	Schipol	Netherlands	Flying	Nostalgia flights
19434	PH-PBA	Aviodome	Amsterdam	Netherlands	Static	
19754	PH-DDZ	Dutch Dakota Association	Schipol	Netherlands	Static	Under restoration
20118	K-688	Military Air Museum	Soesterberg	Netherlands	Static	
20051	ZK-BYF	Silverstream Aeronautical Society	Wellington	New Zealand	Static	
26480	ZK-DAK	Warbirds Association	Aukland	New Zealand	Flying	
33315	ZK-BQK	M.O.T.A.T Museum	Aukland	New Zealand	Static	
34223	NZ3551	RNZAF	Christchurch	New Zealand	Static	At Wigram AB
11750	LN-WND	Dakota Norway	Sandefjord	Norway	Flying	
13749	42-93797	Royal Norwegian Air Force Museum	Gardermoen AFB	Norway	Static	
27110	P2-ANQ	Airport	Port Moresby	Papau New Guinea	Static	
32877	P2-002	Airport	Port Moresby	Papau New Guinea	Static	
4830	OB-R-581		Lima	Peru	Static	
25562	48301	Philippine Air Force Museum	Villamor AB, Manila	Philippines	Static	
19755	43-15289	Air Force Museum	Alverca	Portugal	Static	
9623	5B-CBD	Pylon	Jeddah	Saudi Arabia	Static	
32650	HZ-AAX		Riyadh	Saudi Arabia	Static	
13713	YU-ABB	National Aviation Museum	Belgrade	Serbia	Static	
25480	YU-ABG	National Aviation Museum	Belgrade	Serbia	Static	
12478	KG443	South African Air Force Museum	Swartkop	South Africa	Static	
12586	KG474	South Africa Air Force Museum	Swartkop	South Africa	Static	
20600	T3-36	Air Force Museum	Madrid	Spain	Static	
25464	CR-821	Sri Lanka Air Force Museum	Colombo	Sri Lanka	Static	20 miles south of city
33556	CR-822	Sri Lanka Air Force Museum	Colombo	Sri Lanka	Static	20 miles south of city
9103	SE-APW	Skoklosters Motor Museum	Balsta	Sweden	Static	
13647	SE-CFR	Swedish Air Force Museum	Linkoping	Sweden	Static	
13883	SE-CFP	Flygande Veteraner	Bromma Airport	Sweden	Flying	
42970	SE-EGR	High Chaparral	Hillerstorp	Sweden	Static	Wild West theme park
33393	HB-IRN	Swiss Transport	Luzern	Switzerland	Static	
13620	B-126	Chung Chen Aviation Museum	Taipei	Taiwan	Static	
9651	219789	Royal Thai Police Museum	Bankok	Thailand	Static	Mounted at gate house
32849	76517	Royal Thai Air Force Museum	Bankok	Thailand	Static	Don Muang Airport
13877	YSL52	Turkish Aviation Museum	Istanbul	Turkey	Static	
1911	EI-AYO	Science Museum	Wroughton, WILTS	UK	Static	
2108	N4565L	390th Bomb Group Mem. Museum	Framlington, Suffolk	UK	Static	
9836	FD938	Airborne Forces Youth Initiative	Middle Wallop	UK	Flying	
10200	ZA947	BBMF	Coningsby, LINCS	UK	Flying	
12472	KG437	Restaurant	Fleet, HAMPS	UK	Static	Part in the bar
19047	F-GEFU	Booker	High Wycombe, Bucks.	UK	Static	Cockpit section only
19347	G-DAKS	Aces High	North Weald, ESSEX	UK	Flying	
19975	G-BHUB	Imperial War Museum	Duxford, Cambridge	UK	Static	
26717	G-AMPP	Aces High	North Weald, ESSEX	UK	Static	Used for movie filming
27209	G-AMSM	Brenzett Aero	Brenzett, KENT	UK	Static	Cockpit section only
32918	KN448	Science Museum	London	UK	Static	Cockpit section only
33335	KN645	Aerospace Museum	Cosford, W. Mid	UK	Static	
33419	KP208	Airborne Forces Museum	Aldershot, Hants	UK	Static	

MSN	IDENT	LOCATION	CITY	COUNTRY	STATUS	REMARKS
1910	N16070	Pinal Air Park	Marana, AZ	US	Flying	United Airlines DC-3
1918	N17332	American Airpower	Midland, TX	US	Flying	
1983	N18111	MARC	Memphis, TN	US	Static	
2000	N18124	NASM	Washington, DC	US	Static	
2015	N101ZG	War Eagles Air Museum	Santa Teresa, NM	US	Flying	
2105	N11L	Richmond County Museum	Augusta, GA	US	Static	
2144	N21728	Henry Ford Museum	Dearborne, MI	US	Static	
2180	N1690	Allied Air Force Museum	Allentown, PA	US	Static	Queen City Airport
2193	N600RC	Florida Military Aviation Museum	Clearwater, FL	US	Static	D-Day markings
2202	N12978	C.R. Smith Museum	Fort Worth, TX	US	Static	Flagship Knoxville"
2245	N138D	Museum of Flight	Seattle, WA	US	Static	
3269	N760	Museum of Science and Industry	Los Angeles, CA	US	Static	
3294	N1945	Denver Aerospace Science Museum	Denver, CO	US	Static	
4085	N33639	MARC	Altanta, GA	US	Static	
4201	41-7723	Pima Air Museum	Tucson, AZ	US	Static	
4433	N193DP	Museum of Flying	Santa Monica, CA	US	Flying	
4574	N101Z	Alaska Transport & Industry	Palmer, AK	US	Static	
4790	N34FL	MARC	West Palm Beach, FL	US	Static	
4864	N1301	Edwards AFB	Edwards AFB, CA	US	Static	
4877	N569AR	Museum of Flying	Santa Monica, CA	US	Static	
4894	N763A	Prarie Aviation Museum	Bloomington, IL	US	Static	Ozark Airline colors
4900	N56V	Richmond County Museum	Augusta, GA	US	Static	
6337	N15748	Museum of Flight	Seattle, WA	US	Static	
9358	12418	U.S. Naval Aviation Museum	Pensecola, FL	US	Static	Que Sera Sera"
9530	42-23668	Beale AFB	Marysville, CA	US	Static	Museum closed
9619	12436	U.S. Army Aviation Museum	Dothan, AL	US	Static	Fort Rucker
11762	42-68835	McClellan AFB	Sacramento, CA	US	Static	
11903	N54608	Florida Military Aviation Museum	Clearwater, FL	US	Static	
11928	42-108808	Dyess Air Park	Abilene, TX	US	Static	Restricted access
12508	42-108866	Pate Museum of Transport	Fort Worth, TX	US	Static	
12683	N65162	State Fairgrounds	Oklahoma City, OK	US	Static	Pylon
12686	42-92841	Dover AFB Historical Center	Dover, DL	US	Static	Restricted access
12852	N16602	American Warbird Company	Nut Tree, CA	US	Flying	
13004	42-92127	Elsworth AFB Museum	Rapid City, SD	US	Static	
13050	N90830	Kalamazoo Aviation	Kalamazoo, MI	US	Static	
13227	N64604	Weisbod Aircraft Museum	Pueblo, CO	US	Static	
13741	42-93790	Army Parachutist's School	Fort Benning, GA	US	Static	
13752	42-93800	Bonanzaville USA	West Fargo, ND	US	Static	
13860	N293WM	National Warplane Museum	Geneseo, NY	US	Flying	
19054	N3239T	Valiant Air Command	Titusville, FL	US	Flying	Tico Belle"
19066	N47060	World Aircraft Museum	Calhoun, GA	US	Static	
19320	N41	Kulis ANG	Anchorage, AK	US	Static	
19458	42-100995	National Atomic Museum	Albuquerque, NM	US	Static	
19666	43-15200	Alaskan Historical and Transportion	Palmer, AK	US	Static	
19797	43-15331	National Museum of Transport	St. Louis, MO	US	Static	
19976	42-510	Hurlburt Field Memorial Park	Ft. Walton Beach, FL	US	Static	Displayed as gunship
19978	N62376	Oregon Museum of Science & Industry	Portland, OR	US	Static	
20045	43-15579	March Field Museum	Riverside, CA	US	Static	
20101	43-15635	National Museum of Transport	St. Louis, MO	US	Static	
20443	43-15977	Castle AFB	Atwater, CA	US	Static	
20596	43-16130	8th Air Force Museum	Shreveport, LA	US	Static	
20835	43-16369	World Aircraft Museum	Calhoun, GA	US	Static	
25359	43-48098	Strategic Air Command Museum	Bellevue, NB	US	Static	
25676	43-48415	Kelly AFB	San Antonio, TX	US	Static	
25824	BuNo 17278	Marine Corps Air-Ground Museum	Quantico, VA	US	Static	
26193	43-48932	82nd Airborne Division Museum	Fort Bragg, NC	US	Static	
26218	43-48957	Warner-Robins AFB	Macon, GA	US	Static	

MSN	IDENT	LOCATION	CITY	COUNTRY	STATUS	REMARKS
26268	N232GB	Georgia Historical Aviation Museum	Stone Mountain, GA	US	Static	
26273	N219GB	Tinker AFB Airpark	Oklahoma City, OK	US	Static	Restricted access
26388	43-49127	Maxwell AFB	Montgomery, AL	US	Static	
26408	N151ZE	American Airpower	Midland, TX	US	Static	
26467	43-49206	Altus AFB	Altus, OK	US	Static	Restricted access
26531	43-49270	Grissom AFB	Peru, IN	US	Static	
26542	43-49281	Hill Aerspace Museum	Ogden, UT	US	Static	
26583	N33	Minnesota ANG	Minneapolis, MN	US	Static	
26597	43-49338	Chanute AFB	Rantoul, IL	US	Static	
26616	43-49355	Charleston AFB	Charleston, SC	US	Static	
26703	43-49442	Warner-Robins AFB	Macon, GA	US	Static	
26768	43-15174	USAF Museum	Dayton, OH	US	Static	
26787	N827NA	Fairchild AFB	Spokane, WA	US	Static	Restricted access
26874	N229GB	Mid-Atlantic Air Museum	Reading, PA	US	Static	
26968	N237GB	North Dakota ANG	Fargo, ND	US	Static	
27080		MARC	Caldwell, NJ	US	Static	
27113	43-49852	Bishop	Honolulu, HI	US	Static	
32789	44-76457	Stout Field	Indianapolis, IN	US	Static	
32794	44-76462	Pope AFB	Fayetteville, NC	US	Static	
32818	Bu#39103	USAF Armament Museum	Ft. Walton Beach, FL	US	Static	
32834	44-76502	McChord AFB	Tacoma, WA	US	Static	
32914	710Z	Combat Air Museum	Topeka, KS	US	Static	
33003	44-76671	Lackland AFB	San Antonio, TX	US	Static	
33048	N8704	Yankee Air Force	Ypsilanti, MI	US	Static	
33170	BuNo 99831	Marsh Aviation	Mesa, AZ	US	Flying	
33216	N2312G	MARC	Nashville, TN	US	Static	
33345	N227GB	American Airpower Heritage	Midland, TX	US	Flying	
33359	N34	FAA	Oklahoma City, OK	US	Storage	
34177	45-916	Baker Aviation School	Miami, FL	US	Static	
34189	45-928	MARC	Farmingdale, NJ	US	Static	
34236	N8040L	Escadrille	Cambridge, MA	US	Flying	
34344	45-1074	Pima Air Museum	Tucson, AZ	US	Static	
43321	BuNo 50835	MCAS El Toro	Santa Ana, CA	US	Static	C-117D
43322	BuNo 50821	U.S. Naval Aviation Museum	Pensacola, FL	US	Static	
43324	BuNo 50834	Marine Corps Air-Ground Museum	Quantico, VA	US	Static	C-117D
43363	BuNo 50826	Pima Air Museum	Tucson, AZ	US	Static	C-117D
4984		Venezuelan AF	Maracay	Venezuela	Static	
12386	YV-T-RTC	Venezuelan AF	Maracay	Venezuela	Static	
19335	YV-O-MC1	Transport	Caracas	Venezuela	Static	

Appendix 5
Basler BT-67 Specifications

Comparison of Turbo-67 and Piston-engined DC-3

	BT-67	Piston-engined DC-3
Engines	Pratt & Whitney (Canada) PT6A-67R (1281 shp)	Pratt & Whitney R-1830 (1200 hp)
Propellers	Hartzell (5-blade, 115 inches)	Hamilton Standard (3-blade, 138 inches)
Weight (pounds)		
Maximum Take-Off	28,750	26,900
Cargo-Basic Operating Weight	15,750	17,815
Maximum Useful Load	13,000	9,085
Maximum Fuel Capacity (gallons)		
Standard	772 (5,172 pounds)	800
Long-range tanks	1542 (10,332 pounds)	N/A
Cruise Speed (knots)		
Maximum cruise (12,500 feet)	205 (95% torque)	173 (700 hp)
Standard cruise (12,500 feet)	199 (90% torque)	160 (600 hp)
Low cruise	176 (70% torque)	N/A
Fuel Flow (gallons/hour)		
Maximum cruise	152	119
Standard cruise	145	100
Low cruise	122	N/A
Range (nautical miles)		
Standard fuel	950 (80% torque)	1160
Long-range fuel	2140 (80% torque)	N/A
Single-engine ceiling (feet)	14,000 @ 27,000 pounds	9,000 @ 26,200 pounds

(as provided by Basler Turbo Conversions, Inc.)

Order Form

TELEPHONE ORDERS: Call Aero Vintage Books at **(916) 684-7028**. Please have your VISA or MASTERCARD ready.

FAX ORDERS: Fax this form to **(916) 684-7028**. Include your VISA or MASTERCARD information, including expiration date.

POSTAL ORDERS: Mail a copy of this form to:

Aero Vintage Books
P.O. Box 1508
Elk Grove, California 95759-1508

AVAILABLE FROM AERO VINTAGE BOOKS:

Douglas DC-3: Sixty Years and Counting by Ed Davies, Scott A.Thompson, Nicholas A. Veronico (160 pages, 200 photos, some color) **$24.95** Published by Aero Vintage Books.

B-17 In Blue: The Flying Fortress in U.S. Navy and U.S. Coast Guard Service by Scott Thompson (120 pages, 152 black and white photos) **$16.95** Published by Aero Vintage Books.

Final Cut: The Post-War B-17 Flying Fortress by Scott A. Thompson (212 pages, 275 photos, some color) **$12.95** Published by Pictorial Histories Publishing Company.

Wreck Chasing: A Guide to Finding Aircraft Wrecks by Nicholas A. Veronico, (80 pages, 64 black and white photos) **$9.95** Published by Pacific Aero Press.

Wreck Chasing II: Commercial Aircraft by Nicholas A. Veronico, with Ed Davies, Donald B. McComb, and Michael McComb, (128 pages, some color) **$19.95** Published by World Transport Press

F4U Corsair: Combat, Development, and Racing History of the Corsair by Nicholas A. Veronico with John M. and Donna Campbell (144 pages, 130 photos, 50 color) **$24.95** Published by Motorbooks International.

DEALER INQUIRIES WELCOME

PHONE, FAX, OR MAIL THIS FORM

NAME ______________________________
ADDRESS ______________________________
CITY ______________________ **STATE** ______ **ZIP** ________

Please send:

____ copies of **Douglas DC-3** at **$24.95** per copy ____
____ copies of **B-17 in Blue** at **$16.95** per copy ____
____ copies of **Final Cut** at **$12.95** per copy ____
____ copies of **Wreck Chasing** at **$9.95** per copy ____
____ copies of **Wreck Chasing II** at **$19.95** per copy ____
____ copies of **F4U Corsair** at **$24.95** per copy ____

Sales Tax: Books shipped to California addresses add **7.75%** sales tax ____
Shipping: **$3.50** for first book, **$1.00** for each add'l book ____

VISA MasterCard

TOTAL ORDER $______

☐ CHECK OR MONEY ORDER PAYABLE TO **AERO VINTAGE BOOKS**
☐ PLEASE CHARGE MY VISA OR MASTERCARD:

ACCOUNT NUMBER: ______________________ EXPIRES: ________
SIGNATURE ______________________________